# GREAT
## Economists
## since Keynes

# GREAT
## Economists
## since Keynes

*AN INTRODUCTION TO THE
LIVES & WORKS OF ONE HUNDRED
MODERN ECONOMISTS*

Second edition

# MARK
# BLAUG

*Professor Emeritus, University of London,
Professor Emeritus, University of Buckingham
and Visiting Professor, University of Exeter, UK*

**Edward Elgar**
Cheltenham, UK • Northampton, MA, USA

Published by
Edward Elgar Publishing Limited
8 Lansdown Place
Cheltenham
Glos GL50 2HU
UK

Edward Elgar Publishing, Inc.
6 Market Street
Northampton
Massachusetts 01060
USA

First edition published by Wheatsheaf Books Ltd
Second edition 1998


A catalogue record for this book
is available from the British Library


**Library of Congress Cataloguing-in-Publication Data**
Blaug, Mark.
    Great economists since Keynes : an introduction to the lives and works of one hundred modern economists / Mark Blaug. — 2nd ed.
    Includes bibliographical references and index.
    1. Economists—Biography. I. Title.
HB76.B55  1998
330'.092'2—dc21                               97-37217
  [B]                                             CIP


ISBN 1 85898 692 3 (cased)

Typeset by Manton Typesetters, 5–7 Eastfield Road, Louth, Lincolnshire LB11 7AJ, UK.
Printed and bound in Great Britain by MPG Books Ltd, Bodmin, Cornwall

# Contents

# Preface to the First Edition

This book is addressed to those who are studying economics for the first time, who hear their teachers dropping names like Friedman, Galbraith, and Samuelson, and want to know something about these modern economists and why they are considered important. This book describes the careers and contributions of 100 famous economists, each one of whom has left a mark on twentieth-century economics.

Why 100 and not 200 or 300? The number 100 is arbitrary: we have to draw the line somewhere and 100 is a round number. Similarly, I have interpreted 'modern' to mean living or recently deceased and I have interpreted 'recently deceased' to mean 'since 1970'; obviously, this cut-off date is as arbitrary as the number 100. In short, words like 'famous' and 'modern' cannot be defined so as to satisfy everyone. Needless to say, this is my own personal list of the 100 great names in modern economics and another author might have drawn up a slightly different list. Nevertheless, I feel sure that a referendum among living economists would endorse 90 and perhaps even 95 per cent of my list.

This book can be consulted like a reference book; every entry is self-contained and, hopefully, self-explanatory. However, it can also be read continuously from beginning to end, in which case it will provide a virtual survey of schools of and approaches to modern economics.

Mark Blaug, 1985

# Preface to the Second Edition

This book came out in 1985, over ten years ago. It was my personal list of 100 great names in modern economics, describing their careers and contributions in brief dictionary-type entries. The Royal Swedish Academy of Sciences confirmed most of my choices by their annual awards over the last decade of the Nobel Prize in Economics, or more correctly the 'Bank of Sweden Prize in Economic Sciences'. Thus, the Prize went to Franco Modigliani in 1985, James Buchanan in 1986, Robert Solow in 1987, Ronald Coase in 1991, Gary Becker in 1992, Robert Fogel and Douglass North in 1993, Robert Lucas in 1995, and all these will be found in my list of 100 most eminent economists. However, the Prize also went to Richard Stone in 1984, Maurice Allais in 1988, Trygve Haavelmo in 1989, Harry Markowitz, Merton Miller and William Sharpe in 1990, John Harsanyi, John Nash and Reinhard Selten in 1994 and James Mirrlees and William Vickrey in 1996 and none of these are found in this book. But that only goes to emphasise the point I made in the preface to the first edition of the book: any list like mine is arbitrary and all one can claim is that other economists would select, not the same 100, but at least 90 or 95 of the names. I think that that claim is confirmed by the Nobel Prize awards: in seven years out of twelve, the Swedish Academy of Science agreed with me about who are the greatest economists of our times.

Nevertheless, I had it wrong, so to speak, five times out of twelve, and that left me with a problem: should I alter my roll call of 100 outstanding modern economists to bring it into line with the opinions of the Swedish Academy, or should I stick to my guns and stay with my original list? I have opted for the latter course because to do anything else would turn the book into an attempt to read the mind of the Swedish judges. But if this book has any merit at all, it is that of expressing the purely subjective opinion of one (hopefully well-informed) consumer of economic writings.[1] In short, the list of

1 For another subjective list of 150 major economists by two well-informed Canadian consumers of economic writings, see M.M. Beaud and G. Dostaler, *Economic Thought since Keynes: A History and Dictionary of Major Economists* (Edward Elgar, 1995). For a purely objective list of 1,000 eminent economists as judged by their frequency of citations, see my *Who's Who in Economics: A Biographical Dictionary of Major Economists, 1700–1986* (MIT Press, 1986).

100 names is the same in the second as in the first edition of this book but all the entries are revised and up-dated.

This book is addressed, in the first instance, to students but it is also aimed at members of the general public who feel the need to repair gaps in their knowledge about the House that Economists have built. Economics may not be the Queen of the Sciences but it is one of the most fascinating of all the social sciences, and here, between the covers of one volume, are thumb-nail sketches (and photographs) of the ideas and lives of 100 leaders of the economic profession. They make up a 'coat of many colours' and do not even agree among themselves about what economics is all about. Is economics an attempt to theorise about economic systems with a rigour and elegance that resembles work in nuclear physics, or is it instead a series of practical maxims about how to steer an economic system into desirable directions, or perhaps is it both of these at one and the same time, blending theory and application in an understanding of the workings of an economic system? There are elements of all of these approaches in the biographical portraits that follow. Let the reader make up his or her own mind.

Mark Blaug, 1998

# Acknowledgements

In all but thirty-two cases the sources of the photographs are the economists themselves. In the remaining cases I would like to express my appreciation to the following individuals and organisations for making available to me photographs in their possession:

The American Economic Association (A. Gerschenkron, H. Hotelling, H.G. Johnson, T.C. Koopmans, A.P. Lerner, F. Machlup, J. Marschak, R.A. Musgrave, T. Scitovsky, J. Viner); Fabian Bachrach (F.H. Knight); Basil Blackwell Publisher (J.R. Hicks); Cambridge University Press (M. Morishima); Department of Economics, University of Chicago (P.H. Douglas); G.R. Feiwel (M. Kalecki); P. Gaskell, Trinity College, Cambridge University (M.H. Dobb, P. Sraffa); Dorothy Hahn (K.J. Arrow, F. Hahn, R.M. Solow); Harvard University News Office (A.H. Hansen, S. Kuznets); Institute of Social Studies, Netherlands (J. Tinbergen); *Journal of Law and Economics* (R.H. Coase); Keystone Press Agency (R.G. Hawtrey, A.M. Okun); Ramsey and Muspratt Collection (J. Robinson); H.C. Recktenwald (R. Frisch, R.F. Harrod); O. Steiger (B.G. Ohlin); News and Information Office of the University of Texas at Austin (W.W. Rostow); Margit von Mises (L.E. von Mises).

# List of Entries

* Deceased.

# Adelman, Irma (1930– )

Irma Adelman has made distinguished contributions to the development of computable general equilibrium models for developing planning and has collaborated with Cynthia T. Morris in a pioneering attempt to employ new techniques of multivariate analysis to study the interactions among economic, social, and political forces in the process of economic development. Latterly, she has also attempted to quantify the trade-off between economic growth and inequality in income distribution in particular countries.

Her first book was a purely theoretical survey of *Theories of Economic Growth and Development* (Stanford University Press, 1961; 2nd edn, 1974) in which she attempted to express the ideas of some of the major economists of the past (Adam Smith, David Ricardo, Karl Marx, and Joseph Schumpeter) by means of a single but comprehensive mathematical model of the growth process. Next came *The Theory and Design of Economic Development* (Johns Hopkins University Press, 1966), edited with E. Thorbecke, which contained one of her many efforts to construct a computable planning model for a Third World country, in this case, Korea. But her present reputation was only firmly established with the publication of *Society, Politics, and Economic Development: A Quantitative Approach* (Johns Hopkins University Press, 1967), co-authored by C.T. Morris, which announced a new interdisciplinary framework for the quantitative analysis of the causal factors in the development process. *Society, Politics and Economic Development* analysed the statistical association between various indicators of economic development and a large variety of economic, social and political factors responsible for economic development, using cross-section data for forty-three developing countries. Adelman and Morris employed a statistical tool rarely used by economists, 'factor analysis', which has the virtue of grouping a large body of data into a smaller number of 'factors' that are capable of providing the explanations. Their findings drew attention to a number of elements that had not hitherto been regarded by development economists as critical to the development process, such as the degree of political stability and the degree of 'sophistication' of financial markets in a country. *Society, Politics and Economic Development* was followed first by *Comparative Patterns of Economic Development, 1850–1914* (Johns Hopkins University Press, 1988), again with C.T. Morris, and then by *Economic Growth and Social Equity in Developing Countries* (Stanford University Press, 1973), which applied a similar technique to the same data base in an effort to explain the shares of income accruing to the poorest households in developing countries; it demonstrated that economic growth as such does not automatically raise the income shares of the poor, even when the countries in question are semi-developed rather than underdeveloped, thus contradicting the famous Kuznets inverse-U relationship (see Kuznets, S.). The lessons of that book are amply displayed in one of Adelman's most readable and controversial articles, 'Development Economics: A Reassessment of Goals', *American Economic Review*, May 1975, a summary of her book *Redistribution before Growth: A Strategy for Developing Countries* (Martinus Nijhoff, 1978). A more recent book on *Income Distribution Policy in Developing Countries: A Case Study of Korea* (Stanford University Press, 1977), with S. Robinson, provides a specific case study of the possible conflict between equity and growth in the Third World.

Adelman was born in 1930 in Romania but took all her degrees from the University of California, Berkeley: a BS in 1949 (at the age of nineteen!), an MA in 1950, and a PhD in 1955. She began teaching at Berkeley in 1955, joined the staff at Stanford University in 1962, moved to Johns Hopkins University and, finally, to Northwestern University in 1966, where she became a professor. In 1971 she spent a year at the World Bank in Washington as Senior Economist in the Bank's Development Research Center. The following year she became a Professor of Economics at the University of Maryland. In 1977–8 she was a Fellow at the Netherlands Institute for Advanced Study in the Humanities and Social Sciences. Finally, in 1979, she returned to the University of California, Berkeley, to become Professor of Agricultural Resource Economics, a post she holds to this day. She was elected as Vice-President of the American Economic Association in 1979.

*Primary Literature*
I. Adelman, 'Confessions of an Incurable Romantic', in J.H. Kregel (ed.), *Recollections of Eminent Economists*, vol. 2 (Macmillan, 1989).

# Alchian
# Armen A.
# (1914–   )

Armen Alchian is best known to students for his introductory text-book, *University Economics* (Wadsworth, 1964; 3rd edn, 1972 abridged as *Exchange and Production*, Wadsworth, 1969; 2nd edn, 1983), written jointly with W.R. Allen, which stands out among all of its rivals by a consistent emphasis on the actual or potential role of markets as a device for organising economic life, making due allowance for the transaction and information costs involved in creating markets and the divisible or indivisible benefits to individual economic agents of operating markets.

To his fellow economists, however, Alchian is the author of a small but influential series of articles: as modern economists go, Alchian writes little but makes every publication count. His *Economic Forces at Work* (Liberty Press, 1977) reprints eighteen of his masterful papers, including such gems as 'Uncertainty, Evolution and Economic Theory' (1950) which suggested a new Darwinian justification for some of the standard assumptions of economic theory; 'The Meaning and Validity of the Inflation induced Lag of Wages' (1960), with R.A. Kessel, which exploded the myth that past inflations had accelerated economic growth by redistributing income in favour of profits; and 'Information Costs, Pricing and Resource Unemployment' (1969), which provides an explanation for Keynesian 'unemployment equilibrium' without invoking Keynes's assumption of rigid wages. 'Production, Information Costs, and Economic Organization' (1972), co-authored by H. Demsetz, is another one of Alchian's immensely influential papers: it is almost the first to take up the suggestion of R.H. Coase (q.v.) that transaction costs are the key to the creation of business firms and to think through the implications of that idea for the employment relationship between labour and management (see Demsetz, H.).

'Uncertainty, Evolution and Economic Theory', the first of these papers, must number among the five or ten most cited articles of post-war economics. Do businessmen really strive to maximise profits? If they do, certain things follow about pricing policies and the effects of particular taxes on output and price. So we can check on whether they do by investigating the impact of taxes. But such research is difficult and so, alternatively, we may try asking businessmen just what does motivate their activities. But direct inquiries of motives are as difficult and ambiguous in their results as studies of the impact of taxes. What Alchian suggested instead was the study of the 'survival process': the price system itself is a Darwinian mechanism that selects the 'fit' and rejects the 'unfit', where 'fitness' is judged in terms of the ability to make greater profits than your competitors. Not all businessmen maximise profits but those who fail to do so go bankrupt and hence, in time, we observe only profit-maximisers. This argument serves to justify the general assumption of profit maximisation without having to argue each and every counter-example. No wonder then that Alchian's article achieved immediate fame and was repeatedly invoked by Milton Friedman in an even more famous article, 'Essay on the Methodology of Positive Economics' (*Essays in Positive Economics*, University of Chicago Press, 1953), which argued that the validity of economic theories did not depend on making 'realistic' assumptions about the motivations of economic agents.

Similarly, Alchian's 'Information Costs, Pricing and Resource Unemployment' was the beginning of all later 'job search' theories of unemployment. Alchian's original insight was to note that it takes time to gather information about job opportunities at various wage rates and that time is costly; hence, much, and perhaps all, observed unemployment is simply the lengthening of search-time as job offerings become scarcer, being a rational response to rising information costs. One implication of this argument is that the existence of unemployment benefits causes still more unemployment, but this is only one of many of the controversial implications of job search theories (see Phelps, E.S.). Hence, as elsewhere, Alchian has opened up vistas that others have spent years exploring more fully. There can be no greater compliment than this.

Alchian was born in Fresno, California, in 1914 and his entire life has been spent in the State of California: a BA in 1936 and PhD in 1944 from Stanford University, a post as economist with the Rand Corporation in Santa Monica (1947–64), and, finally, a professorship at the University of California, Los Angeles, since 1958.

# Arrow, Kenneth J. (1921– )

Economists are not unaccustomed to brilliant doctoral dissertations by relatively unknown youngsters – witness Samuelson's *Foundations* and Becker's *Economics of Discrimination* – but Kenneth Arrow's doctoral thesis, *Social Choice and Individual Values* (Wiley, 1951; 2nd edn, Yale University Press, 1963), is in a class by itself. Employing the notational system of symbolic logic, at the time unfamiliar to economists, Arrow proposed to solve a question in politics which no economist and few political scientists had ever posed: suppose all individuals can rank all states of the world in order of preference, is it possible to find a voting rule that will always select one of those states as 'most preferred'?

The most popular voting rule, majority choice, may easily fail to express a unique social preference. Consider, for example, the simple case where three individuals A, B, and C are asked to vote for three alternative states of the world, $x$, $y$, and $z$. Now suppose A prefers $x$ to $y$ and $y$ to $z$, B also prefers $y$ to $z$ but instead prefers $z$ to $x$, whereas C like B prefers $z$ to $x$ but like A prefers $x$ to $y$. It is easily checked that $x$ wins over $y$ by the two votes of A and C, $y$ wins over $z$ by the two votes of A and B, but, unfortunately, $x$ does not therefore win over $z$ because $z$ in turn wins over $x$ by the two votes of B and C. In other words, in this simple case of three voters and three alternative options, the democratic method of majority choice leads to a stalemate.

What Arrow now demonstrated was that this stalemate can occur, not just under a constitution based on the principle of majority rule, but under every conceivable constitution except that of dictatorship: it is logically impossible to add up or otherwise combine the choices of individuals into an unambiguous social choice except by rigging the 'constitution', for example, by confining all choices to two and only two options, either directly or indirectly through political parties and parliamentary representatives.

Arrow's 'impossibility theorem' appeared to have such startling consequences for both political philosophy and welfare economics that literally hundreds of papers have been written to refute it. But Arrow's theorem has withstood all technical criticisms and has never been decisively challenged on its own grounds. Its significance for welfare economics, however, is frequently misunderstood as implying the impossibility of a 'social welfare function' (see Bergson, A.). But Arrow's 'constitutional function' is not identical with Bergson's 'social welfare function'. Bergson's 'social welfare function' says that a competitive equilibrium can achieve any Pareto-optimal solution (see Lerner, A.P.), provided the original endowments of income in the economy are altered by lump-sum transfers of income: the social welfare function expresses the community's agreement on the size and direction of these transfers. Obviously, there is no sense in which it is impossible to form such a function. However, if we ask: how are we to get the community's agreement on lump-sum income transfers?, then indeed Arrow's 'constitutional function' becomes directly relevant. In short, the 'impossibility theorem' is a theorem about politics, not economics.

After making his name with *Social Choice and Individual Values*, Arrow joined forces with Gerard Debreu to rework the standard 'existence proofs' for general equilibrium, principally in a classic paper, 'Existence of Equilibrium for a Competitive Economy', *Econometrica*, July 1954. Leon Walras, the nineteenth-century inventor of general equilibrium theory, believed that one can prove the existence of simultaneous equilibrium in all the markets of an economy simply by counting equations and unknowns to make sure that one has as many known demand-and-supply equations as unknown prices to be determined. It had long been known that an adequate proof must go beyond counting equations and unknowns but a rigorous proof of the existence of a general equilibrium solution had nevertheless defeated everyone before Arrow and Debreu.

By using new mathematical techniques, Arrow and Debreu discovered that the existence of multi-market equilibrium under conditions of perfect competition requires forward markets in all goods and services, that is, markets in which we can pay today to obtain delivery tomorrow or accept delivery today for the promise of payment tomorrow. This finding threw doubt on the practical significance of general equilibrium theory and much of Arrow's work was concerned to demonstrate that general equilibrium theory was nevertheless 'robust', that is, of relevance even to economies with missing forward markets. This is the burden of a later book, *General Competitive Analysis* (Holden-Day, 1971; Oliver & Boyd, 1971), co-authored with Frank Hahn.

In the interim between the original article with Debreu in the 1950s and the book with Hahn in the 1970s, Arrow's work concentrated on the implications of risk aversion for economic activity as it relates to medical and other kinds of insurance. *Essays in the Theory of Risk-bearing* (North-Holland, 1971) sums up his work in this area. Optimal inventory and optimal social investment policies have been other interests, as reflected in *Studies in the Mathematical Theory of Inventory and Production* (Stanford University Press, 1958), authored jointly with S. Karlin and H. Scarf, and *Public Investment, the Rate of Return, and Optimal Fiscal Policy* (Johns Hopkins University Press, 1970), authored jointly with M. Kurz. *The Limits of Organization* (W.W. Norton, 1974) is less well known than his other works, but undeservedly so. A much-studied article, 'The Economic Implications of Learning by Doing, *Review of Economic Studies*, June 1962, marked Arrow's contribution to the modern theory of economic growth. Finally, he was one of the four authors of a famous paper on 'Capital–Labor Substitution and Economic Efficiency', *Review of Economics and Statistics*, August 1961, which introduced the economics profession to the CES (constant elasticity of substitution) production function, the first step beyond the Cobb–Douglas production function in over thirty years (see Douglas, P.H.). These papers and some 100 others are available in his six volumes of *Collected Papers* (Harvard University Press, 1983–5).

Born in New York City in 1921, Arrow graduated from City College, New York in 1940 at the early age of nineteen. He went on to do postgraduate work in statistics at Columbia University under Harold Hotelling (q.v.) but wartime service in the US Air Force interrupted his studies for almost five years. Returning to Columbia after the war, there were further delays before he hit on social choice as the topic of his thesis. He joined the Cowles Commission in Chicago in 1947 (see Marschak, J.) and then moved to Stanford University in 1949, becoming a professor at Stanford in 1953. In 1968 he took up a professorship at Harvard University, only to move back again to Stanford in 1979. He has been honoured throughout his career but increasingly so in the latter years: President of the Econometric Society in 1956, winner of the John Bates Clark medal of the American Economic Association for the most distinguished work by an economist under the age of forty in 1957, President in turn of the Econometric Society in 1956, the Institute of Management Sciences in 1963, the American Economic Association in 1973, and the Western Economic Association in 1980, a recipient of honorary degrees from nine universities, and, to cap it all, the Nobel Prize in Economics, shared jointly with John Hicks in 1972.

*Primary Literature*
K.J. Arrow, 'My Evolution as an Economist', in W. Breit and R.W. Spencer (eds), *Lives of the Laureates: Ten Nobel Economists* (MIT Press, 1990); K.J. Arrow, 'I Know a Hawk from a Handsaw', in M. Szenberg (ed.), *Eminent Economists: Their Life Philosophies* (Cambridge University Press, 1992).

*Secondary Literature*
C.C. von Weizsäcker, 'Kenneth Arrow's Contributions to Economics', in H.W. Spiegel and W.J. Samuels (eds), *Contemporary Economists in Perspective*, vol. 1 (JAI Press, 1984); G.R. Feiwel (ed.), *Arrow and the Foundations of the Theory of Economic Policy* (Macmillan, 1987); G.R. Feiwel (ed.), *Arrow and the Ascent of Modern Economic Theory* (Macmillan, 1987); B.S. Katz (ed.), *Nobel Laureates in Economic Sciences: A Bibliographical Dictionary* (Garland Publishing, 1989).

# Bain, Joe S. (1912–91)

Joe Bain's *Barriers to New Competition: Their Character and Consequences in Manufacturing Industries* (Harvard University Press, 1956) was one of the first studies clearly to identify and measure barriers to entry into industries and to treat them, not just as an important dimension of market structure, but as having a predictable effect on the conduct and performance of business firms. 'Barriers to entry' may take the form of large setting-up costs but they may also consist of the threat to cut prices and to impose large losses on newcomers. Monopoly power is desirable for the sake of the higher profits it brings but these high profits also attract new entrants, which tends to erode profits. It is open to question, therefore, whether entry barriers actually result in above-average profit rates. Bain was in fact one of the first to test the widely held belief that profit rates are higher in concentrated industries, a topic which has since attracted an enormous literature. Finally, Bain has also repeatedly attacked the even more widely held thesis that monopoly, oligopoly, or simply concentration of industry is always and everywhere the result of technical economies of scale either in production or in marketing; frequently, it is the result of a product innovation and the subsequent, cumulative advantages of being the first in the field; at other times, it is simply the result of public regulation, discouraging new entrants into the industry. Bain's many *Essays on Price Theory and*

*Industrial Organization* (Little, Brown, 1972) virtually constitute by themselves an entire course in industrial organisation.

Early in his career, he published an intermediate economic textbook entitled *Pricing, Distribution and Employment: Economics of an Enterprise System* (Henry Holt, 1948; 2nd edn, 1953). Later, he wrote an intermediate text on *Industrial Organization* (Wiley, 1959; 2nd edn, 1968, amplified into *Industrial Organisation: A Treatise*, with T. David Qualls (JAI Press, 1987, 2 vols), which rapidly became the prototype textbook of industrial organisation economics. He also authored, together with R.E. Caves and J. Margolis, a study of *Northern California's Water Industry: The Comparative Efficiency of Public Enterprise in Developing a Scarce Natural Resource* (Johns Hopkins University Press, 1966).

Bain was born in 1912 in Spokane, Washington, and received his BA from the University of California, Los Angeles in 1935, and his MA and PhD from Harvard University in 1939 and 1940 respectively. He started teaching at the University of California, Berkeley, in 1939 and became a Professor of Economics at Berkeley in 1945. He remained at Berkeley during the entire thirty-six years of his academic career, except for a year at Harvard University in 1951–2, retiring in 1975.

He was a member of the Editorial Board of the *American Economic Review* during 1951–4, was elected as Vice-President of the American Economic Association in 1968, and was designated a Distinguished Fellow of the Association in 1982.

*Secondary Literature*
W.G. Shepherd, 'Bain, Joe Staten', in J. Eatwell, M. Milgate and P. Newman (eds), *The New Palgrave: A Dictionary of Economics*, vol. 1 (Macmillan, 1987).

# Baumol, William J. (1922– )

William Baumol is best known for the 'sales maximisation' hypothesis, the first rigorously formulated theory of the behaviour of business firms with objectives other than profit maximisation, and the 'unbalanced growth' model, which demonstrates that the unequal opportunities for technical progress in different sectors of the economy serves to explain the chronic fiscal problems of cities, educational systems, performing arts organisations, etcetera. He is almost as well known, however, as a brilliant expositor of ideas who translates the mysteries of management science and operations research into the language of economics. His best-selling intermediate textbook, *Economic Theory and Operations Analysis* (Prentice-Hall, 1961; 4th edn, 1977), has long acted as an effective bridge between students of business practice and students of economics. Moreover, in countless articles, he has made recent developments in mathematical economics accessible to literary economists, while contributing at the same time to our understanding of the history of mathematical economics.

The 'sales maximisation' hypothesis was the outcome of Baumol's consultancy work in the business world. In his experience, firms did not respond to changing conditions in the ways predicted by orthodox theory. What they seemed to be doing was to maximise sales revenue almost regardless of cost outlays. In the final analysis, of course, cost outlays do matter and, therefore, Baumol hypothesised that firms behave as if they are trying to maximise sales, subject to the condition that minimum profit targets are being met. Thus, firms operating in an expanding market do not behave in the same way as would a profit-maximising firm; nor do they respond to a decline in demand in the same way as a profit-maximising firm. Baumol's hypothesis was rigorously spelled out on lines identical to the textbook theory and this is precisely why it made an impact on the profession out of all proportion to the impact of earlier critics of the profit-maximising theory of the firm. The implications of the sales maximisation hypothesis have been further explored by others and the upshot of the discussion is that the standard theory of profit maximisation no longer stands alone as an explanation of short-run price determination: it must be replaced, or at least complemented, by the theory of sales maximisation.

Baumol was born in 1922 in New York City. He took his BSS from the College of the City of New York in 1942, and his PhD from the University of London in 1949. His PhD thesis on *Welfare Economics and the Theory of the State* (Harvard University Press, 1965) was an early statement of the significance of 'market failure' under perfect competition. He began teaching at the London School of Economics in 1947 but left in 1949 to join the faculty of Princeton University, where he became a professor in 1954. Since 1971 he has also held a joint appointment at New York University.

He was the author of *Economic Dynamics: An Introduction* (Macmillan, 1951; 2nd edn, 1959), a path-breaking introductory textbook on economic models expressed in difference equations. *Business Behavior, Value and Growth* (Harcourt, Brace & World, 1959; 2nd edn, 1966) reprinted the famous paper on sales maximisation. In 1966, he published, jointly with W.G. Bowen, an influential book on *The Performing Arts: The Economic Dilemma* (Twentieth Century Fund, 1966), the argument of which was generalised in a later essay, 'Macroeconomics of Unbalanced Growth: The Anatomy of Urban Crisis', *American Economic Review*, June 1967. This was followed by *Precursors in Mathematical Economics: An Anthology* (London School of Economics, 1968), with S.M. Goldfeld, in which the editorial notes are brief masterpieces in the history of economic thought. *The Theory of Environmental Policy* (Prentice-Hall, 1975), with W.E. Oates, and *Economics, Environmental Policy and the Quality of Life* (Prentice-Hall, 1979), with W.E. Oates and S.A. Batey Blackman, are major works on pricing-solutions to environmental problems, a subject which has become a dominant theme of Baumol's work in the last decade. More recently still, he has published a major book on the structure of industries, *Contestable Markets and the Theory of Industry Structure* (Harcourt, Brace, Jovanovich, 1982), with J.C. Panzar and R.D. Willig, which has already generated a lively controversy. His *Productivity and American Leadership: The Long View* (MIT Press, 1989), with S.A. Batey Blackman and E.N. Wolff, and *Entrepreneurship, Management and the Structure of Payoffs* (MIT Press, 1993) are further testimonies of his abiding interest in industrial organisation. Finally, his *Economics: Principles and Policy* (Harcourt Brace Jovanovich, 1979), with A.S. Blinder, is one of the four or five introductory texts in economics that have stood the test of time. His numerous journal papers are collected in *Selected Economic Writings of William J. Baumol*, ed. E.E. Bailey (New York University Press, 1976) and *Microtheory: Applications and Origins* (MIT Press, 1986).

Baumol was President of the Eastern Economics Association in 1978, President of the Association of Environmental and Resource Economists in 1979, Vice-President and then President of the American Economic Association in 1967 and 1981, and has received honorary degrees from several American and European universities. He is also a talented wood sculptor and painter, who has exhibited his paintings at galleries around the world.

*Primary Literature*
W.J. Baumol, 'On the Career of a Microeconomist', in J.A. Kregel (ed.), *Recollections of Eminent Economists, 2* (Macmillan, 1989).

*Secondary Literature*
E.E. Bailey and R.D Willig, 'William Baumol', in W.J. Samuels (ed.), *New Horizons in Economic Thought* (Edward Elgar, 1992); R. Towse (ed.), *Baumol's Cost Disease: Arts and Other Victims* (Edward Elgar, 1997).

# Becker,
# Gary S.
# (1930– )

Gary Becker is one of the most original minds in modern economics and his writings have the unique quality of opening up new horizons in economic analysis by relating widely observed but apparently unconnected phenomena to the operation of some single, general principle. He did it first in his doctoral dissertation, *The Economics of Discrimination* (University of Chicago Press, 1957; 2nd edn, 1971), in which he attempted to square the competitive model of labour markets with the observed facts of pay differentials between white and black workers by the simple device of introducing a 'taste' for discrimination into the utility functions of both employers and employees; this book at first fell on deaf ears but eventually it sparked off a whole series of explanations to account for the persistence of racial and sexual earning differences in labour markets. He did it a second time when he developed some earlier hints by others (see Mincer, J.) into a general theory of human capital formation via schooling and labour training; his book *Human Capital* (Columbia University Press, 1964; new expanded edn, University of Chicago Press, 1993), served as the starting point for what has been aptly described as the 'human investment revolution in economic thought', which swept over economics in the 1960s. He did it a third time with 'Crime and Punishment: An Economic Approach', *Journal of Political Economy*, March/April 1968, which suggested the startling view that crime is just another occupation which some people take up for perfectly rational reasons, given the expected benefits of crime, the expected costs of crime in terms of the likelihood of arrest and punishment, and their particular risk-preferences. And he did it a fourth time in 'A Theory of the Allocation of Time', *Economic Journal*, September 1965, a paper which explored the division of labour among members of a family, a social institution which economics had hitherto almost totally neglected.

Becker has built on this last article ever since, adding first the decision to have children, then the decision to give those children education, and, finally, the initial decision to marry and the ultimate decision to dissolve the marriage by divorce, culminating in a complete explanation of virtually all aspects of family behaviour. *The Economic Approach to Human Behaviour* (University of Chicago Press, 1976), his first statement of that theory, has since been followed by an even more comprehensive *Treatise on the Family* (Harvard University Press, 1981). Becker's 'new economics of the family' parts company with the traditional conception of the family as a one-person consumption unit and instead views the family as a multi-person production unit, literally producing 'joint utility' with the aid of inputs consisting of the time, skills and knowledge of different members of the family, after which the theory of production can be usefully applied to household behaviour.

Except for twelve years at Columbia University (1957–69), Becker has spent his entire academic career since his first teaching appointment in 1954 at the University of Chicago and his work is generally regarded as typical of the outlook of the Chicago School. Now, the 'Chicago School' usually implies a belief in markets as a solution to most economic problems and a conviction that the market mechanism, despite the enormous growth of government activity, is in fact the dominant mode of economic organisation in the Western world. It may also imply the belief that the economist's standard assumption of 'economic man', a rational agent who always seeks to maximise his advantages, is capable of explaining all aspects of human behaviour and not simply economic behaviour. It is the latter rather than the former belief which characterises Becker's contributions to economics and which has sometimes been greeted with accusations of 'empire-building' and 'intellectual imperialism'. It is too early to say whether this accusation is justified since here, as elsewhere in economics, the proof of the pudding is in the eating and what economists do successfully ultimately determines what is or is not economics. Suffice it to say that Becker has opened up an area of research that was formerly the sole concern of sociologists, anthropologists, and psychologists and, in so doing, has done more to extend the boundaries of economics than almost any other economist.

Becker was born in Pottstown, Pennsylvania, in 1930, completed his BA from Princeton University in 1951 and his PhD from the University of Chicago in 1955. He became a professor at Columbia University in 1960 at the age of thirty and has held a professorship at Chicago since 1970. He is a founding member of the National Academy of Education, and won the distinguished John Bates Clark medal of the American Economic Association in 1967, also serving as a President of the Association in 1987. He was named Vice-President of the Mont Pèlerin Society in 1989 and was awarded the Nobel Prize in Economics in 1992.

*Secondary Literature*
J.R. Shackleton, 'Gary S. Becker: The Economist as Empire-Builder', in J.R. Shackleton and G. Locksley (eds), *Twelve Contemporary Economists* (Macmillan, 1981; Wiley, Halsted Press, 1981).

# Bergson,
# Abram
# (1914– )

Abram Bergson made his name as a graduate student at the age of twenty-four with a classic paper on welfare economics, 'A Reformulation of Certain Aspects of Welfare Economics', *Quarterly Journal of Economics*, February 1938 – and this was his second published paper! What he accomplished in this essay was, first of all, to write down what he called a 'social welfare function', a precise formulation of what economists mean by 'social welfare'. Bergson's 'social welfare function' is a function only of the utility or welfare of individuals and the problem is: how are we to add up such diverse things as the welfare of individuals? If utility or welfare were measurable in 'cardinal numbers' – I know that I like apples better than pears and I even know that I like them twice as much as pears – the problem would be half-solved but there would still remain the question of interpersonal comparisons of utility – yes, I know my cardinal preference for apples over pears and you know yours but how can we compare each other's cardinal preferences? However, 'cardinal' utility had fallen out of favour with economists by 1938 and the standard assumption, to which Bergson was also committed, was that utility is only measurable in 'ordinal' numbers of 'more' or 'less', not how much or how much less. So the problem of the social welfare function is : how do we add up the welfare of individuals when each individual has his own unique ordinal system of preferences for different commodities?

What Bergson demonstrated in this article was that the adding-up problem is only solvable if we attach weights to each individual's welfare; since the market mechanism does not generate such interpersonal weights (other than dollars of income), we must presumably establish them through the ballot box. He then asked himself what could be said about social welfare without attaching interpersonal weights to the individual welfare functions and how much more could be said if there were agreement about how to compare the welfare of different individuals. In other words, he introduced the now familiar distinction between the 'efficiency' and the 'equity' effects of an economic change by showing that propositions about maximum social welfare require definite value judgements about the incomes accruing to different individuals as a result of the change.

In effect, Bergson's paper created what soon became known as the 'new' welfare economics (see Hicks, J.R.; Kaldor, N.; Lerner, A.P.), which avoided both the 'cardinal' measurement of utility and interpersonal comparisons of welfare. Bergson subsequently applied the New Welfare Economics to the famous debate about market socialism in the 1930s (see Hayek, F.A.; Lerner, A.P.) and the measurement of the welfare losses of monopoly under capitalism; these and other influential papers on applied welfare economics are reprinted in his *Essays in Normative Economics* (Harvard University Press, 1966) and *Welfare, Planning and Employment: Selected Essays in Economic Theory* (MIT Press, 1982).

Work in welfare economics was only half, or less than half, of Bergson's lifetime output. Beginning with *The Structure of Soviet Wages: A Study in Socialist Economics* (Harvard University Press, 1944), and going on to *The Real National Income of Soviet Russia since 1928* (Harvard University Press, 1961), *The Economics of Soviet Planning* (Yale University Press, 1964), *Productivity and the Social System: The USSR and the West* (Harvard University Press, 1978), and *Planning and Performance in Socialist Economies: The USSR and Eastern Europe* (Unwin Hyman, 1989), Bergson became one of America's leading experts on the Soviet economy and, in particular, on the measurement of national income in the USSR. As Director of the Russian Center at Harvard University from 1964–8 and 1977–80, he encouraged countless studies of the Soviet economy and bred a whole generation of American Sovietologists.

Bergson was born in 1914 in Baltimore, Maryland, and received his BA in 1933 at the age of nineteen from Johns Hopkins University. He took his MA in 1935 and his PhD in 1940 from Harvard University. After teaching at the University of Texas from 1940–2, he worked as chief of the Russian Economic Subdivision of the US Office of Strategic Services during World War II. After the war, he joined the economics faculty at Columbia University. In 1956 he left Columbia to become Professor of Economics at Harvard University where he remained until retirement in 1981.

He was a Member of the Social Science Advisory Board of the US Arms Control and Disarmament Agency 1966–73 and Chairman of the Board 1971–3. He won an Award for Distinguished Contributions to Soviet Studies from the American Academy of Arts and Sciences in 1975 and an honorary degree from the University of Windsor in 1979. He has lectured widely at universities all over the USA and Europe.

*Primary Literature*
A. Bergson, 'Recollections and Reflections of a Comparativist', in M. Szenberg (ed.), *Eminent Economists: Their Life Philosophies* (Cambridge University Press, 1992).

*Secondary Literature*
M. Ellman, 'Bergson, Abram', in J. Eatwell, M. Milgate and P. Newman (eds), *The New Palgrave: A Dictionary of Economics*, vol. 1 (Macmillan, 1987).

# Boulding, Kenneth Ewart (1910–93)

Kenneth Boulding's writings throughout his long career constantly tended to enlarge the scope of economic science in an effort to work towards a more general social science of which traditional economics would only be a part, albeit an important part. Born in Liverpool, England, in 1910 in a deeply religious Methodist family, Boulding turned to Quakerism as a young man and remained a passionate if unorthodox Christian all his life. He gained a scholarship to Oxford University in 1928, graduated in 1931, and immediately published his first paper in economics in the prestigious *Economic Journal* edited by Keynes – he was twenty-two years old. A fellowship took him across the Atlantic for two productive years at Chicago and Harvard. After a spell at Edinburgh University, he returned permanently to America, teaching at Colgate University, New York (1937–41), Fisk University (1942–3), Iowa State College and McGill University (1943–9), the University of Michigan (1949–77) and finally, from 1977, the University of Colorado, retiring in 1980. At Colgate, he published *Economic Analysis* (Harper, 1941; 4th edn, 1966), an introductory textbook, the first half of which is remarkable in showing how far one can go in economics by using no tool more complicated than that of demand and supply. Oddly enough, there is not so much as a mention of Keynes in the first edition of the book; Keynes only makes an appearance in the second edition, published in the same year as Samuelson's more successful *Economics: An Introductory Analysis* (1948). *Economic Analysis* went through several editions, reaching its final form with the fourth edition of 1966 in which Boulding, like Samuelson before him, claimed to have blended Keynesian and neoclassical economic theory into a coherent and lasting synthesis.

During World War II, Boulding adhered steadfastly to pacifism and was forced in consequence to resign his wartime post as economist with the Economic and Financial Section of the League of Nations, Princeton (1941–2). The close of the war saw the publication of *The Economics of Peace* (Prentice-Hall, 1945), the first of a whole series of books displaying the characteristic Boulding style of using simple models as metaphors to convey overarching themes that stretch the very boundaries of economics. *A Reconstruction of Economics* (Wiley, 1950) urged the subject down a new theoretical path, emphasising stocks rather than flows, assets rather than incomes, and the share of wages and profit in national income, rather than the prices of labour and capital. The book fell on deaf ears, being in some sense too original and too out of step with the pro-Keynesian temper of the times.

The year before, he received the John Bates Clark medal of the American Economic Association, given every other year to 'that American economist under the age of forty who is adjudged to have made a significant contribution to economic thought and knowledge'. Having now been officially admitted to the front ranks of living economists, his efforts seemed increasingly to move away from the traditional concerns of economists. *The Organizational Revolution* (Harper, 1953) was a maverick study, which largely explored the ethical implications of Big Business. *Image* (University of Michigan Press, 1961) was a contribution to the philosophy of the social sciences, exploring the images we conjure up to study social behaviour. Next came *Conflict and Defence: A General Theory* (Harper & Row, 1962), *The Meaning of the Twentieth Century* (Harper & Row, 1965) and *Ecodynamics* (Sage, 1978), both of which represented his abiding concern to integrate the economic concept of price equilibrium with the biological concept of ecological equilibrium. His 1966 paper, 'The Economics of the Spaceship Earth', in H. Jarrett (ed.), *Environmental Quality in a Growing Economy*, (Johns Hopkins University Press), with its striking image of the earth as a closed system, was perhaps more responsible than any other publication for the explosion of environmental economics in the late 1960s. Later, Boulding became preoccupied at the University of Colorado with the development of *A Preface to Grants Economics: The Economy of Love and Fear* (Praeger, 1981). The 'exchange system' studied in standard economics, Boulding argues, is only one of the three major modes of organising social life. The other two are the 'threat system' of war and the 'integrative system' of Grants Economics, that is the one-way gifts of money, goods, and services, represented by unilateral government transfer payments, bequests, charitable donations, and the like. Moreover, such one-way transfers are not exceptions but rather represent indispensable complements to the two-way transfers of the 'exchange system'. Grant Economics then is the study of the role of gifts in modern economies.

Boulding's lifetime output has been enormous: more than a dozen books and over one thousand articles. His *Collected Papers*, eds F.R. Glahe and L. Singell (Colorado Associated University Press, 1971, 1973, 1974, 1975) runs to five volumes, and there was enough incidental material left over to make a sixth volume: *Beast, Ballads, and Bouldingisms*, ed. R.P. Beilock (Transaction Books, 1980). Despite Boulding's frequently expressed disdain for standard economics, he was named President of the American Economic Association in 1968. He also served as President of the Society for General System Research from 1955 to 1959 and the Association for the Study of the Grants Economy from 1970 to 1989. He nevertheless paid a high price for his wide-ranging interests: his fellow economists respected him, enjoyed his doggerels (he never stopped writing rhymed poetry), but rarely read his books with the attention they deserve. He has remained to this day the Great Outsider among modern economists, a voice crying in the wilderness. It may be that for all his path-breaking explorations in general systems theory, ecological interactions, and the like, his ideas lacked the relevance to immediate circumstances and the fund of researchable hypotheses that makes for a 'school' of thought.

*Primary Literature*
K.E. Boulding, 'Kenneth E. Boulding', in P. Arestis and M. Sawyer (eds), *A Biographical Dictionary of Dissenting Economists* (Edward Elgar, 1992); K.E. Boulding, 'From Chemistry to Economics and Beyond', in M. Szenberg (ed.), *Eminent Economists: Their Life Philosophies* (Cambridge University Press, 1992).

*Secondary Literature*
C.E. Kerman, *Creative Tension: The Life and Thought of Kenneth Boulding* (Basic Books, 1974), ch. 5; L. Silk, *The Economists* (Basic Books, 1974), ch. 5; A. Rappoport, 'Boulding, Kenneth Ewart', in J. Eatwell, M. Milgate and P. Newman, *The New Palgrave: A Dictionary of Economics*, vol. 1 (Macmillan, 1987).

# Bowles, Samuels (1939– )

Samuel Bowles is a leading 'radical' economist and a prominent figure of the Union of Radical Political Economics, a professional association of dissenting economists which publishes the *Review of Radical Political Economics*. Bowles was not always a radical: *Planning Educational Systems for Economic Growth* (Harvard University Press, 1969) and *Notes and Problems in Microeconomic Theory* (Markham, 1970; North-Holland, 1980), with D. Kendrick and P. Dixon, are perfectly orthodox books in the economics of education and advanced microeconomics. But somewhere in the late 1960s, notably in a frequently cited paper, 'Schooling and Inequality from Generation to Generation', *Journal of Political Economy*, May/June 1972, a new radical note made its appearance.

More recently Bowles with Gintis and other radical economists has developed the concept of the incomplete employment contract into a veritable alternative paradigm of 'contested exchange', alternative that is to the Walrasian concept of mutually beneficial exchange. *Understanding Capitalism: Competition, Command and Change in the US Economy* (Harper & Row 1985, 1985), with R.C. Edwards, *Democracy and Capitalism* (Basic Books, 1986), with H. Gintis, and *After the Waste Land: A Democratic Economics for the year 2000* (M.E. Sharpe, 1991), with T. Weisskopf and D. Gordon, set forth a new microeconomic foundation to the analysis of contemporary capitalism and a new macroeconomic forecast of its future development.

The publication of *Schooling in Capitalist America* (Basic Books, 1976), written jointly with H. Gintis, marked a complete break with orthodox economics. In this work, Bowles and Gintis argued in favour of the 'correspondence thesis' – the organisation and reward system of schools in a capitalist economy 'corresponds' with or virtually duplicates the organisation and reward system of factories – and reinterpreted the entire history of American education as a response to business pressure on the schools, concluding that effective educational reform is possible only under a regime of participatory socialism. The book has been widely translated and has become a minor best-seller, at least among sociologists if not economists. More recently, Bowles and Gintis have turned their attention to Marxian economics, arguing that it stands in need of serious revision, among which are its obsession with the labour theory of value and its neglect of the family as an economic institution. One of their important papers, 'Structure and Practice in the Labor Theory of Value', *Review of Radical Economics*, March 1981, reveals them as being miles away from the orthodox Marxists of yesterday (see Dobb, M.H.). One difference is their stress on sexual and racial discrimination in labour markets as being necessary and not incidental features of capitalism. Since the employment contract is 'incomplete' (see Demsetz, H.) and since the conflict of interest between workers and capitalists is irreconcilable – a typical Marxian element in the argument – capitalists must prevent concerted action by workers to realise their common interests because, once that happens, the work force is uncontrollable. The golden rule for controlling the work force is to 'divide and conquer'. Hence, argue Bowles and Gintis, capitalism cannot dispense with sexual, racial and ethnic discrimination between workers.

Bowles was born in 1939 in New Haven, Connecticut. He obtained his BA from Yale University in 1960 and his PhD from Harvard University in 1965, his doctoral dissertation being an early version of his first book, *Planning Educational Systems*. He began teaching at Harvard in 1971. In 1974, he left Harvard to head the Department of Economics at the University of Massachusetts, Amherst.

He was a Member of the Editorial Board of the *Review for Radical Political Economics* 1974–6, and has been a Member of the Steering Committee of the Center for Popular Economics since 1978.

*Primary Literature*
S. Bowles, 'Samuel Bowles', in P. Arestis and M. Sawyer (eds), *A Biographical Dictionary of Dissenting Economists* (Edward Elgar, 1992).

# Buchanan,
# James M.
# (1919– )

James Buchanan is the founder of 'public choice theory', the economic study of nonmarket decision-making or, to put it simply, the attempt to complete the theory of market exchange with a corresponding theory of the functioning of political markets. What makes public choice theory economics and not just fancy political science is that it is squarely based on the standard economist's assumption of man as a rational, utility-maximising agent. Individuals agree to assign the monopoly of force in society to a government because they believe it will serve their self-interest; in so doing, they accept a set of rules, a constitution. Why and how such rules are adopted, and whether some rules are better than others, is the subject of Buchanan and Gordon Tullock's path-breaking book, *The Calculus of Consent: Logical Foundations of Constitutional Democracy* (University of Michigan Press, 1962).

The economic analysis of constitutional choice is only part of public choice theory. In a long series of books – *Public Finance in a Democratic Process* (University of North Carolina Press, 1966), *The Demand and Supply of Public Goods* (Rand McNally, 1968), *Cost and Choice* (Markham, 1969; University of Chicago Press, 1979), *Theory of Public Choice: Political Applications of Economics* (University of Michigan Press, 1972), with R.P. Tollison, *The Limits of Liberty* (University of Chicago Press, 1975), *Freedom in Constitutional Contract* (Texas

A&M University Press, 1977), *Democracy in Deficits: The Political Legacy of Lord Keynes* (Academic Press, 1977), with R.E. Wagner, and *The Reason of Rules: Constitutional Political Economy* (Cambridge University Press, 1985), both with G. Brennan *The Power to Tax* (Cambridge University Press, 1980), – Buchanan has employed the theory to attack virtually every aspect of public sector economics, including the political process which lies behind the determination of tax and spending levels.

One constant theme is the notion that all costs are basically subjective, that opportunity costs exist inside people's heads, that they are only identical to prices paid in the market in long-run perfectly competitive equilibrium. This makes mincemeat of the standard doctrine of marginal cost pricing of public utilities (see Hotelling, H.; Lerner, A.P.) and more or less takes us back to square one in applied welfare economics. As a matter of fact, Buchanan takes the view that economists have not so far talked much sense about public finance.

Early in his career, Buchanan's work was deeply influenced by his study of certain nineteenth-century European and particularly Italian writers on public finance whose approach to questions of taxation was totally different from that of leading Anglo-American writers: the European authors emphasised a concept of government based on mutual agreement among citizens in which taxes are seen as 'payments' for services rendered by government. In consequence, Buchanan has argued that unanimity is the only really defensible 'calculus of consent' but that a political democracy based on majority rule may nevertheless be freely chosen by everyone if minority rights are adequately protected. The question then becomes that of discovering those constitutional rules which preserve the original consensus. Buchanan has no difficulty in showing that the growth of government activity in recent years has departed widely from this 'optimal' constitution and his writings, therefore, abound in suggestions for additional constitutional constraints on government and its multifarious agencies. Indeed, he has called for a 'constitutional revolution' to reassess the entire spectrum of constitutional rights of individuals.

Buchanan was born in Murfreesboro, Tennessee, in 1919 and has never completely lost a touch of Southern drawl in his speech. He received his BA from the University of Middle Tennessee in 1940, his MA from the University of Tennessee in 1941, and his PhD from the University of Chicago in 1948. In 1955 he spent a year in Italy as a Fulbright Scholar to study the European tradition of public finance. Returning from Italy in 1956, he became a Professor of Economics and Director of the Thomas Jefferson Center of Political Economy at the University of Virginia and proceeded to lay the foundations of public choice theory. In 1962, having published *The Calculus of Consent*, he founded the Public Choice Society with Gordon Tullock and promoted a new journal called *Public Choice*, which stimulated others to work in the field. In 1969, Buchanan became a Professor and Director of the Center for Study of Public Choice, first at the Virginia Polytechnic Institute and State University and then at George Mason University in Fairfax, Virginia. A President of the Southern Economic Association in 1963, a Vice-President of the American Economic Association in 1972, President of the Mont Pèlerin Society from 1984 to 1986, Buchanan has lectured at universities all over the world, while producing a steady flow of articles and books which have gradually enlarged the scope of public choice theory to the point where it now forms a recognised and well-defined sub-discipline within economies. In 1986 he received the Nobel Prize in Economics.

Some would argue that public choice theory is too preoccupied with normative questions of how collective choices *ought* to be made instead of addressing the positive questions of the *actual* effects of government behaviour on the economy. But whatever the ultimate verdict on public choice theory, there can be little doubt that it now forms a definite tradition connected with other straws in the wind, such as the economic theory of property rights (see Alchian, A.A.; Demsetz, H.), the economics of law (see Posner, R.A.) and the economics of organisations (see Simon, H.A.).

*Primary Literature*
J. Buchanan, 'Better than Ploughing', in J.A. Kregel (ed.), *Recollections of Eminent Economists*, vol. 2 (Macmillan, 1985); J. Buchanan, 'Born Again Economist', in W. Breit and R.W. Spencer (eds), *Lives of the Laureates: Ten Nobel Economists* (MIT Press, 1990).

*Secondary Literature*
G. Locksley, 'Individuals, Contracts and Constitutions: the Political Economy of James M. Buchanan', in J.R. Shackleton and G. Locksley (eds), *Twelve Contemporary Economists* (Macmillan, 1981; Wiley,

Halsted Press, 1981); D.G. Mueller, 'On Buchanan', in H.W. Spiegel and W.J. Samuels (eds), *Contemporary Economists in Perspective*, vol. 2 (JAI Press, 1984); D. Reisman, *The Political Economy of James Buchanan* (Macmillan, 1988); T. Romer, 'On James Buchanan's Contribution to Public Economics', *Journal of Economic Perspectives*, Fall 1988; L. Rittenberg, 'James McGill Buchanan', in B.S. Katz (ed.), *Nobel Laureates in Economic Sciences* (Garland, 1989).

# Burns,
# Arthur F.
# (1904–87)

As Chairman of the Board of Governors of the Federal Reserve System 1970–8, Arthur Burns presided throughout the 1970s over America's struggle against rising inflation in the face of chronic unemployment. The Chairman of the Fed. is always in the hot-seat of monetary policy in the United States but Burns' intimate knowledge of the Washington scene, aided by three years as Chairman of President Eisenhower's Council of Economic Advisors in the 1950s and a year as personal adviser to President Nixon in the late 1960s, allowed him to promote the post into that of the maker and breaker of the US government's economic policy. For those eight years, he simply was the most powerful economist in the USA.

It is doubtful that he would ever have reached this summit of power in policy-making were it not for the fact that he had earlier established a firm reputation as an authority on business cycles. His massive book, *Measuring Business Cycles* (National Bureau of Economic Research, 1946), co-authored with W.C. Mitchell, crowned a decade of work at the National Bureau on 'reference cycles', distilling the large number of statistical indicators of booms and slumps into a single signal of the turning points in business cycles. Although the book was vigorously attacked by Tjalling Koopmans as 'Measurement Without Theory', *Review of Economics and Statistics*, August 1947, the indicators selected by Burns and Mitchell have continued to dominate business cycle forecasting ever since. When Mitchell died in 1948, Burns inherited his mantle and stood alone as America's leading expert on business cycles.

Burns was born in Stanislau, Austria, in 1904 but his family emigrated to the United States when he was ten years of age. All his university degrees were acquired at Columbia University in New York, as were all his teaching appointments: BA in 1925, MA in 1925, and PhD in 1934 with a doctoral dissertation on *Production Trends in the United States since 1870* (Princeton University Press, 1934). He joined the National Bureau as a Research Associate in 1930 and, after an early career at Rutgers University from 1930 to 1943, he was appointed Professor of Economics at Columbia University in 1944, a post which he held for twenty-one years. In the late 1940s he emerged as one of the keenest American critics of Keynes, not because of any inherent logical defects in Keynes' theories, but rather because of the haste with which Keynes and Keynesians rushed towards policy conclusions on the base of theories which, Burns felt, had not yet been decisively tested. National Bureau pamphlets, such as *Economic Research and the Keynesian Thinking of Our Times* (1946) and *The Instability of Consumer Spending* (1952), as well as a number of articles published as *Frontiers of Economic Knowledge* (Princeton University Press, 1954), conveyed Burns' sceptical attitude to the grandiose claims of the Keynesian system.

In 1957 he became President of the National Bureau and two years later he was President of the American Economic Association. He continued to write on business cycles, his last serious essay on that subject appearing in 1969, *The Business Cycle in a Changing World* (Columbia University Press, 1969). Even during his tenure as chief of the Fed. from 1970 to 1978, he never stopped writing and speaking. *Reflections of an Economic Policy Maker* (American Enterprise Institute, 1978) is a collection of his speeches and testimony during this eight-year period. He served as American Ambassador to West Germany, from 1981 to 1985.

*Secondary Literature*
G.H. Moore, 'Burns, Arthur F.', in D.L. Sills (ed.), *International Encyclopaedia of the Social Sciences*, vol. 16 (The Free Press, 1979); R. Sobel, *The Worldly Economists* (The Free Press, 1980), chs 3, 8; G. Moore, 'Burns, Arthur Frank', in J. Eatwell, M. Milgate and P. Newman, *The New Palgrave: A Dictionary of Economics*, vol. 1 (Macmillan, 1987).

# Chenery, Hollis B. (1918– )

Hollis Chenery has been a key figure in the quantification movement that swept through development economics in the late 1950s and '60s. In a classic essay, 'Patterns of Industrial Growth', *American Economic Review*, September 1960, he employed international comparative analysis to demonstrate that economic growth is characterised by systematic changes in the structure of production in different industries and sectors of economic activity. A similar method also underlies his major text in input–output analysis, *Interindustry Economics* (Wiley, 1959), written jointly with P. Clark, and a later book, written with R. Syrquin, *Patterns of Development, 1950–1970* (Oxford University Press, 1975).

'Patterns of Industrial Growth' showed that self-sustaining economic growth is largely a function of industrialisation and that industrialisation is usually associated with a declining proportion of agricultural goods in a country's total exports. This finding was widely interpreted as justifying an import-substitution industrialisation strategy for Third World countries but this interpretation of the paper was largely an abuse of Chenery's findings. Another one of Chenery's influential papers was 'Capital–Labor Substitution and Economic Efficiency', *Review of Economics and Statistics*, August 1961, written jointly with K.J. Arrow and others, which, inaugurated the CES (constant elasticity of substitution) production function, and thus brought to an end the 'tyranny' of the Cobb–Douglas production function (see Douglas, P.H.).

Chenery went on subsequently to employ the concept of systematic patterns of economic development in the construction of planning models for different types of Third World countries, as in *Studies in Development Planning* (Harvard University Press, 1971), *Structural Change and Development Policy* (Oxford University Press, 1979) and *Industrialisation and Economic Growth: A Comparative Study* (Oxford University Press, 1976). *Redistribution with Growth: An Approach to Policy* (Oxford University Press, 1974), of which he was one of the many authors, reflects a long-standing concern with the distributional aspects of development strategies and, in particular, the possible conflicts between the goals of efficiency and equity: the argument of the book is that the conflict between efficiency and equity can be avoided in the Third World by appropriate development strategies.

Chenery was born in 1918 in Richmond, Virginia. He obtained a BS in mathematics from the University of Arizona in 1939, another BS in engineering from the University of Oklahoma in 1941, an MA in economics from the University of Virginia in 1947, and a PhD in economics from Harvard University in 1950. He began teaching at Stanford University in 1952, becoming a full professor there in 1961. He was an Assistant Administrator at the US Agency of International Development in Washington from 1960 to 1965, then a Professor of Economics at the Center of International Affairs, Harvard University from 1965 to 1970, and, finally, an economic adviser to President McNamara of the World Bank from 1970 to 1972. In 1972 he became Vice-President in Charge of Development Policies at the World Bank, a post which he held until 1982. Returning to Harvard as a professor, he retired from teaching in 1988. He is a Council Member of the Econometric Society and the recipient of an honorary doctorate from the Netherlands School of Economics.

# Clower, Robert Wayne (1926– )

Robert Clower's essay, 'The Keynesian counter-revolution: A Theoretical Appraisal' (1965), reprinted in his own collection of readings in *Monetary Theory* (Penguin, 1969) and in many other anthologies, ranks as one of the most important papers, if not the most important paper, published on macroeconomics in the last two or three decades. What Clower did was to provide the first convincing microeconomic explanation of how equilibrium is achieved in a Keynesian model despite the fact that there is unemployment in labour markets. The traditional interpretation of Keynes argues that Keynes must have supposed that money wages cannot fall because of, say, union resistance and that prices in general never fall sufficiently to lower real wages and thus to encourage more employment. But this interpretation was never very persuasive and is not in fact directly supported by anything Keynes himself said. Clower, however, managed to account for Keynes' 'unemployment equilibrium' by introducing the 'dual decision hypothesis'.

Clower began by distinguishing 'notional' demand from 'effective' demand. Notional demand is the demand of households at prices which reflect a full employment equilibrium. If the economic system fails to reach full employment equilibrium, however, some households will find that their actual incomes have fallen below their 'notional' incomes and they will therefore reduce their consumption expenditures to conform to the constraints imposed by their actual incomes. Demand functions which take these constraints into account are 'effective' demand functions. Thus, when there is considerable unemployment, the excess supply of labour at the going real wage rate is not matched by an equivalent excess 'effective' demand for goods and services because some 'notional' excess demand has been eliminated by the reallocation of expenditure reflecting the constraint of reduced incomes. Those deviations from full employment equilibrium are spread throughout all markets via the multiplier process. Producers now will receive the wrong price signals, which will not necessarily induce the adjustment that leads to full employment equilibrium. The labour market would be cleared if money wages were reduced but such wage reductions are not communicated to employers as an increase in effective demand for output. In consequence, labour markets are cleared by adjusting employment to unchanged wages, instead of wages being adjusted to unchanged employment levels. In short, economic adjustments now depend more on income than on relative prices because all exchange is disequilibrium exchange at 'false prices'. Or, to put it differently, what is important in pre-Keynesian economics is not the assumption of perfect competition but the much less widely noted assumption that all prices adjust instantaneously to clear markets. Once we get away from the rather special case of instantaneously adjusted prices, there is no longer any presumption that the workings of the price system will lead automatically to the elimination of shortages and surpluses in all markets and thus to full employment.

There has been much discussion as to whether Clower is right to assert that Keynes had something like the 'dual-decision hypothesis' at the back of his mind. But whatever the verdict on that question, the field of macroeconomics has never been quite the same since the publication of Clower's essay (q.v.) A. Leijonhufvud expanded Clower's argument into a full-scale treatise and many others have since adopted the notion of the dual-decision hypothesis, income-constrained processes, false trading at disequilibrium prices, and quantity rather than price-adjustments as the microfoundations of a Keynesian-type macroeconomics (see Okun, A.). More recently, he has gone on to expand on the theme that the instability of economic systems can only be explained by a Marshallian rather than a Walrasian account of market processes:

see *Money and Markets: Essays by R.W. Clower*, ed. D.A. Walker (Cambridge University Press, 1984).

Clower was born in Pullman, Washington, in 1926. He received his BA in 1948 and his MA in 1949, both from Washington State University. In 1952, he received another MA from the University of Oxford, followed many years later by a doctorate from Oxford in 1978. He began teaching at Washington State University in the early 1950s and in 1957 moved to Northwestern University shortly before publishing his first book, *Introduction to Mathematical Economics* (Richard D. Irwin, 1957), co-authored with D.W. Bushaw. In 1961 he took a year off to direct an economic survey of Liberia, which resulted in a book, *Growth Without Development: An Economic Survey of Liberia* (Northwestern University Press, 1966), co-authored with G. Dalton and others. He became a Professor of Economics at Northwestern University in 1963. After two years as Visiting Professor at the University of Essex in England and Makerere College, Uganda, he left Northwestern University in 1971 and taught at various universities in Australia, Canada, and Italy, before returning in 1978 to his *alma mater*, Washington State University. In 1980 he moved again to the University of California, Los Angeles, and from there to the University of South Carolina in 1986, where he resides today.

He is the author of an intermediate textbook in *Microeconomics* (Richard D. Irwin, 1972), co-authored with J.F. Due, and another, *Intermediate Microeconomics* (Harcourt Brace Jovanovich, 1988), with P. Graves and R. Sexton. He was managing editor of *Economic Issues* from 1973 to 1980 and was until 1984 Chief Editor of the *American Economic Review*, the leading American economics journal.

# Coase, Ronald Harry (1910– )

Ronald Coase has published one book, *British Broadcasting: A Study in Monopoly* (Longmans Green, Harvard University Press, 1950), and eighteen articles in a long academic career, but his reputation rests securely on only two of these articles: 'The Nature of the Firm', *Economica*, November 1937, his very first published paper, and 'The Problem of Social Cost', *Journal of Law and Economics*, October 1960. The paper on the nature of the firm posed an innocent question which had never been asked before – why do business firms exist at all? – and drew from it an amazing series of implications by a process of pure deduction. The argument went roughly as follows: the purchase or hire of factors of production requires the drawing up of contracts, and the process of employing factors in the production of goods and services requires a knowledge of prices, both of which involve the using up of real resources; when the cost of such market transactions reaches a certain level, it pays to replace the market mechanism by a centralised organisation operated on hierarchical principles called a 'firm'; but the costs of coordinating inputs rises as the firm grows larger, thus setting a limit to the size of the firm; beyond that size, therefore, additional transactions are farmed out to other, smaller firms.

The paper attracted little attention when it first appeared. The full impact of Coase's revolutionary idea of focusing on the costs of using the market has only lately become evident as economists have moved increasingly towards an analysis of the economics of the family and other non-profit, non-market institutions.

The second essay on 'The Problem of Social Cost' is like no other paper by an economist: it contains no diagrams or equations, it is full of quotations from lawyers and judges, and it proceeds in large part by examining the logic of Pigou's famous analysis in *Economics of Welfare* (1920) of the spillover costs imposed on farmers by steam locomotives and on households by factory chimneys. Such cases of spillover costs were regarded by Pigou as exemplifying what we would now call 'market failure', requiring government intervention to raise the private costs of the activity up to their true social costs. Coase challenged Pigou's conclusions with a double-barrelled argument. First, if property rights in all the relevant resources are clearly assigned and if all the economic agents involved can get together to negotiate with one another – 'transaction costs are negligible' – the agents themselves will be motivated to enter into voluntary agreements to shift the costs of pollution from the victims to the perpetrators. Second, and more surprisingly, under these circumstances it can be shown that the value or composition of national income is unaffected by the precise pattern of liability for pollution as determined by private negotiations; this second proposition has gone down in the literature as 'the Coase theorem'. Finally, Coase argued that, even if transaction costs are so high as to make the Coase theorem irrelevant, there is still no presumption that government intervention will improve matters, 'government failure' must be weighed against 'market failure'. This, and some of his other famous papers, are published together in *The Firm, the Market and the Law* (University of Chicago Press, 1988) and *Essays on Economic and Economists* (University of Chicago Press, 1994).

It is rare for a single article to generate an entire branch of economics, much less two branches of economics, but the Economics of Property Rights (see Demsetz, H.) and the Economics of Law (see Posner, R.A.), two rapidly growing sub-disciplines within economics in the last decade or so, can be traced directly to Coase's article on social cost and his editorship from 1964 to 1982 of the *Journal of Law and Economics*.

Coase was born in Willesden, London, in 1910 and entered the London School of Economics as a commerce student in 1929. He graduated in 1932, taught for a while at the London School of

Economics, and then moved on to the Dundee School of Economics in Scotland, followed by two years at the University of Liverpool, and returning to the LSE in 1935, where he taught until 1951. Receiving his doctorate from the University of London in 1951, he emigrated to the United States. Seven years as a professor at the University of Buffalo (1951–8) were followed by six years at the University of Virginia (1958–64). In 1964 he moved to the University of Chicago from which he retired in 1979. Upon retirement, he was elected as a Distinguished Fellow of the American Economic Association: he was awarded the Nobel Prize in Economics in 1991, proving once and for all that one can be a great economist even if publishing little and even if one never writes a single mathematical equation. He remains active today as Senior Fellow in Law and Economics at the University of Chicago Law School.

*Secondary Literature*
K.G. Elzinga, 'Coase, R.H.', in D.L. Sills (ed.), *International Encyclopaedia of the Social Sciences*, vol. 16 (The Free Press, 1979); S.G. Medema, *Ronald H. Coase* (Macmillan, 1994); S.G. Medema (ed.), *The Legacy of Ronald Coase in Economic Analysis* (Edward Elgar, 1995, 2 vols).

# Debreu, Gerard (1921– )

Gerard Debreu was born in Calais, France, in 1921 and studied mathematics in his youth, graduating from the University of Paris in 1946. He was a member of the irreverent 'Bourbaki' group in France in the early post-war period, a set of young French mathematicians who set about reconstructing the logical foundations of mathematics, publishing all their works jointly under the name of a non-existent genius called 'Henri Bourbaki'. In 1948, he came to the USA on a Rockefeller Foundation Fellowship and in 1950 he joined the Cowles Commission at the University of Chicago (see Marschak, J.). He began to collaborate with Kenneth Arrow (q.v.) and together they published an epoch-making paper, 'Existence of an Equilibrium for a Competitive Economy' (1954), in which they provided a definitive mathematical proof of the existence of general equilibrium, using topological methods hitherto unknown in economics. It is easy to scoff at these and other attempts to prove the possibility of a unique solution of a general equilibrium system of demand and supply equations. Obviously, in the real world unique prices and quantities are somehow determined in all markets and one might think that the economist's time is better spent discovering how markets produce a unique solution than in worrying whether a set of simultaneous equations is mathematically solvable. Nevertheless, general equilibrium theories are used in all branches of modern economics and unless one were sure that a general equilibrium model possessed a solution, one could never confidently employ general equilibrium analysis. Furthermore, proofs of the existence of a general equilibrium solution depend on certain restrictive conditions, and these conditions may throw light on the way in which multimarket equilibrium is actually attained in the real world. Indeed, the Arrow–Debreu paper did illuminate some aspects of real world competition (see also Hahn, F.).

In 1955, Debreu moved with the rest of the Cowles Commission to Yale University, where he remained as an Associate Professor until 1960. In 1959, he published his masterpiece, *Theory of Value: An Axiomatic Analysis of Economic Equilibrium* (Wiley, 1959; Yale University Press, 1971), a slim book which has ever since marked the ultimate stage of mathematical sophistication which economists can reach; using set theory and topology rather than calculus and matrix algebra, he succeeded in restating all the traditional results of competitive price theory with maximum economy and precision; it is a work which makes no concessions to those who can only think in words but which has, nevertheless, had a considerable influence on the verbal exposition of ideas in economic textbooks.

Debreu has since published a large number of technical papers on what is called 'existence theorems', seeking to relax the stringent assumptions required to prove the existence of general equilibrium under competitive conditions, while also addressing the quite separate question of the speed at which actual economies converge on a general equilibrium solution. W. Hildenbrand (ed.), *Mathematical Economics: Twenty Papers of Gerard Debreu* (Cambridge University Press, 1981) reprints a selection of these essays.

Debreu left Yale University in 1960 and is today Professor of Economics and Mathematics at the University of California, Berkeley. He was President of the Econometric Society from 1969 to 1971, a Fellow since 1970 of the American Association for the Advancement of Science, and President of the American Association in 1990. But the honour which must have given him most pleasure is that of Chevalier of the French Legion of Honour in 1976 because he remains, for all his years in America, recognisably French in speech, food habits, and personal charm. However, even that honour was capped in 1983 by the award of the Nobel Prize in Economics.

*Primary Literature*
G. Debreu, 'Random Walk and Life Philosophy', in M. Szenberg, *Eminent Economists: Their Life Philosophies* (Cambridge University Press, 1992).

# Demsetz, Harold (1930– )

It is not clear who deserves credit for the discovery of the theory of property rights, although it is clear that it all started from Ronald Coase's (q.v.) famous paper on 'The Problem of Social Cost'. Coase had shown that the failure of markets to produce efficient outcomes is frequently due to the impossibility of defining property rights over the unintended by-products of economic activity because the number of agents involved is so large that the required 'transaction costs' – the costs of organising a market in economic transactions – are prohibitive. What are 'transaction costs'? They are the costs of making deals: the costs of obtaining information to draw up contracts; the costs of writing the contracts and the costs of monitoring to ensure that the terms of the contracts are carried out. Coase had established the significance of transaction costs but he had failed nevertheless to generalise this insight into a comprehensive statement of the emergence of clearly specified property rights as a precondition for the functioning of markets. It was this generalisation which was first achieved by Demsetz's brilliant paper, 'Toward a Theory of Property Rights', *American Economic Review*, May 1967.

Property rights depend on transaction costs and these in turn depend on the costs of obtaining information in markets. The theory of property rights and the theory of information costs are therefore intimately related, a point which is best illustrated by the employment contract in labour markets. The employment contract is by its nature 'incomplete' in the sense that the contract states what the worker is to be paid and how long he or she is to work but fails to specify the pace and intensity of the work effort. Workers may be threatened with the 'stick' of unemployment and persuaded with the 'carrot' of promotion but that is only effective if their performance on the job is constantly monitored. Thus, the employment relationship is essentially an information problem. In a path-breaking paper, 'Production, Information Costs, and Economic Organization' *American Economics Review*, December 1972, Demsetz and A.A. Alchian (q.v.) argued that the employment relationship, superficial appearances notwithstanding, may be conceived as a type of voluntary exchange between employers offering a 'fair day's pay' and employees offering a 'fair day's work'. In other words, labour markets require, in A. Okun's (q.v.) memorable phrase, 'an invisible handshake' to take the place of 'the invisible hand' that regulates the operation of other markets. This theory of the incomplete employment contract, also known as 'implicit contract' theory or the 'principal–agency problem', has now been taken up by a number of other economists working in both labour economics and macroeconomics.

Other topics which have been illuminated by Demsetz with the aid of the theory of property rights are the role of advertising as a form of market rivalry and the regulation of public utilities as a device for remedying market failures. Demsetz's entire output has taken the form of articles in journals and chapters in books, reprinted in *The Organization of Economic Activity* (Basil Blackwell, 1988–9, 2 vols). A set of lectures, *Economic, Legal and Political Dimensions of Competition* (North-Holland, 1982) sum up his life's work to date.

He was born in Chicago, Illinois, in 1930. He received his BA from the University of Illinois in 1953, followed by a Master's degree in business administration in 1954 and a PhD in economics in 1959, both from Northwestern University. He became a Professor of Economics at the University of Chicago in 1963, leaving in 1971 to become Senior Research Fellow at the Hoover Institution, Stanford, where he remained until 1977. In 1978, he became a professor at the University of California, Los Angeles, a post he holds to this day. He has been an active member of the Mont Pèlerin Society ever since 1955.

# Denison, Edward F. (1915–92)

Edward Denison is the 'father' of Growth Accounting or Sources-of-Growth Analysis, a technique of decomposing the observed growth of national income into its constituent elements so as to throw light on the causes of economic growth. It begins with the use of a Cobb–Douglas production function (see Douglas, P.H.) to estimate the physical contribution of labour and capital to national output. This method usually produces a large 'residual' of unexplained output and much of the 'art' of growth accounting lies in the way the residual is then broken down into its various elements, namely, improvements in the quality of both labour and capital, interindustry shifts of resources, economies of scale, lags in the application of knowledge, and so forth.

Growth accounting has come in for a good deal of criticism, largely because of its failure to base the technique on any well-established and generally accepted theory of growth but it enjoyed a decade of unparalleled success in the 1960s, being applied by Denison himself and by innumerable followers to the study of growth in many countries around the world, both rich and poor, both capitalist and communist. One of Denison's most famous findings – the expansion of education in the United States during the years 1929–59 alone accounts for as much as 23 per cent of America's annual growth rate in that period – contributed substantially to the explosion of public spending on education in the 1960s, suggesting as it did that schooling is a major factor in the acceleration of a country's growth rate. Quite apart from his work on growth accounting, however, Denison has also participated actively in official work on national income accounting in the United States, contributing in particular to the improved measurement of changes in the capital stock.

Denison was born in Omaha, Nebraska, in 1915. He completed his BA at Oberlin College in 1936 and went on to take an MA in 1938 and a PhD in 1941 at Brown University. Upon receiving his doctorate, he joined the Office of Business Economics of the US Department of Commerce, eventually becoming an assistant director. He spent twenty-one years at the Department of Commerce, the last six of which were combined with the post of Associate Director of Research at the Committee of Economic Development, a private research foundation. In 1962, he published his first book, *The Sources of Economic Growth in the United States and the Alternatives before Us* (Committee for Economic Development, 1962), which launched the subject of growth accounting. He left government service in the same year and joined the Brookings Institution in Washington D.C., as a Senior Fellow.

His second book, *Why Growth Rates Differ: Postwar Experiences in Nine Western Countries* (Brookings Institution, 1967), altered the perspective of growth accounting from explaining growth in one country to explaining differences in the levels and rates of growth of different countries. The results of this book were more ambiguous than the results of the earlier study of US growth; for example, the amount of education embodied in the labour force did not account for much of the inter-country differences in observed growth rates and for any of the differences to the low growth rate of the US economy. Denison's next three books returned to his original theme of growth in a single country: *Accounting for United States Economic Growth, 1929–1960* (Brookings Institution, 1974), *How Japan's Economy Grew So Fast* (Brookings Institution, 1976), co-authored with W.K. Chung, and *Accounting for Slower Economic Growth: the United States in the 1970s* (Brookings Institution, 1979). Leaving the Brookings Institution in 1978, Denison rejoined the Department of Commerce as Associate Director of National Economic Accounts. Since then, he has published two further books: *Trends in American Economic Growth, 1929–82* (Brookings Institution, 1985) and *Estimates of Pro-*

*ductivity Changes by Industry: An Evaluation and an Alternative* (Brookings Institution, 1989).

Denison was Vice-President of the American Economic Association in 1978 and a Fellow of the American Academy of Arts and Sciences, the American Statistical Association, and the International Association for Research in Income and Wealth. His career proves that one can go far in economics without ever holding an academic job. On the other hand, one must add that there are not many Denisons in the economics profession.

# Dobb,
# Maurice H.
# (1900–76)

Maurice Dobb was the foremost Marxist economist of the Western world all through the 1930s, '40s. and '50s and he and Paul Baran of Stanford University were the only Marxist economists before the war to hold a teaching position at a leading American or British university. Moreover, unlike Baran, Dobb was no free-wheeling, do-it-yourself Marxist but one who held to the Moscow line through-out his mature career, not just on matters of politics but also on questions of theory. Nevertheless, the outstanding quality of his critical writings on standard economics, his exposition of the fine points in Marxian theory, his historical work on the Soviet economy and the development of capitalism, and, latterly, his analysis of development planning in Third World countries were such as to earn him a respectful hearing everywhere. His gentle, old-world charm disarmed even those who were prepared to attack him be-fore meeting him. His literary style was always elegant but complex and even convoluted; this lent a certain fuzziness to his writings, which only helped him to attract still more readers.

He was born in 1900 in England and took his BA in 1922 at the University of Cambridge. Enrolling at the London School of Economics as a graduate student, he earned his doctorate in only two years with *Capital, Enterprise and Social Progress* (Routledge, 1925), a study of entrepreneurship which is still worth reading. He took up a lectureship at Cambridge University in 1924 and spent the rest of his academic life there as Reader in Economics until his retirement in 1967. He has already joined the newly formed Communist Party of Great Britain in 1922 and he remained an open and acknowledged party member until his death in 1976.

His first post-doctoral work was *Russian Economic Development since the Revolution* (Routledge & Kegan Paul, 1928), a book which he subsequently revised and enlarged on a number of occasions under the title of *Soviet Economic Development since 1917* (Routledge & Kegan Paul, 6th edn, 1966). For some time it reigned supreme as almost the only serious study of Soviet economic development; the fact that it provided a subtle apology for Stalinism, justifying every one of Stalin's actions, did it no harm in the inter-war years. Subsequent editions revealed some qualifications to Dobb's argument but even the last edition more or less vindicates highly centralised planning, emphasis on heavy industry, forced collectivisation of agriculture, in short, the entire pattern of Soviet development since the 1917 Revolution.

After a short, now forgotten book on *Wages* (Nisbet, 1928), his next contribution was *Political Economy and Capitalism* (Routledge & Kegan Paul, 1937); International Publishers, 1945), a series of essays employing Marxian concepts to expose the weaknesses of orthodox economics, which many of his admirers regard as his major work. But his most influential work was *Studies in the Development of Capitalism* (Routledge & Kegan Paul, 1946), which was designed to demonstrate that Marx was as good an economic historian as he was an economist. Dobb's analysis in that book of the transition from feudalism to capitalism in Western Europe, laying special emphasis on the emergence of a propertyless class of wage earners, has been the basis of a heated debate between Marxists ever since; see *The Transition from Feudalism to Capitalism*, ed. M. Dobb and P.M. Sweezy (New Left Books, 1976). There followed a number of books on economic development: *An Essay on Economic Growth and Planning* (Monthly Review Press, 1960, 2nd edn, 1963), *Economic Growth and Underdeveloped Countries* (Lawrence & Wishart, 1963), and *Papers on Capitalism, Development and Planning* (Routledge & Kegan Paul, 1967). He went back to the economics of socialism, which had cropped up repeatedly in his previous writings, in *Economic Theory and Socialism: Collected Papers* (Routledge & Kegan Paul, 1955, 2nd edn, 1965) and *Welfare Economics and the Economics of Socialism* (Cambridge University Press, 1969).

In 1951, he collaborated with Piero Sraffa, (q.v.) in editing the *Works and Correspondence of David Ricardo*, and this experience, reinforced by the publication of Sraffa's *Production of Commodities by Means of Commodities*, led him gradually to the view that 'true' economics did not start with Marx but rather with Ricardo and that the entire history of economics can be divided into two main lines of approach: the Ricardo–Marx–Sraffa line of analysis of the determination of the 'economic surplus' and the Smith–Walras–Arrow–Debreu line of general equilibrium analysis of price determination. His last book, *Theories of Value and Distribution since Adam Smith* (Cambridge University Press, 1973), is an attempt to document this point of view, which, it must be said, is highly debatable.

*Primary Literature*
M. Dobb, 'Random Biographical Notes', *Cambridge Journal of Economics*, 2 (2), 1978.

*Secondary Literature*
J. Eatwell, 'Dobb, Maurice H.', in D.L. Sills (ed.), *International Encyclopaedia of the Social Sciences*, vol. 16 (The Free Press, 1979); B. MacFarlane, 'On Dobb', in H.W. Spiegel and W.J. Samuels (eds), *Contemporary Economists in Perspective*, vol. 2 (JAI Press, 1984); A Sen, 'Dobb, Maurice Herbert', in J. Eatwell, M. Milgate and P. Newman (eds), *The New Palgrave: A Dictionary of Economics*, vol. 1 (Macmillan, 1987); B.J. McFarlane and H.B. Pollitt, 'Maurice Herbert Dobb', in P. Arestis and M. Sawyer (eds), *A Biographical Dictionary of Dissenting Economists* (Edward Elgar, 1992).

# Domar,
# Evsey D.
# (1914–    )

Evsey Domar is the co-inventor with Roy Harrod (q.v.) of the so-called 'Harrod–Domar model' of dynamic equilibrium. Harold arrived there first but Domar's starting point was in many ways more natural. In Harrod, a change in current investment causes a change in current income via Keynes' multiplier' and then this change in current income induces a further change in current investment – this is the so-called 'accelerator'. Domar realised, however, that investment also generates extra productive capacity, which cannot be productively employed unless income rises in the *next* period, which in turn requires still more investment, and so forth, the point being that the requirements for steady-rate, period-by-period growth are different from those of static, one-period equilibrium. Domar has described how he came to start thinking about all this. He was attending a class in 1941–2 at Harvard University taught by Alvin Hansen (q.v.) and was puzzled by a diagram in Hansen's *Fiscal Policy and Business Cycles*, which showed the effect of a constant stream of investment on national income: 'It appeared to me strange that such a stream resulted in a constant rather than a rising income, and an investigation of this puzzle resulted in a paper on the public debt ['The "Burden of the Debt" and the National Income', 1944], which in turn led to the other essays.' The public debt paper and others written in the 1940s, in which Domar applied the rate of growth as an analytical device to a number of specific economic problems, are reprinted in his *Essays in the Theory of Economic Growth* (Oxford University Press, 1957). This volume also contains a fascinating discussion of a model of economic growth published by the Soviet economist G.A. Feldman, as early as 1928, which bears an amazing resemblance to the Harrod–Domar growth model.

Domar was born in 1914 in Lodz, Russia (now Poland). He grew up in Manchuria, Russia, where he eventually attended the State Faculty of Law in Harbin, Manchuria (1930–1). In 1936, he entered the University of California, Los Angeles, as an undergraduate, obtaining his BA in economics in 1939. He then took an MA in mathematics at Michigan University in 1941. Turning back to the study of economics, he obtained an MA in 1943 and a PhD in 1947 from Harvard University.

He worked first as an economist with the Board of Governors of the Federal Reserve System (1943–6), then taught at the Carnegie Institute of Technology (1946–7), the University of Chicago (1947–8), Columbia University (1951–5), and Johns Hopkins University (1955–8), finally becoming a Professor of Economics at the Massachusetts Institute of Technology in 1958, until his retirement in 1984. He was a recipient of the John R. Commons award of Omicron Delta Epsilon in 1965, a Vice-President of the American Economic Association in 1970, and a President of the Association of Comparative Economics in 1970.

In recent years, Domar's interest has shifted to the working of the Soviet economy, in particular to 'The Soviet Collective Farm as a Producer Co-operative', *American Economic Review*, September 1966, a type of economic organisation in agriculture which has been widely imitated in the Third World. He has also turned his attention to historical modelling on a grand scale, as evidenced by his much-discussed paper on 'The Causes of Slavery or Serfdom: A Hypothesis', *Journal of Economic History*, March 1970. These and other papers appeared as *Capitalism, Socialism, and Serfdom: Essays by Evsey Domar* (Cambridge University Press, 1989).

*Primary Literature*
E.D. Domar, 'How I Tried to Become an Economist', in M. Szenberg (ed.), *Eminent Economists: Their Life Philosophies* (Cambridge University Press, 1992).

# Dorfman, Robert (1928– )

Robert Dorfman's early work applied the principles of operations research to economic problems, and one of his youthful articles, 'Mathematical, or "Linear" Programming: A Non-mathematical Exposition', *American Economic Review*, December 1953, taught the technique of linear programming to an entire generation of economists (see Koopmans, T.C.). This article was the starting point of a longer and extended treatment in a classic textbook, *Linear Programming and Economic Analysis* (McGraw-Hill, 1958), which Dorfman wrote jointly with Paul Samuelson (q.v.) and Robert Solow (q.v.) it can still be read with profit today as one of the best intermediate texts in price theory of the entire post-war period.

Dorfman's capacity for explaining complex material in simple language was employed once again in another widely read essay, 'An Economic Interpretation of Optimal Control Theory', *American Economic Review*, December 1969, another mathematical technique which appears to have obvious application in economics. Subsequently, Dorfman turned his attention to cost-benefit analysis and, in particular, the assessment of natural resource and environmental policies. *Designs of Water Resource Systems* (Harvard University Press, 1962), with A. Maass and others, and a book of readings on the *Economics of he Environment* (W.W. Norton, 1972), edited with N.S. Dorfman, are expressions of this interest in the application of economic principles to ecological questions. A beautiful survey article, 'Forty Years of Cost-Benefit Analysis', in R. Stone and W. Peterson (eds), *Economic Contributions to Public Policy* (Macmillan, 1978) summed up his view of where we are in cost-benefit analysis. He has also written an effective pamphlet-long introduction to economics, *Prices and Markets* (Prentice-Hall, 1967; 2nd edn, 1978). A collection of his best essays is about to appear under the title *Economic Theory and Public Decision* (Edward Elgar, 1997).

Dorfman was born in New York City in 1916 and received his BA in 1936 and MA in 1937 from Columbia University. He went on to do a PhD at the University of California, Berkeley, in 1950, at which date he also joined the teaching staff. Earlier, he worked as a Senior Statistician at he US Office of Price Administration (1941–3) and an Operation Analyst with the US Air Forces (1943–50). In 1955, he left Berkeley to become Professor of Economics at Harvard University; he remained at Harvard until his retirement in 1984.

He was President of the Institute of Management Science in 1965, Member of the Executive Committee of the American Economic Association during 1968–71, and Vice-President of the Association of Environmental Resource Economists in 1980.

# Douglas, Paul H. (1892–1976)

Paul Douglas was an influential US Senator from the State of Illinois during the years 1948–66 but, despite his distinguished legislative career, it is not this which gave him fame as an economist. It was rather his discovery (actually a rediscovery) of the 'Cobb–Douglas production function' in 1928. Capitalising on earlier work by Charles W. Cobb, a fellow mathematician-economist, Douglas succeeded in estimating a statistical equation expressing the physical output of the manufacturing sector as a function of its labour and capital inputs; from this equation, he deduced the relative shares of manufacturing output that competition would assign to labour and capital respectively and found that this deduction agreed remarkably closely with the observed shares of wages and profits in manufacturing income. At first this was regarded as a curious result, a puzzle requiring a solution rather than an established truth. However, others replicated his findings for different countries, for different time periods, and for the economy as a whole. No wonder that Douglas, surveying the work done in the field during the preceding twenty years in a presidential address to the American Economic Association in 1947, was driven to the conclusion that economics had at long last formulated genuine 'laws of production'.

But it was still early days for the Cobb–Douglas production function. It was only in the 1950s with the rise of the theory of economic growth that it came into its own as a single expression for the production processes of an entire economy. The exercise of estimating Cobb–Douglas production functions became a veritable intellectual industry, providing material for endless doctoral dissertations in economics. Douglas himself was amazed to learn in old age that there was still life left in his pet equation after fifty years. His last professional article, written at the age of eighty-four, the year of his death, says it all: 'The Cobb–Douglas Production Function Once Again', *Journal of Political Economy*, October 1976.

The Cobb–Douglas production function is in many ways a highly restricted type of production function. Production functions may be characterised by a single statistic, the elasticity of substitution, that is, the percentage change in the relative amounts of the inputs employed in production resulting from a given percentage change in their relative prices. For a Cobb–Douglas production function, the elasticity of substitution is always equal to unity, and this (we learn in intermediate courses in economics) means that the relative shares of income accruing to the factors of production will remain constant whatever are the relative supplies of the factors. However, in recent years, the Cob–Douglas production function has been superseded by the so-called 'CES' production function (see Chenery, H.B.) in which the elasticity of substitution may assume any value provided it is a constant value, and the 'VES' production function, in which even constancy is abandoned: the elasticity of substitution may assume any value and indeed a variable value for different input combinations. The singular obsession of economists with the Cobb–Douglas production function has thus finally come to an end. At the same time, there has developed a healthier, more sceptical attitude towards the whole exercise of estimating aggregate production functions for the economy as a whole.

Douglas was born in Salem, Massachusetts, in 1892 but spent his childhood and adolescence in Maine. He graduated from Bowdoin College in 1913 and then took graduate work under John Bates Clark at Columbia University, receiving his MA in 1915 and his PhD in 1921. He started his teaching in 1916 at the University of Illinois and, after short spells at Reed College and the University of Washington, took up a post as professor at the University of Chicago in 1920, where he remained, apart from wartime service as a private in the marines, until 1948 when he left to take up a seat in the US Senate. It was during a three-year leave of absence at Amherst

College in 1924–7 that he met Cobb and began to work on production functions. When his third term in the US Senate ended in 1966, he taught for three more years at the New School for Social Research in New York City, retiring in 1969 at the age of seventy-seven.

His first important book was *Real Wages in the United States, 1890–1926* (University of Chicago Press, 1930; Kelley & Millman, 1966) but it was dwarfed by *The Theory of Wages* (University of Chicago Press, 1934; Kelley & Millman, 1957) which contained some of the first empirical work in modern times on the supply of labour as well as a superb survey of the history of wage theory, culminating in his own statistical vindication of marginal productivity theory. His writings implied that little could be done to affect wages by unions, minimum wage laws, or other forms of government intervention, but his public life contradicted these implications. As a converted Quaker, he was always active in the American Friends Service Committee and as a Senator he fought for family allowances, unemployment insurance, old age pensions, and union protection legislation. He never adequately discussed the tensions between his academic views and his political life and his *Economy in the National Government* (University of Chicago Press, 1952) and *Ethics in Government* (University of Chicago Press, 1952; Greenwood Press, 1972) shed little light on this puzzle.

*Secondary Literature*
G.C. Cain, 'Douglas, Paul H.', in D.L. Sills (ed.), *International Encyclopaedia of the Social Sciences*, vol. 18 (The Free Press, 1979); P.H. Douglas, *In the Fullness of Time: The Memoirs of Paul H. Douglas* (Harcourt, 1972); C.G. Clark, 'Douglas, Paul Howard', in J. Eatwell, M. Milgate and P. Newman (eds), *The New Palgrave: A Dictionary of Economics*, vol. 1 (Macmillan, 1987).

# Downs, Anthony (1930– )

Anthony Downs' outstanding study, *An Economic Theory of Democracy* (Harper & Row, 1957), was the first sign of the type of 'intellectual imperialism' that was soon to characterise post-war economics, whereby the territory of other social sciences, such as political science, sociology, and anthropology, were invaded and occupied by economists. Downs made the simple assumption that political parties are motivated, not by the 'good' of society as a whole, but by the aim of maximising their electoral vote. From this central assumption, added to the assumption of 'selfish' voters who reckon the costs of obtaining information about political candidates and platforms, he deduced a surprising number of the observed characteristics of party politics in a democracy, such as the tendency of multiparty systems to degenerate into a two-party system and for most voters to abstain from voting in elections. In short, what he demonstrated was that the standard utility-maximising assumptions of economic theory are perhaps as powerful in generating predictions about political behaviour as they are in generating predictions about economic behaviour.

Downs' book was even constructed like a book on economic theory. In the first part, the logical structure of political decision-making is considered in a world with 'perfect information': the goal of political parties is to gain and keep office and the goal of voters is to maximise their own utility, and everyone is perfectly informed about the effects of government action. The second part drops this assumption of perfect foresight and explores the impact of uncertainty on the behaviour of parties and voters. Finally, the third part examines the ways in which information costs influence political behaviour. We are therefore brought slowly from the abstract world of the first part to something like the real world of the last part.

Downs' book raised a storm of controversy in political science and political sociology. Its influence can still be seen in public choice theory (see Buchanan, J.M.; Tullock, G.), although public choice theory is largely concerned with the normative aspects of political decision-making, whereas Downs was always insistently 'positive' in his approach, seeking, that is, to explain observed patterns of behaviour. He has gone on to apply his original framework to the current operations of government in *Inside Bureaucracy* (Little, Brown, 1967) and to the analysis of racial segregation in US cities in *Racism in America* (US Civil Rights Commission, 1970). More recently, he has turned his attention to the analysis of *Urban Problems and Prospects* (Rand McNally, 1970; 2nd edn, 1976) and *Federal Housing Subsidies* (Heath-Lexington, 1973), followed by *Opening Up the Suburbs: An Urban Strategy for America* (Yale University Press, 1973), *Rented Housing in the 1980s* (Brookings Institution, 1983), and *Revolution in Real Estate Finance* (Brookings Institution, 1985).

Downs was born in Evanston, Illinois, in 1930 and received his BA in Political Theory and International Relations from Carleton College in 1952. He took his MA in 1953 and his PhD in 1956, both from Stanford University. From 1959–77, he was Chairman of the Real Estate Residents Corporation. Today he is a Senior Fellow of the Brookings Institution in Washington.

# Feldstein, Martin (1939– )

Martin Feldstein's career has ranged from quantitative studies in health economics to theoretical and empirical analysis of social insurance programmes (old-age pensions, unemployment compensation, and health insurance), not to mention the effects of public tax, transfer and spending policies on private capital formation. In short, his scope has been so wide as to defy summary in terms of a central focus. Nevertheless, his work has returned again and again to the intended and unintended consequences of the welfare state.

*Economic Analysis for Health Service Efficiency* (North-Holland, 1967), *Health Care Economics* (Wiley, 1979), and *Hospital Costs and Health Insurance* (Harvard University Press, 1981) are representative of his lifelong interest in health economics. *Capital Taxation* (Harvard University Press, 1981), *Inflation, Tax Rules, and Capital Formation* (Chicago University Press, 1981), *Behavioral Simulation Methods in Tax Policy Analysis* (Chicago University Press, 1981), *The Effects of Taxation on Capital Accumulation* (University of Chicago Press, 1987) and *Taxes and Capital Formation* (University of Chicago Press, 1987) bring together his numerous papers on the effects of taxes on capital formation. Much of his work on social insurance programmes also takes the form of articles, which have not so far been brought together between hard covers.

On unemployment compensation, for example, Feldstein has argued that the existing system acts to raise 'the natural rate of unemployment' (see Friedman, M.) by lowering the price of *not* working to unemployed workers and by inducing employers to lay off workers during periods of slack demand, knowing that workers prefer waiting to be recalled to their old job rather than to undertake a painful search for a new one. Feldstein estimated that fully half of temporary layoffs in the American economy can be attributed to the current level of unemployment compensation and he has proposed to make unemployment benefits taxable like income from work at an increasing rate as the duration of unemployment lengthens. This view of the unemployment problem as basically a 'job search' problem (see Phelps, E.S.) has met with the ironic reply that ill health cannot be cured by imposing an illness tax on all those who report symptoms to their doctor. Feldstein agrees that not all reported unemployment can be reduced to voluntary job refusals by the unemployed and he has matched his proposal to tax unemployment benefits with the proposal to issue training 'vouchers' to teenage entering the labour market for the first time, which they could 'cash' with firms who promised to provide them with work experience and on-the-job training.

Feldstein was born in 1939 in New York City. He received his BA from Harvard University in 1961 and his BLitt and PhD from the University of Oxford in 1963 and 1967. He taught at Nuffield College, Oxford, during 1965–7 and became a Professor of Economics at Harvard University in 1967, a post which he still holds today. Since 1977, he has also been President of the National Bureau of Economic Research at Cambridge, Massachusetts. In the same year, at the age of thirty-eight, he was awarded the John Bates Clark Medal of the American Economic Association for 'many significant contributions, covering an astonishing array of economic methods and problems... the economics of medical and hospital care... problems in benefit-cost analysis, public investments, taxation, social security, time preference and interest rates, asset holding under certainty, charitable donations, bequests, production functions, labor supply, unemployment, and inflation'. The sheer quantity of his output is illustrated by the fact that in that single year, 1977, he authored and co-authored as many as fourteen articles. He was Chairman of President Reagan's Council of Economic Advisers from 1982 to 1984. An article in the *Economic Journal*, September 1992, looks retrospectively at his experience, of 'Economic Advising in the United States'.

# Fogel,
# Robert W.
# (1926– )

The publication of Fogel's *Railroads and American Economic Growth: Essays in Econometric History* (Johns Hopkins University Press, 1964) marked the arrival of 'cliometrics' or the New Quantitative Economic History, which marries the axioms of neoclassical economics to the principles of statistical inference in order to ask such counterfactual questions as: what would have been the rate of American economic growth if the railroads had never existed? To those who objected to this very question, the answer was that all historical investigations in fact pose counterfactual questions, implicitly rather than explicitly.

In the vigorous debate that surrounded the rise of the New Economic History, Fogel stood firm in defence of his methods, as is made clear by his *Reinterpretation of American Economic History* (Harper & Row, 1971), with S.L. Engerman, and *'Scientific' History and Traditional History* (Yale University Press, 1982), with G.R. Elton. Moreover, having overturned most previous studies of the economic effects of the American railroads in the nineteenth century, Fogel joined forces with S.L. Engerman to re-examine the economics of American slavery. *Time on the Cross: The Economics of American Negro Slavery* (Little, Brown, 1974) is perhaps the most controversial book that has ever been published in American history, on a subject known for its furious controversies. Endorsing the thesis of a classic article by A.H. Conrad and J.R. Meyer, 'The Economics of Slavery in the Ante-Bellum South', *Journal of Political Economy*, April 1958, which first contested the orthodox view that slavery was an inefficient and unprofitable mode of production, Fogel and Engerman proceeded to attack anyone who upheld the orthodox view as racist and to insist that slavery was so efficient that only an extra-economic force like the Civil War could have brought about its downfall. Their book has been frequently translated and the literature of critical commentaries over less than a decade is now much longer than the book itself; see his *Without Consent or Contract: The Rise and Fall of American Slavery* (W.W. Norton, 1989) and *Without Consent or Contract: The Rise and Fall of American Slavery. Evidence and Method*, 2 vols (W.W. Norton, 1991), with S.L. Engerman *et al.*

It would be misleading to describe Fogel's contributions to economic history as merely reinterpreting the past in a provocative manner. Much of his work has focused on the retrieval of data from historical archives: he has reconstructed time series for the American economy going back to the eighteenth century of such variables as fertility and mortality rates, the female participation rate, migration rates, mobility rates, and savings ratios.

Fogel was born in New York City in 1926. He received a BA from Cornell University in 1948, an MA from Columbia University in 1960, and a PhD from Johns Hopkins University in 1963, by which time he had already published his first book on *The Union Pacific Railroad: A Case in Premature Enterprise* (Johns Hopkins University Press, 1960). He started teaching at Johns Hopkins University in 1958 but moved in 1959 to the University of Rochester. In 1964 he joined the University of Chicago, where he became a Professor of Economic History in 1965. In 1968 he combined this with a professorship at the University of Rochester, leaving both posts in 1975 to become a professor at Harvard University. He returned to the University of Chicago, however, in 1981 to become Director of the Walgreen Foundation as well as Director of the Center of Population Economics.

He was President of the Economic History Association in 1977, President of the Social Science History Association in 1980, and has been a Program Director of the National Bureau of Economic Research since 1978. He was awarded the Nobel Prize in Economics in 1993, along with Douglas North (q.v.).

# Friedman, Milton (1912– )

As a result of his regular column in *Newsweek* (1966–84), his TV documentary series *Free to Choose*, and the adoption by many governments around the world of his doctrine of 'monetarism', Milton Friedman is probably the only living economist that absolutely everybody has heard of. He is, however, much more than an economic journalist and media personality. His numerous articles and books are studied by all serious students of economics and his many contributions to technical economics won him the Nobel Prize in Economics in 1976. Finally, as all those who have ever seen him in the flesh will testify, he is the greatest stand-up debater in the economic profession. This is all the more surprising in that his appearance is against him – he is short and has a thin, nasal voice – and so is his mild and courteous manner: but within a few minutes of any public discussion in which he is involved, the remorseless style of his arguments begins to make its effect and by the end of the debate there is never any doubt about the winner.

Milton Friedman was born in New York City in 1912, the son of poor Jewish immigrants, earned his BA from Rutgers University at the age of twenty, his MA from the University of Chicago in 1933, and his PhD from Columbia University in 1946. After a long spell at Columbia before and after World War II, interrupted by wartime service with the division of Tax Research at the US Treasury and short spells at Wisconsin and Minnesota, he joined the University of Chicago in 1948, where he remained all his working life until his retirement in 1979. He was an adviser to Barry Goldwater in the unsuccessful presidential campaign in 1964 and subsequently advised President Nixon in 1968 and President Reagan in 1988. Despite endless rumours to the contrary, he never acted as a consultant to the Junta in Chile. He served as President of the American Economic Association in 1967 and President of the Mont Pèlerin Society 1970–2, having played an active role in the Society alongside its founder Friedrich Hayek (q.v.) since 1947. He also served as a member of the Economic Policy Advisory Board in 1981. He is currently a Senior Research Fellow at the Hoover Institution in Stanford, California.

Friedman's early training was in statistics and so were his first publications. He made his name in 1946 with his doctoral dissertation (co-authored with Simon Kuznets) on *Income of Independent Professional Practice* (National Bureau of Economic Research, 1946). This was followed in 1953 by *Essays in Positive Economics* (University of Chicago Press, 1953), which included a series of famous papers published in the late 1940s and early '50s on the methodology of economics (see Alchian, A.A.), the Marshallian demand curve, and the marginal utility of income. Such was his standing in the profession even at this early date that he was awarded the John Bates Clark Medal of the American Economic Association in 1951, just a year before reaching the age of forty. His professional reputation was placed beyond any doubt, however, by *A Theory of the Consumption Function* (Princeton University Press, 1957), which re-interpreted the Keynesian concept of the consumption function by relating it to lifetime instead of current income. For its ingenious manipulation of data and its reconciliation of apparently conflicting evidence, this book must rank as one of the masterpieces of modern econometrics. *Capitalism and Freedom* (University of Chicago Press, 1962) revealed Friedman's gifts for writing popular economics, crusading in readable language for such ideas as a 'negative income tax', a volunteer army, freely floating exchange rates, and 'educational vouchers' in the effort to show that the market mechanism is capable of solving almost all the outstanding social problems of our times. *An Economist's Protest: Columns in Political Economy* (Thomas Horton & Daughters, 1975), *There Is No Such Thing as a Free Lunch* (Open Court, 1983), *Bright Promises, Dismal Performance: an Economist's Protest* (Harcourt

Brace Jovanovich, 1983), but above all, *Free to Choose: A Personal Statement* (Harcourt Brace Jovanovich, 1980, Penguin, 1980), co-authored with his wife, Rose Friedman, provide additional examples of Friedman's positive genius for teaching applied economics.

It was only in *Studies in the Quantity Theory of Money* (University of Chicago Press, 1956) that Friedman turned decisively towards monetary economics, resuscitating the old discredited 'quantity theory of money' and giving new life to the anti-Keynesian doctrine that 'money matters'. According to the quantity theory of money, the price level in an economy depends essentially on the supply of money, that is, coins, notes and checking deposits in banks. Friedman argued, first of all, that every dramatic change in the level of prices has always been preceded in the past by a dramatic change in the rate of growth of the money supply, and second, that downturns and upturns in the total level of economic activity are always sparked off by sharp changes in the money supply. Since he doubted the ability of governments to achieve 'fine tuning', his preferred remedy was a legislative rule, linking the rate of growth of the money supply automatically to the rate of growth of real GNP. In practice, however, he was willing to settle for a 'discretionary' policy that gave priority to monetary policy over fiscal policy.

Friedmanite 'monetarism' was given authority by the publication of a stupendous *Monetary History of the United States, 1867–1960* (Princeton University Press, 1963), co-authored with A.J. Schwartz, which announced, among its many other findings, the startling notion that the Great Depression of the 1930s was largely the outcome of the bungling monetary policies of the Federal Reserve System. Next came his presidential address to the American Economic Association. 'The Role of Monetary Policy', *American Economic Review*, March 1968, which introduced the profession to the now famous concept of 'the natural rate of unemployment' – the minimum level of unemployment that can be sustained without provoking ever-increasing inflation – in the attempt to account for the phenomenon of 'stagflation', that is the simultaneous occurrence of unemployment and inflation. Stagflation is difficult to explain in terms of orthodox Keynesian theory and Friedman seized on it in attempting to demonstrate the bankruptcy of Keynesian economics. The central element in his explanation was the notion that price inflation depends on wage inflation, which in turn depends critically on the expectations of wage earners about future changes in the price levels. Once workers have come to expect a given rate of price inflation, any attempt by the government to reduce the level of unemployment by expansionary fiscal policies creates pressures to raise money wages, thus neutralising the reduction in unemployment while generating still more inflation. In technical language, the long-run 'Phillips Curve' (see Phillips, A.W.) is vertical at the rate of unemployment at which the labour market is effectively cleared; this rate is called 'the natural rate' because it is determined by real factors – impediments to labour mobility, barriers to occupational entry, restrictions on lay-offs, etc. – which cannot be altered quickly by macroeconomic policies. In *A Theoretical Framework for Monetary Analysis* (Columbia University Press, 1971) and 'Nobel Lecture: Inflation and Unemployment', *Journal of Political Economy*, June 1977, Friedman continued to elaborate these ideas, arguing that the new problem was not 'stagflation' but 'slumpflation', that is, *rising* levels of unemployment occurring simultaneously with *rising* rates of price inflation; in short, the long-run 'Phillips Curve' has become positively inclined.

It took exactly twelve years for the Keynesian Revolution to be incorporated into textbooks of elementary economics. Milton Friedman equalled Keynes' record: the natural-rate hypothesis was announced in 1967 and eleven years later Robert J. Gordon, a neo-Keynesian rather than a monetarist, published *Macroeconomics* (Little, Brown, 1978; 2nd edn, 1981), an intermediate textbook which is entirely organised around the central concept of 'the natural rate of unemployment'.

Milton Friedman is still active, although eighty-five years of age. In 1982 he supplemented his *Monetary History* by a new blockbuster on *Monetary Trends in the United States and the United Kingdom* (University of Chicago Press, 1982), co-authored with A.J. Schwartz; see also his Monetary Mischief: Episodes in Monetary History (Harcourt Brace Jovanovich, 1992). In the meantime, economists continue to argue about 'monetarism', its meaning, its practical relevance, and the precise relationship between Friedman's 'monetarism' and supply-side economics of the Reagan–Thatcher variety.

*Primary Literature*
M. Friedman, 'My Evolution as an Economist', in W. Breit and R.W. Spencer (eds), *Lives of the Laureates: Ten Nobel Economists* (MIT Press, 1990).

*Secondary Literature*
L. Silk, *The Economists* (Basic Books, 1976), ch. 2; R. Sobel, *The Worldly Economists* (The Free Press, 1980), chs 6 and 8; J. Burton, 'Positively Milton Friedman', in J.R. Shackleton and G. Locksley (eds), *Twelve Contemporary Economists* (Macmillan, 1981; Wiley, Halsted Press, 1981); A. Horsch and N. De Marchi, *Milton Friedman: Economics in Theory and Practice* (University of Michigan Press, 1990); R.J. Gordon, ed., *Milton Friedman's Monetary Framework: A Debate with his Critics* (University of Chicago Press, 1974); A. Walters, 'Friedman, Milton', J. Eatwell, M. Milgate and P. Newman (eds), in *The New Palgrave: A Dictionary of Economics*, (Macmillan, 1987) vol. 2; W. Frazer, *Power and Ideas: Milton Friedman and the Big U-turn* (Gulf Atlantic, 1988); J.C. Wood and R.N. Woods (eds), *Milton Friedman: Critical Assessment*, 4 vols (Routledge, 1990).

# Frisch, Ragnar A.K. (1895–1973)

Ragnar Frisch was a pioneer of 'econometrics', a name which he himself coined, that union of mathematical and statistical methods applied to the testing of economic hypotheses which, he firmly believed, would at long last establish economics as a science. He founded the Econometric Society in 1930, edited *Econometrica* from 1933 to 1955, and was awarded the first Nobel Prize in Economics in 1969, jointly with Jan Tinbergen (q.v.) for his services to econometric modelling and measurement. But he was also the nearest equivalent in our times to the economist as Plato's 'philosopher-king': for over thirty years, he exerted an overwhelming influence on economic thought and economic policy in his native country, Norway.

Curiously enough, most of his writings remain unpublished but what he did publish – essays such as 'Propagation Problems and Impulse Problems in Dynamic Economics' (1933), reprinted in R.A. Gordon and L.R. Klein (eds), *Reading in Business Cycles* (Richard D. Irwin, 1965), 'On the Notion of Equilibrium and Disequilibrium', *Review of Economic Studies*, February 1936, and 'Alfred Marshall's Theory of Value', *Quarterly Journal of Economics*, November 1950, and books such as *Theory of Production* (Reidel, 1965; Rand McNally, 1965) and *Maximas and Minimas* (Reidel, 1966) – had the uncanny quality of becoming instant classics. In the closing years of World War II, he took an increasing interest in problems of economic planning, of which *Planning for India* (Asia Publishing House, 1960) and *Economic Planning Studies: A Collection of Essays* (Reidel, 1976) provide only a hazy impression. His macroeconomic 'decision models', as he liked to call them, were large-scale optimisation models, embodying input–output and behavioural equations, which he never managed to put to serious practical use. Nevertheless, he made an impact on the planning literature, not just in Western but also in Eastern Europe, through personal contacts, memoranda to government, letters to colleagues, and unpublished drafts of manuscripts.

Frisch was born in Oslo, Norway, in 1895. He worked as a young man in his father's gold and silver workshops, earning a certificate as a goldsmith, and at the same time he studied economics at the University of Oslo. Upon graduation in 1919, he went to France to prepare his doctoral dissertation in mathematical statistics. After the award of his PhD in 1926, he left, like so many other inter-war European economists, to travel in America on a Rockefeller Foundation Fellowship. Returning to Norway in 1928, he became a lecturer at the University of Oslo but two years later he went back to America as Visiting Professor at Yale University. A new professorship was especially created to bring him back to Norway and in 1931 he was appointed to the Chair of Economics at the University of Oslo, which he held until his retirement in 1965. Throughout the 1930s and again in the early post-war years, he advised the Labour Party of Norway along lines which resembled the ideas of Keynesian policy-makers in Britain and America, except for a greater emphasis on central planning in respect of the key industries of the economy.

*Secondary Literature*
L. Johansen, 'Frisch, Ragnar', in D. Sills (ed.), *International Encylopaedia of the Social Sciences*, vol. 18 (The Free Press, 1979); J.C. Andvig, *Ragnar Frisch and the Great Depression: A Study in the Inter-war History of Macroeconomic Theory and Policy* (Norwegian Institute of International Affairs, 1985); P.N. Rasmussen, 'Frisch, Ragnar Anton Kittel', in J. Eatwell, M. Milgate and P. Newman (eds), *The New Palgrave: A Dictionary of Economics*, vol. 2 (Macmillan, 1987).

# Galbraith, John Kenneth (1908– )

As a celebrity, Galbraith puts every other living economist to shame: Harvard professor, speech writer for Adlai Stevenson, family friend of the Kennedys and personal adviser to President Kennedy, American ambassador to India, Chairman of Americans for Democratic Action, contributor to *Playboy* and the *New York Times*, best-selling author, novelist, popular pundit, much-quoted wit, and tallest (6 feet 8 inches) economist of all times. Friedman television series *Free to Choose* was partly designed to neutralise Galbraith's series *The Age of Uncertainty* but it attracted fewer viewers even though it was arguably better television.

Born in Ontario, Canada, in 1908 among Scottish-Canadian farmers, Galbraith received his first degree from Ontario Agricultural College. In 1932, he crossed the border to take up graduate studies in agricultural economics at the University of California, Berkeley. Taking his PhD in 1936, he was offered an instructorship at Harvard, where he launched upon a study of industrial price rigidities. In 1937, he spent a year at Cambridge University from which resulted a book with H.S. Dennison on *Modern Competition and Business Policy* (Oxford University Press, 1938). Returning to Harvard and later Princeton, he left academic life at the outbreak of World War II to head the Price Section of the Office of Price Administration. Other economists saw wartime rationing and price control as a temporary but necessary evil: Galbraith, however, defended it in *A Theory of Price Control* (Harvard University Press, 1952) as a simple extension of price-fixing by large corporations in peacetime.

After leaving the government in 1943, he alternated between the editorial board of *Fortune* magazine and the directorship of the US Strategic Bombing Survey. In 1949, he was back at Harvard as a professor, finally retiring in 1975. Three years later *A Theory of Price Control* was published alongside *American Capitalism: The Concept of Countervailing Power* (Houghton Mifflin, 1952, 3rd edn, 1962) and it was the latter book which catapulted Galbraith into the best-sellers' list. *American Capitalism* was an optimistic book: it argued that the powerless perfect competitor of textbook optimistic theory had been increasingly replaced by giant organisations (firms, unions, retailing chains, etc.) but that every abuse of economic power on one side of the market generated its own 'countervailing' check on the opposite side, as a result of which consumers were not much worse off than they were under perfect competition.

Galbraith's next book, *The Great Crash 1929* (Houghton Mifflin, 1954; 3rd edn, 1972; Penguin, 1961) was not quite as successful as *American Capitalism* but *The Affluent Society* (Houghton Mifflin, 1958; 3rd edn, 1976; Penguin, 1962) exceeded even the popularity of *American Capitalism*: it became virtually the non-fiction book of the year and its contrast between 'private affluence' and 'public squalor' immediately entered into popular language. The modern consumer, Galbraith argued, is satiated by opulence and is increasingly vulnerable to advertising and salesmanship to create a demand for baubles and trinkets. Such artificial tastes and preferences are none the less treated by economists as if they originated with the individual consumer, thus ignoring the fact that consumer sovereignty has been effectively replaced by producer sovereignty. At the same time, vital public services (roads, schools, museums, low-cost housing, the police, etc.) increasingly demanded by a rich society are starved of revenue because of 'conventional wisdom', such that only the private sector is productive of wealth and that progressive taxation destroys economic incentives. The result is a society which mixes affluence in the private sphere with squalor in the public sphere. The effect of this book was like a bomb-shell: it marked the beginning of the anti-growth movement that ushered in the War on Poverty and the Ecological Movement of the late 1960s and it remains to this day the most widely read book by any modern economist.

After one or two minor publications, 1967 saw the publication of his most ambitious work, *The New Industrial State* (Houghton Mifflin, 1967; 3rd edn, 1978; Penguin 1969). It was once again a picture of modern economic life dominated by Big Business, which in turn is dominated not by stockholders or even nominal managers, but by the new 'techno-structure' of professionally qualified men and women that fill the technical and sales positions, thus providing the crucial knowledge on which all strategic business decisions rest. Many of the separate strands of *American Capitalism* and *The Affluent Society* were picked up and developed afresh in this culminating book of Galbraith's career, supplemented by the afterthought volume *Economics and the Public Purpose* (Houghton Mifflin, 1973; Penguin, 1975). Galbraith was heavily criticised in the debate that broke out over *The New Industrial State* and he did in fact retreat a little, conceding that the giant corporations had not succeeded in totally destroying a significant remnant of small and medium-sized firms in the US economy. Nevertheless, by and large he stuck to his guns, contending that orthodox economics had simply never revised its doctrines in the light of the growth of Big Business. Similarly, his most recent book, co-authored with N. Salinger, *Almost Everyone's Guide to Economics* (Houghton Mifflin, 1978), presents the basic outlines of Galbraithian economics as a genuine alternative to mainstream doctrines.

Galbraith has remained a renegade in the eyes of his fellow economists. They voted him President of the American Economic Association in 1972 but they never stopped criticising his racy style of undocumented assertions, his fond belief in planning and more state control, his contempt for rigorous analysis, his insistence that most economics is simply 'conventional wisdom', and, of course, they find it hard to forgive him for selling in the millions!

*Primary Literature*
J.K. Galbraith, *A Life in Our Times* (Houghton Mifflin, André Deutsch, 1981).

*Secondary Literature*
C.H. Hession, *John Kenneth Galbraith and his Critics* (New American Library, 1972): L. Silk, *The Economists* (Basic Books, 1976), ch. 3; R. Sobel, *The Worldly Economists* (The Free Press, 1980), ch. 4; W. Breit and R.L. Ransom, 'John Kenneth Galbraith: Economists as Social

Critic', in *The Academic Scribblers: American Economists* (Dryden Press, 2nd edn, 1982); D.R. Fusfeld, 'John Kenneth Galbraith', H.W. Spiegel and W.J. Samuels (eds), *Contemporary Economists in Perspective* (JAI Press, 1984); D. Reisman, 'The Dissenting Economist: J.K. Galbraith', in J.R. Shackleton and G. Locksley (eds), *Twelve Contemporary Economists* (Macmillan, 1981); S. Pressman, 'John Kenneth Galbraith', in P. Arestis and M. Sawyer (eds), *Biographical Dictionary of Dissenting Economists* (Edward Elgar, 1992).

# Georgescu-Roegen, Nicholas (1906–94)

Georgescu-Roegen's career shows a steady expansion of outlook and interests from an early phase of highly technical mathematical economics, largely in utility theory and input–output analysis, to a later phase of growth modelling and the ambitious attempt to formulate the principles of 'bioeconomics', a new style of 'dialectical' economic thinking to replace more or less the whole of present-day economics with its 'mechanical' mode of reasoning. The earlier phase is well represented by such famous articles as 'The Pure Theory of Consumer Behaviour', *Quarterly Journal of Economics*, August 1936, and his contributions to *Activity Analysis of Production and Allocation* (Yale University Press, 1951), edited by T. Koopmans and others. The later phase begins with *Analytical Economics: Issues and Problems* (Harvard University Press, 1966) but is more clearly set out in *The Entropy Law and the Economic Process* (Harvard University Press, 1971) and *Energy and Economic Myths: Institutional and Analytical Economic Essays* (Pergamon Press, 1976). Somewhere in the middle are innumerable articles on special problems, such as production theory, the nature of expectations, the anatomy of agrarian economies, and the Marxist prediction of capitalist breakdown. It is only fair to add that Georgescu-Roegen's later books have not been well received, or, rather, have been respectfully received and quickly put away. For various complex reasons, not to mention the difficult style in which they are written and the intimidating references which they contain to theoretical developments in physics and biology, these works have received virtually no critical discussion from economists.

The essence of Georgescu-Roegen's 'bioeconomics' is the notion that production, involving as it does the transformation of what is for all practical purposes a constant stock of matter and energy, must conform to the same Law of Entropy that governs all closed systems: entropy or unavailable matter and energy tends constantly to increase, while available matter and energy tends constantly to decrease. Economic growth only appears superficially to increase output per unit of inputs; in fact, it does so by using up the finite stock of the world's matter and energy. Thus, industrial societies relying on fossil fuels and other mineral inputs are necessarily subject to entropic decay through extraction on the one hand and pollution on the other. It is in this sense that production even with technical progress is subject to historically diminishing returns. The old idea of a 'stationary state' as the terminus of economic growth, a situation in which the economic system replaces itself precisely from time period to time period and does so forever, is a simple impossibility. The implications of this line of thinking are elegantly explored in Georgescu-Roegen's readable article, 'Energy Analysis and Economic Evaluation', *Southern Economic Journal*, April 1979.

Georgescu-Roegen was born in 1906 in Constanza, Romania. He obtained his first degree in mathematics from the University of Bucharest in 1926 and went on to take a doctorate in statistics from the University of Paris in 1930. He started teaching at the University of Bucharest in the same year, becoming a Professor of Statistics there in 1932. In 1947, he emigrated to America and joined the faculty at Harvard University for two years. In 1949, he became a Professor at Vanderbilt University, where he remained until his retirement in 1976.

He was co-editor of the *Enciclopedia Romanei* from 1935 to 1947. He was Associate Editor of *Econometrica* from 1951 to 1968. He was voted a Distinguished Fellow of the American Economic Association in 1971 and won the Earl of Sutherland Prize for Achievement in Research in 1976.

*Primary Literature*
N. Georgescu-Roegen, 'An Emigrant from a Developing Country: Autobiographical Notes', in J.A. Kregel (ed.), *Recollections of Eminent Economists*, vol. 2 (Macmillan, 1989); N. Georgescu-Roegen, 'Nicholas Georgescu-Roegen About Himself', in M. Szenberg (ed.), *Eminent Economists, Their Life Philosophies* (Cambridge University Press, 1992); N. Georgescu-Roegen, 'Nicholas Georgescu-Roegen'; in P. Arestis and M. Sawyer (eds), *A Biographical Dictionary of Dissenting Economists* (Edward Elgar, 1992).

*Secondary Literature*
N. Wade, 'Nicholas Georgescu-Roegen: Entropy, the Measure of Economic Man', *Science*, 31 October 1975; A. Maneschi and S. Zamagni, 'Nicholas Georgescu-Roegen, 1906–1994', *Economic Journal*, May 1997; S. Zamagni, 'Georgescu-Roegen, Nicholas', in J. Eatwell, M. Milgate and P. Newman (eds), The New Palgrave: A Dictionary of Economics, vol. 2 (Macmillan, 1987); P. Mirowski, 'Nicholas Georgescu-Roegen', in W.J. Samuel (ed.), *New Horizons in Economic Thought* (Edward Elgar, 1992).

# Gerschenkron, Alexander (1904–78)

Gerschenkron was one of the many Austrian economists who arrived in America in 1938 as a result of Hitler's invasion of Austria (see also Machlup, F.; Morgenstern, O.). Born in 1904 in Odessa, Russia, his family moved to Vienna after the Russian Revolution where Gerschenkron completed his education, receiving his doctor's degree from the University of Vienna in 1928. His first post was as an Associate of the Austrian Institute of Business Cycle Research, then headed by Friedrich Hayek (q.v.). Leaving for the United States in 1938 on the day of the German invasion, he obtained a post as research assistant and subsequently lecturer at the University of California, Berkeley. In 1944, he joined the research staff of the Federal Reserve System in Washington, having published his first book, *Bread and Democracy in Germany* (Fertig, 1943; 2nd edn, 1966); two years later he became a Professor at Harvard University, where for many years he directed economic research in the Russian Research Center. He retired in 1974 and died in 1978.

In a major article, 'The Soviet Indices of Industrial Production', *Review of Economics and Statistics*, November 1947, and a book, *A Dollar Index of Soviet Machinery Output, 1927–28 to 1937* (Rand Corporation, 1951), he discovered the so-called 'Gerschenkron effect' whereby the choice of the base year for an index of industrial output in a relatively unindustrialised economy largely determines the rate of growth exhibited by that index. Gerschenkron was able to show that Soviet industrial production in the 1930s had been measured by Soviet planners in such a way as to produce the highest rate of growth.

Gerschenkron withdrew from teaching in the Soviet area in 1956 and switched his interest to the causes of growth in nineteenth-century Europe, particularly in the less-developed Balkan and Latin countries of Europe. In *Economic Backwardness in Historical Perspective* (Harvard University Press, 1968), he planted the influential notion of the 'advantage of backwardness', which allows poorer countries to borrow advanced technology from richer countries and thus to leapfrog stages of development. This constituted one of the many objections to the fashionable Rostowian notion of the 1960s (see Rostow, W.W.) that economic growth around the world is marked by a definite succession of 'stages of growth', which all countries are bound to pass through, albeit at different rates. Gerschenkron employed the concept of the 'advantage of backwardness' to throw light on the wholly different role of the state in promoting industrialisation in countries like Russia, Italy and Hungary on the one hand, and France and Germany on the other. In *Europe in the Russian Mirror* (Cambridge University Press, 1970) and *An Economic Spurt that Failed* (Princeton University Press, 1977), he returned to his earlier concern with Soviet economic development in the light of the historical experience of growth in different parts of Europe.

Gerschenkron's encyclopaedic knowledge of Russia and things Russian were legendary around Harvard in the 1950s and '60s. His erudite essay on Pasternak's novel *Doctor Zhivago* in the *New York Review of Books* and his devastating critique of Nabokov's English translation of Pushkin's *Eugene Onegin* in the journal *Modern Philosophy*, 1966, followed by a furious debate with Nabokov which traded blow for blow, are classics of literary criticism in their own right. He became a Distinguished Fellow of the American Economic Association in 1969.

*Secondary Literature*
A. Erlich, 'Gerschenkron, Alexander', in D. Sills (ed.), *International Encyclopaedia of the Social Sciences*, vol. 18 (The Free Press, 1979).

# Haberler, Gottfried (1900–95)

Haberler's *Theory of International Trade, with its Application to Commercial Policy* (Macmillan, William Hodge, 1936) constituted a landmark in the history of international economics because it was the first book which successfully reformulated the old classical theory of comparative costs in the modern language of general equilibrium theory, thus restating more precisely the traditional analysis of the benefits of free trade. In *Studies in the Theory of International Trade* (1937), Jacob Viner (q.v.) took exception to the way Haberler converted the classical conception of costs, based on real sacrifices of human effort, into a perfectly general and hence empty concept of costs as alternative opportunities forgone. Haberler was unconvinced by Viner's criticisms and the debate between them was never decisively resolved, in part because it was not so much a quarrel about the nature of costs as about the respective merits of 'partial' versus 'general' equilibrium analysis. Nevertheless, the drift of professional opinion eventually went Haberler's way.

In 1937, Haberler's next book, *Prosperity and Depression* (League of Nations, 1937; Harvard University Press, 1958), made almost as big an impact as his earlier book on international trade. In this work he reviewed and classified all the prevailing monetary and non-monetary theories of business cycles with the aim of producing a synthetic explanation that would put to rest what was then becoming an almost endless controversy about the causes of booms and slumps. Whether he succeeded in producing everybody's-theory-of-business-cycles is doubtful but his effort certainly put a stop to the proliferation of alternative theories and pointed the way to empirical testing, which soon placed business cycle theory on a more secure footing (see Tinbergen, J.). Since then, Haberler has continued to contribute to the post-war analysis of the causes and cures of inflation, particularly in relation to questions of international monetary reform.

Haberler is one of the many European immigrants who have had a lasting influence on American economics in this century (see also Coase, R.H.; Debreu, G.; Hayek, F.A.; Koopmans, T.C.; Leontief, W.W.; Lerner, A.P.; Machlup, F.; Marschak, J.; Modigliani, F.; and Morgenstern, O.). He was born in Vienna, Austria, in 1900 and received his Bachelor's degree in 1923 and his Doctor's degree in 1925, both from the University of Vienna. After publishing his first book on the theory of index numbers, he travelled to Britain and America on a Rockefeller Foundation Fellowship in 1927–9. In 1928, he began teaching at the University of Vienna but left Austria in 1932 to become a lecturer at Harvard University. From 1934 to 1936, he worked at the League of Nations in Geneva, returning to Harvard in 1936 to become Professor of Economics. He remained at Harvard University until his retirement in 1971. After retirement, he continued to be active as a Resident Scholar at the American Enterprise Institute in Washington until his death in 1995.

He served as President of the International Economic Association in 1950–1, the National Bureau of Economic Research in 1955, the American Economic Association in 1963, Editor of the *Quarterly Journal of Economics* during 1965–70, and a consultant to the US Department of Treasury during 1965–78. He has received honorary degrees from several European universities and was the first economist to win the prestigious Antonio Feltrinelli Prize in 1980. *Economic Growth and Stability* (Nash, 1974) and *The Great Depression of the 1930s: Can It Happen Again?* (American Enterprise Institute, 1981) give the flavour of his thinking, which might be described as that of an economic 'conservative'. His many papers and essays have been collected together in *Selected Essays of Gottfried Haberler*, ed. A.Y.C. Koo (MIT Press, 1985) and *The Liberal Economic Order*, ed. A.Y.C. Koo, 2 vols (Edward Elgar, 1993).

*Secondary Literature*
M. Gillis, R.E. Baldwin, L.H. Officer and T.D. Willet, 'Gottfried Haberler: Contributions upon Entering His Ninth Decade', *Quarterly Journal of Economics*, February 1982.

# Hahn, Frank (1925– )

Frank Hahn is a specialist in general equilibrium theory, a highly technical branch of mathematical economics which investigates the abstract properties of multimarket equilibrium: whether it 'exists'; whether, if it exists, it is 'unique'; and whether, if it is unique, it is also 'stable' both for small and large deviations from equilibrium. Almost every question in economics involves interrelationships between different markets and it is these interrelationships which are the central focus of general equilibrium theory; for that reason alone it is important to clarify the purely logical difficulties in general equilibrium analysis. Moreover, the abstract investigation of general equilibrium theory has thrown light on a number of features of actual economies; for example, why there are forward markets for some but by no means all commodities, or why certain departures from an initial equilibrium diverge from, rather than converge on, a new equilibrium (see Arrow, K.J.; Debreu, G.). Much of Hahn's early technical work was concerned with the problem of introducing money into general equilibrium theory, a difficulty which had defeated many previous efforts to prove the existence of a general equilibrium solution under perfect competition.

Most general equilibrium theorists write for an audience of other economists and do not take time to explain why general equilibrium theory is important. But Hahn has repeatedly struggled to explain the significance of general equilibrium theory to students, as in his Inaugural Lecture at the University of Cambridge, *On the Notion of Equilibrium in Economics* (Cambridge University Press, 1973), in the first readable chapter of an otherwise advanced book, *General Competitive Analysis* (Oliver & Boyd, 1971), written jointly with K.J. Arrow. One of his central arguments was that equilibrium theory merely gives precision to the 200-year old claim of economists that the 'invisible hand' of the competitive market produces order rather than chaos and, under certain specified conditions, a better order than any other conceivable alternative; general equilibrium analysis tells us precisely what these conditions are and therefore explains rigorously why the 'invisible hand' sometimes fails. More recently, Hahn has become an outspoken opponent of 'monetarism' (see Friedman, M.), particularly the version adopted by the Thatcher government in Britain. In his latest book, *Money and Inflation* (Basil Blackwell, 1982), he attacks monetarism on a number of fronts, including its incompatibility with general equilibrium theory: general equilibrium theory does not support the idea that an economy with heavy unemployment can be driven to achieve full employment solely by control of the money supply.

Hahn was born in 1925 in Berlin, Germany. He arrived in Britain in his teens, received his BS in 1945 and his PhD in 1950, both from the London School of Economics. His doctoral dissertation on *The Share of Wages in National Income* (Heinemann, 1969) was years ahead of its time in constructing a macroeconomic theory of income distribution; by the time it was published in 1969, however, the topic was all too familiar and the book therefore made little impact. He started teaching mathematical economics at the University of Birmingham in 1953. In 1960 he moved to the University of Cambridge and became Managing Editor of the *Review of Economic Studies* (1963–7). In 1965 he became Professor of Economics at the London School of Economics, moving back to Cambridge in 1970, where he remained until 1992. He has been a Visiting Professor at the University of Siena in Italy ever since. He was President of the Econometric Society in 1968, the Royal Economic Society in 1986, and is a Corresponding Fellow of the American Academy of Arts and Sciences.

His numerous papers over the years have appeared in a series of books, namely *Money and Inflation* (Blackwell, 1982), *Equilibrium and Macroeconomics* (Blackwell, 1984) and *Money, Growth and Stability* (Blackwell, 1985).

*Primary Literature*
F. Hahn, 'Autobiographical Notes with Reflections', in M. Szenberg (ed.), *Eminent Economists: Their Life Philosophies* (Cambridge University Press, 1992).

# Hansen, Alvin H. (1887–1975)

Alvin Hansen did more than any other economist to bring the Keynesian Revolution to America, and the standard Keynesian emphasis on fiscal rather than monetary policy as the effective answer to mass unemployment owes more to Hansen's interpretation of Keynes than to Keynes himself. His *Fiscal Policy and Business Cycles* (W.W. Norton, 1941) was the first work by a major American economist to support the whole of Keynes' analysis of the causes of the Great Depression and to use it to restate the case for a policy of 'compensatory finance', a continuous effort to stabilise national income by means of deliberately unbalanced government budgets. In his Harvard Seminar on Fiscal Policy, which he taught together with John E. Williams throughout the late 1930s, he infected an entire generation of students, such as Paul Samuelson (q.v.), John Kenneth Galbraith (q.v.), James Tobin (q.v.) and others with a positive attitude to the Keynesian system. In addition, he published a steady stream of books and articles promulgating the new macroeconomics, such as *Monetary Theory and Fiscal Policy* (McGraw-Hill, 1949), *Business Cycles and National Income* (W.W. Norton, 1951; 2nd edn, 1964) and, above all, *A Guide to Keynes* (McGraw-Hill, 1953), a teaching handbook which took the reader through Keynes' *General Theory* chapter by chapter and sometimes paragraph by paragraph.

Hansen made such frequent use of Hicks' IS–LM diagram (see Hicks, J.R.), in which the level of national income and the rate of interest are simultaneously determined in commodity and money markets, that the IS–LM apparatus has ever since been called the 'Hicks–Hansen' synthesis between Keynesian and 'classical' economics. Moreover, on the basis of a few paragraphs in *The General Theory*, Hansen developed a long-run interpretation of Keynes' message, suggesting that the Great Depression was only a symptom of an entire era of chronic stagnation which would keep the capitalist economic system at levels below full employment for decades to come. He never clearly spelled out the 'stagnation thesis' but hinted that declining population growth, the exhaustion of the frontier of new land, and technical change of a capital-saving rather than a labour-saving kind would make it impossible for private investment to absorb all the saving generated by rising income. Hansen has been called 'the American Keynes'; if so, the American Keynes was much gloomier about the long-run prospects of capitalism than the English Keynes.

Hansen was born in 1887 in Viburg, South Dakota, and was educated locally, completing a BS from Yankton College, Dakota, in 1910. For some years he worked as a school teacher, principal, and school superintendent, and then went for graduate training to the University of Wisconsin. He received his doctorate from the University of Wisconsin in 1918 but had started teaching at Brown University two years earlier. In 1919 he moved to the University of Minnesota and in 1937 he came to Harvard as Professor of Political Economy. His first major book was *Business-cycle Theory: Its Development and Present Status* (Ginn, 1927). The next book was *Economic Stabilization in an Unbalanced World* (Harcourt Brace, 1932), a good example of Hansen in his pre-Keynesian days. By 1938 he had been converted to Keynes, as is evident from *Full Recovery of Stagnation?* (W.W. Norton, 1938). In another important book, *State and Local Finance in the National Economy* (W.W. Norton, 1944), written jointly with H.S. Perloff, he drew attention to the perversity of modern state and local tax systems which frequently caused state and local spending to decline in a slump and to increase in a boom against the prevailing trends in federal government spending. Among his last books were *Economic Issues of the 1960s* (McGraw-Hill, 1960) and *The Dollar and the International Monetary System* (McGraw-Hill, 1965) in which the influence of Keynes is still seen as paramount.

In 1933–4, Hansen served as Director of Research for President Roosevelt's Committee of Inquiry on National Policy in International Economic Relations. In 1937–8, Hansen became a member of the President's Advisory Council on Social Security. In 1941–3, he was Chairman of the US–Canadian Joint Economic Committee. He also served as Special Economic Advisor to the Board of Governors of the Federal Reserve System from 1940 to 1945. He was Vice-President of the American Statistical Association in 1937 and President of the American Economic Association in 1939. After his retirement from Harvard University in 1957, Hansen taught as Visiting Professor at the University of Bombay and a large number of American universities virtually to the year of his death at the age of eighty-eight in 1975.

*Secondary Literature*
S.E. Harris, 'Hansen, Alvin', in D.L. Sills (ed.), *International Encyclopaedia of the Social Sciences*, vol. 6 (The Free Press, 1968); W. Breit and R.L. Ransom, 'Alvin H. Hansen: The American Keynes', in *The Academic Scribblers: American Economists in Collision*, (2nd edn. Dryden Press, 1982); R.A. Musgrave, J.H. Williams, G. Haberler, W.S. Salant, P.A. Samuelson, J. Tobin, 'Alvin H. Hansen', *Quarterly Journal of Economics*, February 1976; R.A. Musgrave, 'Hansen, Alvin', in J. Eatwell, M. Milgate and P. Newman (eds), *The New Palgrave: A Dictionary of Economics*, vol. 2 (Macmillan, 1987).

# Harrod, Roy F. (1900–78)

Official biographer of Keynes and leading promoter of Keynesian economics, Harrod's own contribution to economics was to dynamise the Keynesian theory of income determination by converting it into a theory of the requirements of steady-state growth, that is, a growth path which can be sustained indefinitely until it is disturbed by an outside shock. Because Evsey Domar (q.v.) produced a later but similar version of the same theory, it has come to be known as the 'Harrod–Domar growth model'. First sketched in 1939 and then expanded into a book, *Towards a Dynamic Economics* (Macmillan, 1948; 2nd edn, St Martins Press, 1956; Greenwood Press, 1980), Harrod aided by Domar literally turned economics around from its almost total preoccupation with static equilibrium theory, of which the Keynesian system as formulated by Keynes was itself a reflection. In addition, however, Harrod made significant contributions to imperfect competition theory in the 1930s, wrote on the workings of the international monetary system, and stepped outside economics to examine the *Foundations of Inductive Logic* (Macmillan, 1956), in which, like so many philosophers before him, he attempted to solve David Hume's old 'problem of induction'; Harrod regarded this book as his most important achievement – greater than anything he had accomplished in economics.

Harrod was born in Norfolk, England, in 1900 and was educated privately at Westminster School and New College, Oxford University. He was appointed as a lecturer at Christ Church College, Oxford, shortly after his graduation in 1922 and spent the rest of his academic life there, becoming Senior Censor (the effective head of the College) and a member of the governing body of Oxford University. Before taking up his post at Oxford, however, he spent a term at King's College, Cambridge, where he fell under the spell of Keynes. He remained one of Keynes' keenest correspondents and was one of the first to see a draft of Keynes' *General Theory* in 1935, contributing the one and only diagram to appear in the final version of the book. Curiously enough, Harrod's first book *International Economics* (Cambridge University Press, 1933) contained the typically Keynesian concept of the foreign trade multiplier, a year or so ahead of Keynes' own recognition of the role of the multiplier. Harrod's *Life of John Maynard Keynes* (Macmillan, 1951; Kelley, 1969; Penguin, 1972) said much more about the works of Keynes than about his life and must be credited as a major element in the rapid dissemination of Keynes' ideas in the 1950s. More recent biographies of Keynes by Skidelsky and D. Moggridge have shown how much Harrod left out of his *Life of John Maynard Keynes*, the better to promote Keynesianism.

Even as the *General Theory* appeared on the bookstalls, Harrod's *The Trade Cycle: An Essay* (Macmillan, 1936; Kelley, 1965) combined John Maurice Clark's old 'acceleration principle' with Keynes' new 'multiplier' to produce a theory of the rate of change of aggregate demand. Three years later he produced a more mature version of the same idea in 'An Essay in Dynamic Theory', *Economic Journal*, March 1939, thereby effectively inventing modern growth theory. Giving Clark's 'accelerator' a new label, 'the capital–output ratio', and setting the reciprocal of Keynes' 'multiplier', the marginal propensity to save, equal to the average propensity to save, he showed that steady-state or smooth growth required total income to grow at the rate given by the saving rate divided by the capital–output ratio. Around this simple equation, he built up a rich theory in which there are actual growth paths, 'natural' growth paths (that is, full capacity ceilings), and 'warranted' or steady-state equilibrium growth paths; only special circumstances permit the actual growth path to be a warranted one and whenever actual growth departs from warranted growth, the departure is cumulative. In short, steady-state growth is highly unlikely to occur because it is an extremely unstable 'knife-edge' equilibrium.

The post-war publication of *Towards a Dynamic Economics* sparked off a great debate on the 'knife-edge' properties of Harrod's steady-state growth path in which it was argued that both the accelerator and the saving rate were subject to automatic corrective forces that drove the actual growth rate back to the warranted growth rate every time it deviated from it. Harrod's reactions to that debate, in which he stood his ground and made few concessions, can be seen in the later *Economic Dynamics* (Macmillan, St Martins, 1973). His several extremely influential articles on the theory of the firm under conditions of imperfect or monopolistic competition are brought between hard covers in *Economic Essays* (Macmillan, 1952; 2nd edn, St Martins, 1972).

During World War II, Harrod served on Prime Minister Church-ill's private statistical staff. Harrod's *The Prof.: A Personal Memoir of Lord Cherwell* (Macmillan, 1959) is a tribute to that period in which Harrod was associated with the great (Churchill) and the near-great (Lord Cherwell was Churchill's personal scientific adviser). Through-out the 1950s and 1960s, Harrod's journalistic output, quite apart from his more serious publications: Topical Comments: Essays in Dynamic Economics Applied (Macmillan, 1961), *The British Economy* (Macmillan, 1963; Greenwood Press, 1977), *Reforming the World's Money* (Macmillan, St Martins, 1965), *Dollar–Sterling Collaboration* (Atlantic Trade Study, 1968), and *Money* (Macmillan, St Martins, 1969), was so prodigious as to defy belief. In writing so much, he probably diluted the impact he might have had. As a matter of fact, his journalistic writings do not show him off to best advantage, conveying as they do the air of one who feels himself to be in full possession of the whole truth (as laid down by Keynes).

Harrod was Co-editor of the *Economic Journal* 1945–61, President of the Royal Economic Society 1962–4, and was knighted in 1959. He was an adviser to the Conservative Prime Minister Harold Macmillan from 1958 to 1963. He retired from teaching in 1967.

*Secondary Literature*
I.C. Johnson, 'Harrod, Roy F.', D.L. Sills (ed.), *International Encyclo-paedia of the Social Sciences*, vol. 18 (The Free Press, 1979); H. Phelps-Brown, 'Sir Roy Harrod: A Biographical Memoir', *Economic Journal*, March 1980; W. Eltis, 'Harrod, Roy Forbes', in J. Eatwell, M. Milgate

and P. Newman (eds), *The New Palgrave: A Dictionary of Economics*, vol. 2 (Macmillan, 1987).

# Hawtrey, Ralph G. (1879–1975)

Ralph Hawtrey's career proves two things: it is possible for an economist to go on producing articles and books throughout his or her life and it is possible to build a reputation as an economist without holding an academic post. Hawtrey was born in Slough, England, in 1879 and educated privately at Eton and Trinity College, Cambridge, where he obtained a First Class degree in mathematics in 1901. Hawtrey's youth was attended by constant money worries. This seems to have influenced him to opt for security rather than a slow rise up the academic ladder. Upon graduation, he entered the Civil Service, first in the Admiralty and then in the Treasury, where he remained for forty-three years until his retirement in 1947. Only then did he become a Professor of Economics at the Royal Institute of International Affairs, a post which he had until 1952. He was President of the Royal Economic Society from 1946 to 1948 and was knighted in 1956.

His first book, *Good and Bad Trade: An Inquiry into the Causes of Trade Fluctuations* (Macmillan, 1913; Kelley, 1962) was published just before the outbreak of World War I. His last book, *Incomes and Money* (Longmans, Green, 1967) was published in 1967. In between, there were nineteen books, among which *Currency and Credit* (Macmillan, 1919; Kelley, 1950), *The Art of Central Banking* (Macmillan, 1932; Kelley, 1962) and *Capital and Employment* (Macmillan, 1937;

Kelley, 1952) stand out for their influence on banking policy and the thinking of contemporary economists. Throughout his long career, he stood consistently for the view that business cycles are essentially a monetary phenomenon, which must therefore be controlled by regulating credit to wholesalers and retailers via the Bank Rate (or rediscount rate) and not by regulating public expenditure. It is noteworthy that he never contemplated direct control of the money supply as advocated by modern monetarists (see Friedman, M.). But this is in perfect keeping with the times because in the 1930s monetary policy always meant, rightly or wrongly, a policy about the rate of interest and not a policy about money supply targets.

For years Hawtrey held on tenaciously to what Keynes called the 'Treasury View', namely, that expenditures on public works financed by the sale of government bonds do nothing to remedy a depression because they only 'crowd out' private investment, a position which Hawtrey gradually qualified under criticism but never entirely withdrew. Although this placed him firmly in the anti-Keynesian camp, he had a considerable influence on the early development of Keynes' thought, not just in the 1920s but right through the 1930s, and his criticisms were taken seriously both by Keynes and by Keynes' young disciples. In particular, he taught a whole generation of British economists that the demand for idle money balances is a key element in any policy designed to stabilise the level of total economic activity.

Hawtrey's writings over a period of fifty-four years have a remarkable consistency, such that the text alone can never be used to date any of his books. Through all of them runs an unwavering belief in the critical role of short-term interest rates and the pivotal position of 'middlemen' in the economy, pivotal that is for fluctuations in the level of economic activity. But this very consistency also earned him the reputation of being old-fashioned and refusing to move with the times. Prominent as he was in the inter-war years, he came to be ignored increasingly in the post-war era. It is only since his death that he has made a comeback as an early 'monetarist' (see Friedman, M.).

*Secondary Literature*
E.G. Davis, 'R.G. Hawtrey, 1879–1975', in D.P. O'Brien and J.R. Presley (eds), *Pioneers of Modern Economics in Britain* (Macmillan, 1981); P. Deutscher, *R.G. Hawtrey and the Development of Macroeconomics*

(Macmillan, 1990); R.J. Bigg, 'Hawtrey, Ralph George', in J. Eatwell, M. Milgate and P. Newman (eds), *The New Palgrave: A Dictionary of Economics*, vol. 2 (Macmillan, 1987).

# Hayek,
# Friedrich A. von
# (1899–1992)

Hayek's reputation has gone through a remarkable cycle. An eminent exponent of the Austrian theory of business cycles in the 1930s (see Mises, L.E. von), he was worsted in the battle over Keynes' *Treatise on Money* (1930) and retreated into capital theory, an esoteric branch of economics in which few economists then took an active interest (see Knight, F.H.). Even the immensely popular *Road to Serfdom* (Routledge & Kegan Paul, 1944; University of Chicago Press, 1956), an indictment of government intervention in modern economies as representing 'creeping socialism', failed to reinstate him to front ranks. He gave up economics altogether after the war and took up psychology, political philosophy, the philosophy of law, and the history of ideas. And then gradually, his fame as a 'libertarian' began to spread. Since receiving the Nobel Prize in Economics in 1974, shared jointly with Gunnar Myrdal, he has come back to mainstream economics as a leading critic of Keynesianism and an advocate of free banking as the answer to the scourge of inflation. Today he reigns supreme as the kind of moral philosopher and political economist that economics has not seen since Adam Smith.

He was born in 1899 in Vienna, the capital of the Austro-Hungarian Empire, in an academic family. After serving in the army in World War I, he returned to Vienna and entered the Law Faculty of the University of Vienna, taking his *Dr Juris* in 1921. Two years later, he obtained a second doctorate in economics. There followed a brief visit to America, attending courses at Columbia University and working as a research assistant to various American economists. Returning to Vienna in 1924, he and a number of other young promising economists (see also Haberler, G.; Machlup, F.; and Morgenstern, O.) formed a circle under the watchful eye of Ludwig von Mises, whose own private seminar formed a fulcrum of economic discussion in Austria in the 1920s. In 1927, with Mises' support, Hayek became the director of the Austrian Institute for Business Cycle Research and two years later he was admitted as *Privatdozent* (lecturer) to the University of Vienna, the first rank on the ladder of academic success in the Austria of those days.

Shortly thereafter, Lionel Robbins invited him to give some lectures at the London School of Economics. Published under the title *Prices and Production* (Routledge & Kegan Paul, 1931; 2nd edn, Kelley, 1978), these lectures made a considerable stir in the English-speaking world and led to a professorship at the London School of Economics, which lasted eighteen years. According to *Prices and Production*, rising prices in a boom lead to a fall in real wages, which then induces the substitution of labour for machines and a general shortening of production periods; in consequence, interest rates rise, investment falls off and the economy turns down. Conversely, in a slump the rising level of real wages revives investment as labour is displaced and periods of production are lengthened. In this argument, quite contrary to the usual Keynesian reasoning, a rising level of consumption after a certain point reduces rather than increases investment, and vice versa for a falling level of consumption.

Hayek wrote an unfavourable review of Keynes' *Treatise on Money* to which Keynes replied; Piero Sraffa (q.v.) on behalf of Keynes wrote an equally critical review of *Prices and Production*, to which Hayek replied; the controversy was joined by every prominent monetary economist of the day and was only put to rest by Keynes' *General Theory* (1936), which totally altered the terms of the debate.

Hayek continued to work on a by-product of that debate as summed up in his *Profits, Interest and Investment* (Routledge & Kegan Paul, 1939; Kelley, 1978) and *The Pure Theory of Capital* (Macmillan, 1941; University of Chicago Press, 1975). He participated in another controversy, resulting from Mises' denial that a socialist economy could price its goods and services in accordance with the principles of relative scarcity (see Mises, L.E. von), and edited a classic volume on *Collectivist Economic Planning: Critical Studies on the Possibilities of Socialism* (Routledge & Kegan Paul, 1935; Kelley, 1978). He had long shown an expertise in the history of economic thought and now extended it to the history of political ideas: a series of articles on 'scientism', later to appear as *The Counter-revolution of Science* (Free Press, 1952), traced modern collectivist beliefs in economic planning to the eighteenth-century theories of Saint-Simon and August Comte. In 1944, *The Road to Serfdom* won him momentary notoriety as a political thinker and marked the beginning of his later rise to leadership in the world-wide libertarian movement. After the war, he became a frequent visitor at American universities, founded and for twelve years headed the Mont Pèlerin Society, a society of social scientists dedicated to defending the principles of the free market, and published a series of influential essays, published between hard covers in *Individualism and Economic Order* (Routledge & Kegan Paul, University of Chicago Press, 1948).

In 1950, he left Britain and became Professor of Social and Moral Sciences at the University of Chicago. Further works in the history of ideas, including a surprising treatise on psychology, *The Sensory Order: An Inquiry into the Foundations of Theoretical Psychology* (Routledge & Kegan Paul, University of Chicago Press, 1976), led in 1960 to the masterpiece of his 'middle years', *The Constitution of Liberty* (Routledge & Kegan Paul, University of Chicago Press, 1960). This was a major statement of modern liberalism, which shocked many readers by its effective criticism of inheritance taxation and high marginal rates of income taxation. In 1962, Hayek returned to Europe as Professor of Economic Policy at the University of Freiburg in Breisgau, Western Germany. After retirement from Freiburg in 1968, he spent a further nine years in Austria at the University of Salzburg before retiring at long last from academic life – at the age of seventy-eight. He died in 1992.

The Salzburg years witnessed the publication of his final major work, the three-volume study of *Law, Legislation and Liberty* (Routledge & Kegan Paul, University of Chicago Press, 1973, 1976, 1979), capping a career marked by eighteen books, fifteen pamphlets, 142 journal articles and chapters in books, not one of which is shallow, or superficial. Some of his old papers, such as 'Economics and Knowledge', *Economica*, February 1937, have recently been disinterred as opening new vistas that should have been explored earlier, in this paper he argued, quite correctly, that economic theory had never actually demonstrated how the knowledge which economic agents require to achieve equilibrium is generated and communicated among them by the process of competition.

At the heart of many of his later writings is the 'doctrine of unintended social consequences': most of the worthwhile institutions of modern society (markets, courts, the legal system, and even the government itself) are the unintended by-products of individual actions taken for other reasons and never could have been deliberately and consciously created. It follows, according to Hayek, that the least interference with spontaneous individual action there is, the better. This is not an argument for doing nothing but rather an argument for doing little and for doing it gradually. This doctrine of 'least interference' lends itself either to a traditional conservative or to a radical anarchist interpretation. There are young libertarians who would oppose all censorship or regulation of pornography in modern society on Hayekian grounds and yet Hayek himself never went that far in opposing government intervention. Contrariwise, Hayek extended his doctrine to central banking, in *Denationalisation of Money* (Institute of Economic Affairs, 1976), thus clashing with traditional economic liberalism, which always treated state monopoly of the issue of money as an exception to the general rule of laissez-faire. In short, everyone agrees with what Hayek meant in general but there is a large spectrum of answers to what he meant in particular. His last book, *The Fatal Conceit: The Errors of Socialism*, became volume 1 of the *Collected Works of F.A. Hayek*, ed. W.W. Bartley III (Routledge, University of Chicago Press, 1988). When Bartley died, the project was taken over by others. So far, volume 3: *The Trend of Economic Thinking*, ed. W.W. Bartley III and S. Kresge (1991), volume 4: *The Fortune of Liberalism*, ed. P.G. Klein (1992), and volume 9: *Contra Keynes and Cambridge*, ed. B. Caldwell (1995) have appeared and a dozen more volumes are already in the pipeline.

It will take another generation fully to digest Hayek's many and multifaceted contributions to economics and indeed social science as a whole.

*Secondary Literature*
F. Machlup, 'Hayek, Friedrich, A. von', in D.L. Sills (ed.), *International Encyclopaedia of the Social Sciences*, vol. 18 (The Free Press, 1979); N.P. Barry, 'Restating the Liberal Order: Hayek's Philosophi-

cal Economics', in J.R. Shackleton and G. Locksley (eds), *Twelve Contemporary Economists* (Macmillan, 1981; Wiley, Halsted Press, 1981); G.L.S. Shackle, 'F.A. Hayek', in D.P. O'Brien and J.R. Presley (eds), *Pioneers of Modern Economics in Britain* (Macmillan, 1981); R.W. Garrison and J.M. Kirzner, 'Hayek, Friedrich August', in J. Eatwell, M. Milgate and P. Newman (eds), *The New Palgrave: A Dictionary of Economics*, vol. 2 (Macmillan, 1987); J.C. Wood and R.N. Wood, *Friedrich A. Hayek: Critical Assessments*, 4 vols (Routledge, 1991).

# Hicks, John R. (1904–89)

Hicks is one of the half-dozen outstanding economic theorists of the twentieth century: his early work on he marginal productivity theory of distribution, his subsequent contributions to welfare economics (including the so-called 'Hicks–Kaldor compensation test'), his invention of the 'IS–LM' diagram to expound the true meaning of Keynes, his masterpiece *Value and Capital* (Clarendon Press, 1939; 2nd edn, 1953), which taught a whole generation of economists to employ indifference curves and general equilibrium theory, and his more recent synthesising work on growth theory, have all become standard parts of the tool kit of modern economists. Knighted in 1964, joint winner (with Kenneth J. Arrow) of the Nobel Prize in Economics in 1972, and the recipient of a dozen honorary degrees, he always remained curiously shy and diffident in face-to-face conversation. His writings on economics, however, have a literary elegance and an expository clarity that we associate only with great teachers.

Hicks was born in Leamington Spa, England, in 1904. Graduating from Oxford University in 1925, he continued his studies before joining the staff of the London School of Economics in 1926. He left the LSE in 1935 to take up a professorship at Manchester University, where he remained until 1946. Moving to a fellowship and then a professorship at Nuffield College, Oxford, he retired from active academic life in 1965. His first book, *The Theory of Wages* (Macmillan, 1932; 2nd edn, 1963) was ostensibly a book about labour economics but some of its elements, such as the 'elasticity of substitution' and its connection with the relative income shares of labour and capital, proved to have a much wider application to the general theory of distribution. Next came a classic paper with R.G.D. Allen, 'A Reconsideration of the Theory of Value', *Economica*, February 1934, which replaced the then standard marginal utility theory of consumer behaviour with a new indifference theory. An equally famous and endlessly reprinted article, 'Mr Keynes and the "Classics" ', *Econometrica*, April 1937, introduced the IS–LM curve into macroeconomics. Further papers on theoretical welfare economics buttressed Hicks' growing reputation and *Value and Capital* in 1939 placed him indisputably in the front ranks of living theorists.

The IS–LM apparatus is a perfect example of Hicks' unusual ability to synthesise the ideas of other economists. Keynes' *General Theory* (1936) is a confusing book and many who have read it have failed to grasp its central message; it attacks something called 'classical economics' but it is not clear what this is and who these classical economists are. Hicks realised that much of Keynes' book involves a contrast between a market for goods and services, in which planned saving and investment is brought into equilibrium via changes in total income, and a market for money, in which the demand for and supply of money is brought into equilibrium via changes in the rate of interest; moreover, both markets have to be in equilibrium simultaneously in order to produce what Keynes called 'unemployment equilibrium', that is, equilibrium at less than full employment. Hicks therefore invented a diagram with income on the horizontal axis and interest on the vertical axis in which equilibrium in each of the two markets is depicted by a single curve, the intersection of the two curves yielding an 'unemployment equilibrium'. So far, all we have is a geometrical trick. But Hicks went on to show that Keynes took one view of the typical slopes of the IS and LM curves, whereas his predecessors, the 'classics', took another, and it is these differences in beliefs about the slopes of the two sets of curves which accounted for the contrast between Keynes' policy recommendations and those of his predecessors. In other words, the purpose of the IS–LM apparatus must not be misunderstood: it is not a translation of the whole of Keynes into geometry, or a simple summary of Keynes' arguments, but a guide to the *General Theory*, an attempt to say what it means and to show why Keynes produces such novel answers to old questions (see Hansen, A.H.). It has proved to be an amazingly versatile gadget and even recent controversies between monetarists and neo-Keynesians have been conducted in terms of different interpretations of the IS–LM diagram.

Hicks' *Social Framework: An Introduction to Economics* (Clarendon Press, 1942; 4th edn, 1971) enjoyed considerable popularity as a textbook in the early post-war years. *A Contribution to the Theory of the Trade Cycle* (Clarendon Press, 1950) marked Hicks' first attempt at equilibrium dynamics, building on the Harrod–Domar growth model and Samuelson's interaction of the multiplier and the accelerator (see Harrod, R.F.). The first few chapters on demand in *Value and Capital* were revised in *A Revision of Demand Theory* (Clarendon Press, 1956; 2nd edn, 1959) to take account of the 'revealed preference theory' of Paul Samuelson (q.v.). *Capital and Growth* (Oxford University Press, 1965) developed the now well-known contrast between 'fixprice' and 'flexprice' markets, another example of Hicks' skill in inventing labels for fundamental distinctions. *A Theory of Economic History* (Clarendon Press, 1969) revealed a surprising gift for making grand generalisations about centuries of historical development, and *Capital and Time: A New -Austrian Theory* (Clarendon Press, 1973), *The Crisis in Keynesian Economics* (Basil Blackwell, 1974) and *Causality in Economics* (Basil Blackwell, 1979) once again displayed Hicks' innovative skills in growth and monetary economics.

We have said nothing about his work in monetary economics, his half-dozen books and reports on problems of local taxation, co-authored with his wife, Ursula Hicks, who was an expert on public finance in her own right, and the many illuminating prefaces which Hicks was in the habit of writing when his books were reprinted to show how his thinking had changed over the years. His publication record ran to twenty books and over fifty articles, most of which are reprinted in three volumes, *Collected Essays on Economic Theory* (Basil Blackwell, 1981, 1982, 1983), and he never stopped writing, contributing his last posthumous paper on 'The Unification of Macroeconomics', *Economic Journal*, March 1990. Even in 1989 and 1991, two more of his books appeared: *A Market Theory of Money* (Clarendon Press) and *The Status of Economics* (Basil Blackwell). Great economists, like great conductors, seem to be able to continue working right into their seventies and eighties.

*Primary Literature*
J.R. Hicks, 'The Formation of an Economist', in J.A Kregel (ed.), *Recollection of Eminent Economists*, vol. 1 (Macmillan, 1988).

*Secondary Literature*
B. Morgan, 'Sir John Hicks's Contributions to Economic Theory', in J.R. Shackleton and G. Locksley (eds), *Twelve Contemporary Economists* (Macmillan, 1981; Wiley, Halsted Press, 1981); W.J. Baumol, 'Sir John Hick's Contributions to Economics', in H.W. Spiegel and W.J. Samuels (eds), *Contemporary Economists in Perspective*, vol. 1 (JAI Press, 1984); 'Hicks, John Richard', in J. Eatwell, M. Milgate and P. Newman (eds), *The New Palgrave: A Dictionary of Economics*, vol. 2 (Macmillan, 1987); J.C. Wood and R.N. Wood (eds), *Sir John Hicks: Critical Assessments*, 4 vols (Routledge, 1989).

# Hirschman, Albert O. (1915– )

Albert Hirschman is a master of what has been has been called 'lateral thinking': looking at an old problem from a new, unexpected angle. He has performed this conjuring trick in countless articles and, in particular, in two deservedly famous books: *The Strategy of Economic Development* (Yale University Press, 1958; 2nd edn, 1961) and *Exit, Voice and Loyalty: Responses to Decline in Firms, Organizations and States* (Harvard University Press, 1970).

In the first, he rejected the then fashionable view that Third World countries must develop by a carefully managed process of 'balanced growth', insisting, first, that economic growth is typically unbalanced, and, second, that development planning is only effective when it concentrates its efforts on key industries with ample backward and forward 'linkages' to other industries. A backward linkage refers to the inputs which an industry employs, which connect it with the producers of raw materials, machinery, and semi-finished goods; a forward linkage refers the output which an industry sells to other industries rather than to final consumers; thus, the leather tanning and hide industry is a key industry in Hirschman's terminology, whereas the shoe industry is not. The arguments of the book were illustrated by the development experiences of Latin America, a subject to which he returned in *Journeys Toward Progress: Studies of Economic Policy-making in Latin America* (Twentieth Cen-

109

tury Fund, 1963), *Development Projects Observed* (Brookings Institution, 1967), and *A Bias for Hope: Essays on Development and Latin America* (Yale University Press, 1971).

*The Strategy of Economic Development* proved to be one of the most influential books on economic development published in the 1950s. The notion that successful growth is 'balanced' in the sense of marching on all fronts – consumer goods expanding at the same rate as investment goods, agriculture growing at the same rate as manufacturing, etc. – was one of the results of the early mathematical theories of economic growth, and what Hirschman in fact accomplished was to separate development economics as a discipline concerned with the actual growth experiences of poor countries from growth theory as a subject concerned with the abstract characteristic of growth models.

In the second of Hirschman's major books, *Exit, Voice and Loyalty*, he considered how people react to a deterioration in, say, the quality of a firm's performance; traditional theory says they 'exit', but Hirschman reminded us that they sometimes use 'voice', attempting to change rather than escape from an objectionable situation. Employing this contrast of 'exit' versus 'voice', complicated by the opposite force of 'loyalty', he proceeded to illuminate a vast number of issues in business behaviour, industrial organisation, and even political science. Further implications of this apparatus are explored in his *Essays in Trespassing: Economics to Politics and Beyond* (Cambridge University Press, 1981), a collection of fourteen essays echoing almost every one of Hirschman's themes. He has also written a fascinating account of eighteenth-century thinking about commercial civilisation with a self-explanatory sub-title: *The Passions and the Interests: Political Arguments for Capitalism before its Triumph* (Princeton University Press, 1977). *Rival Views of Market Society and Other Essays* (Viking Penguin, 1986) brings together essays that followed from *The Passions and the Interests*. A more recent book is *The Rhetoric of Reaction: Perversity, Futility, Jeopardy* (Harvard University Press, 1991), a book which reflects the Reagan–Thatcher decade of the 1980s.

Hirschman was born in 1915 in Berlin, Germany. He was an undergraduate student at the Sorbonne in Paris and then the London School of Economics in the mid-1930s, obtaining his doctorate in 1938 from the University of Trieste. In 1941 he came to the United States on a Rockefeller Foundation Fellowship. After wartime service in the American army, he joined the Federal Service Board in

Washington in 1946 as Chief of the Western European Section and published his first book, *National Power and the Structure of Foreign Trade* (University of California Press, 1945, 1980). In 1952, he went to Latin America as financial adviser to the National Planning Board in Bogota, Columbia; two years later, he left the Board but stayed on in Columbia as a private economic consultant. In 1956, he took his first academic appointment as Research Professor at Yale University (1956–8), followed by a professorship in International Economics at Columbia University (1958–64), a professorship in Political Economy at Harvard University (1964–74), and, finally, a professorship in economics at the Institute for Advanced Study, Princeton University in 1974 until his retirement in 1985. He received an honorary degree from Rutgers University in 1978 and was a recipient of the Frank E. Seidman Distinguished Award in Political Economy in 1980.

*Primary Literature*
A.O. Hirschman, *A Propensity to Self-subversion* (Harvard University Press, 1995).

*Secondary Literature*
C.K. Wilber and K.P. James, 'Albert Hirschman', in W.J. Samuels (ed.), *New Horizons in Economic Thought* (Edward Elgar, 1992); M.S. McPherson, 'Hirschman, Albert Otto', in J. Eatwell, M. Milgate and P. Newman (eds), *The New Palgrave: A Dictionary of Economics*, vol. 2 (Macmillan, 1987).

# Hotelling, Harold (1895–1973)

Harold Hotelling, a pioneer of mathematical economics and the inventor of many statistical methods now found in textbooks on multivariate analysis, is one of those modern economists whose impact depends entirely on a relatively small number of journal articles. Again and again, Hotelling studied the literature on some questions, published his findings in a single paper, and then turned his attention to a wholly different question. Thus, in 1929 he published a short essay on 'Stability in Competition', *Economic Journal*, March 1929, in which he forged an unexpected link between the idea of non-price competition and the geographical location of rival firms or retail outlets, demonstrating that profit maximisation automatically causes the rivals to locate near to each other; he went on to argue that this 'principle of minimum differentiation' (as Kenneth Boulding (q.v.) was later to call it) might account not only for the similarity of so many competing products but also for the similarity of the programmes of competing political parties. This paper launched a stream of articles by others on the economics of location, which formed an important ingredient in the Monopolistic Competition Revolution which swept through economics in the early 1930s (see Robinson, J.)

Similarly, a few years later, Hotelling applied the calculus of variations, a mathematical technique common to physics but then uncommon to economics, to obtain the socially optimum rate of extraction of an irreplaceable natural resource. This paper on 'The Economics of Exhaustible Resources', *Journal of Political Economy*, April 1931, was rediscovered after the oil crisis of 1973 and stimulated much of the work of the 1970s on the economics of depletable resources. Finally, in 1938 Hotelling's best-known paper on 'The General Welfare in Relation to Problems of Taxation and of Railway and Utility Rates', *Econometrica*, July 1938, provided a mathematical vindication of the principle that publicly owned or regulated firms should price their products at marginal costs, in consequence of which the marginal-cost-pricing rule became the first commandment of the 'new' welfare economics (see Lerner, A.P.).

These are three examples of Hotelling's extraordinary power to fire off great ideas in all directions, a power which he displayed on at least five or six other occasions, not just in economics (see *The Collected Economics Articles of Harold Hotelling*, ed. A.C. Darnell, Springer-Verlag, 1980), but also in statistics. He was responsible for the development of two specific statistical techniques – 'principal components analysis' and 'canonical correlation analysis' – and made important contributions to many areas of statistical theory.

Hotelling was born in Fulda, Minnesota, in 1895 and worked as a journalist on a local paper after completing high school in Seattle. In 1916 he entered the University of Washington to study journalism, earning his bachelor's degree in 1919. As an undergraduate, he discovered his flair for mathematics and went on to take an MA in mathematics from the University of Washington in 1921, followed by a PhD from Princeton University in 1924. He started teaching at the Food Research Institute of Stanford University in 1924, where he began to publish his first papers on mathematical statistics. In 1927, he became an Associate Professor of Mathematics at Stanford University, moving to Columbia University in 1931 to become Professor of Economics. He stayed at Columbia for fifteen of his most productive years, moving for the last time in 1946 to establish a new department of statistics at the university of North Carolina. He reached retirement age in 1966.

He was an honorary fellow of the British Royal Statistical Society, a Distinguished Fellow of the American Economic Association (1965), President of the Econometric Society (1936), President of the Institute of Mathematical Statistics (1941), and the recipient of several honorary degrees from American universities.

*Secondary Literature*
R.W. Pfouts and M.R. Leadbetter, 'Hotelling, Harold', in D.L. Sills (ed.), *International Encyclopaedia of the Social Sciences*, vol. 18, (The Free Press, 1979); H. Hotelling, *The Collected Economic Articles of Harold Hotelling* (ed. A.C. Darnell, (Springer-Verlag, 1990).

# Isard,
# Walter
# (1919–  )

Walter Isard is one of those lucky economists who found an almost totally neglected area, the economics of location, made it his own, developed its implications for general economics, and subsequently promoted it into a more comprehensive field of research known as 'regional science', which straddles the boundaries between economics, geography, and operations research. Location theory, the theory of the spatial location of economic activity, is in fact a very old branch of economic studies, which has its place, along with so much of the rest of economics, in *The Wealth of Nations* (1776) by Adam Smith. But it largely disappeared from mainstream economics in the nineteenth century, although for some strange reason it never entirely died out among German-speaking economists.

Isard reviewed the entire history of this subject in his first book, *Location and Space Economy* (Technology Press, Wiley, 1956), in which he complained that the whole of classical and neoclassical economics had confined itself to analysing 'a wonderland of no spatial dimensions' in which firms locate their plants without regard to transport costs and sell to markets without regard to the area of sale. A number of German economists in the nineteenth and early twentieth centuries, however, worked on the problem of the optimum location of a plant and, at the same time, on the analysis of market sales areas. These two sides of location theory – the cost-oriented analysis of optimum plant location and the demand-oriented analysis of sales areas – were finally brought together in the Monopolistic Competition Revolution of the 1930s with its notion of spatial product differentiation as one of the sources of a firm's monopolistic power of price-making (see Hotelling, H.; Robinson, J.). Isard traced much of the traditional neglect of this rich heritage of spatial competition theory to the fact that classical location theory is expressed in the outdated language of partial equilibrium – one market at a time – and the last sections of his book were therefore devoted to restating the whole of classical location theory in the language of general equilibrium.

In more recent years, Isard has moved increasingly away from classical location theory. Responding to a growing interest in the 'agglomeration economies' that characterise economic activity in urban centres and the problems of backward regions in America and elsewhere, he turned instead to input–output analysis and the regional 'multipliers' of Keynesian macroeconomics. *Methods of Regional Analysis* (MIT Press, 1960), written with others, and *Regional Input–Output Study* (MIT Press, 1971), co-authored with T. Langford, led up to *Introduction to Regional Science* (Prentice-Hall, 1975), the first of many textbooks to come in this still-growing area of research. *Spatial Dynamics and Optimal Space-Time Development* (North-Holland, 1979), co-authored with P. Liossatos and others, testifies to Isard's continued activity in the field. Isard's brainchild, regional science, has by now become a discipline of its own, which, it is only fair to add, has virtually moved out of economics. His other interest in peace science and the settlement of conflicts shows up in books such as *Conflict Management: Analysis and Practical Management Procedures*, with C. Smith (Ballinger Press, 1982), *Arms Races, Arms Control and Conflict Analysis* (Cambridge University Press, 1988) and *Understanding Conflict and the Science of Peace* (Basil Blackwell, 1992). *Selected Papers of Walter Isard*, ed. C. Smith, 2 vols (New York University Press, 1990) reprints some of his 200 articles on regional science and peace economics.

Isard was born in Philadelphia, Pennsylvania, in 1919, the son of a German immigrant family. He took his BA from Temple University in 1939 and his MA and PhD from Harvard University in 1941 and 1943 respectively. After teaching for several years at Harvard, he was invited by the University of Pennsylvania in 1956 to form a new Department of Regional Science. Isard stayed at Pennsylvania until 1979 when he moved to Cornell University to become Professor of Regional Science and Peace Science. He has been honoured with degrees from a number of American and European universities. He has edited the *Journal of Regional Science* since its inception in 1960.

# Johnson, Harry G. (1923–77)

Harry Johnson was notorious in his lifetime as a living machine for producing economic literature: during a relatively short career of twenty-seven years, he produced over five hundred academic papers, one hundred and fifty book reviews, thirty-five books and pamphlets, and hundreds of newspaper articles, many of which were written on trains and aeroplanes; so prodigious was his output that articles by him continued to appear years after his death, conveying the uncanny impression that he was still hard at it in Heaven. Moreover, almost nothing he wrote was tossed off. On the contrary, the average quality of his output was astonishingly high, synthesising apparently unrelated contributions by others and restating previous results with a verve that made them stand out like new. But writing was only one of his many activities. He travelled ceaselessly to conferences around the world and lectured at universities up and down Europe, America, Africa and Asia. His frantic energy was fuelled by wood-carving and alcohol, producing the one while listening and consuming the other while writing.

One of his earliest contributions was a savage review of James Meade's *Theory of International Economic Policy* (1951), and international economics remained throughout his life the subject on which he was a recognised expert. But *International Trade and Economic Growth: Studies in Pure Theory* (Harvard University Press, 1958),

*Money, Trade and Economic Growth: Survey Lectures in Economic Theory* (Allen & Unwin, Harvard University Press, 1962), and *Aspects of the Theory of Tariffs* (Allen & Unwin, Harvard University Press, 1971) were complemented by his work in monetary economics, as evidenced by *Essays in Monetary Economics* (Allen & Unwin, 1967), *Further Essays in Monetary Economics* (Harvard University Press, 1972), *Inflation and the Monetarist Controversy* (North-Holland, 1972), *Macroeconomics and Monetary Theory* (Gray-Mills, Aldine, 1972), *The Theory of Income Distribution* (Gray-Mills, 1973), and *Selected Essays in Monetary Economics* (Allen & Unwin, 1978). Other pedagogic contributions were *The Two-sector Model of General Equilibrium* (Allen & Unwin, 1971) and *General Equilibrium Analysis: A Microeconomic Text*, with M.B. Kraus (Allen & Unwin, 1974). But he also wrote a brilliant book on *Economic Policies toward Less Developed Countries* (Brookings Institution, Allen & Unwin, 1967) and his many sparkling essays on such wide-ranging questions as advertising, brain drain, scientific research, the Keynesian Revolution, student protest, nationalism, human capital theory, minimum wage legislation, and incomes policies are brought together in *The Canadian Quandary* (McGraw-Hill, 1963; Carleton Library, 1977), *On Economics and Society* (University of Chicago Press, 1975) and *The Shadow of Keynes* (University of Chicago Press, Basil Blackwell, 1978), written jointly with his wife, Elizabeth S. Johnson.

Johnson was born in Toronto, Canada, in 1923 and graduated from the University of Toronto at the age of twenty in 1943. He began his academic career straightaway as an Acting Professor of Economics at St Francis Xavier University in Nova Scotia. After military service in the Canadian infantry, he crossed the Atlantic to take another BA at the University of Cambridge in 1946. He became an instructor at the University of Toronto in the same year, earned an MA in 1947 and then topped it off by an MA at Harvard University in 1948. Returning to England, he became a Fellow at King's College, Cambridge, where he taught until 1956, moving that year to the University of Manchester as Professor of Economics. Collecting together his by now formidable list of published papers into a book, *International Trade and Economic Growth*, he gained a doctorate with it from Harvard University in 1958. The following year, he joined the University of Chicago as Professor of Economics, a post which he combined with a commuting professorship at the London School of Economics during the years 1966–74 and the Graduate

Institute for International Studies in Geneva, Switzerland, during the years 1976–7. He was made a Distinguished Fellow of the American Economic Association in 1977, received honorary degrees from seven British and Canadian universities and served as President-Elect of the Eastern Economic Association in 1975–6 and Vice-President of the American Economic Association in 1976. He was editor or co-author of a large number of journals: *Review of Economic Studies*, *The Manchester School*, *Economica*, the *Journal of Political Economy* and the *Journal of International Economics*. He died in Geneva in 1977 at the age of fifty-three.

His writings are characterised by the use of geometric rather than algebraic illustrations and proofs, the rigorous application of a general equilibrium framework to the analysis of economic problems, a zeal for exploring the policy implications of analytical concepts, and a general suspicion of vulgar Keynesianism, interventionism, and collectivism in all its varieties. While contributing to positive international economics, his passionate concern to provide policy-relevant economics drove him towards applied welfare economics, and most of his best work on optimum tariffs in the face of retaliation, culminating in the concept of the so-called 'scientific tariff', emphasised the welfare gains and losses of 'second-best' departures from free trade. In monetary economics, he was largely responsible for the introduction of money into the barter model of early growth theorists. In his later years, he bent all his efforts towards the development of 'the monetary approach to the balance of payments', the view that balance-of-payments policies must always be accompanied by domestic credit policies designed to influence the demand for money, editing (with J.A. Frenkel) two sets of papers embodying the latest research in the field: *The Monetary Approach to the Balance of Payment* (Allen & Unwin, University of Toronto Press, 1976) and *The Economics of Exchange Rates* (Addison-Wesley, 1978). He always held a curiously ambivalent attitude to 'monetarism' (see Friedman, M.): in one of his most famous papers, 'The Keynesian Revolution and the Monetarist Counter-revolution', *American Economic Review*, May 1971, he ridiculed the scientific pretensions of monetarism and predicted its imminent decline, and yet in the field of international economic relations he was a major advocate of the view that 'money matters'.

*Secondary Literature*
J.N. Bhagwati and J.A. Frenkel, 'Johnson, Harry G.', in D.L. Sills (ed.), *International Encyclopaedia of the Social Sciences*, vol. 18 (The Free Press, 1979); J.A. Frenkel, 'Johnson, Harry Gordon', in J. Eatwell, M. Milgate and P. Newman (eds), *The New Palgrave: A Dictionary of Economics*, vol. 2 (Macmillan, 1987).

# Jorgenson, Dale W. (1933– )

Dale Jorgenson has been largely responsible for the formulation of the neoclassical theory of investment, based on the rental price of capital services, and for the explanation of productivity change in terms of new technology embodied in additional investment. In old-style production theory, new technology is conceived as being 'disembodied' in the sense of somehow being independent of increases in capital and labour. This was always recognised as an unrealistic view but it proved difficult to model a process in which capital changes form as it accumulates. In a series of famous papers – 'Capital Theory and Investment Behavior', *American Economic Review*, May 1963, 'The Embodiment Hypothesis', *Journal of Political Economy*, February 1966, and 'The Explanation of Productivity Change', *Review of Economic Studies*, 34, 1967, the latter written jointly with Z. Griliches – Jorgenson succeeded in showing that technical change can be meaningfully analysed as an investment process in the improvement of the capital stock, so that 'capital', like wine, is a matter not just of amount but also of 'vintage'. In another much-quoted paper, 'Econometric Studies of Investment Behavior: A Review', *Journal of Economic Literature*, December 1971, he summed up what is now known about the determination of private investment. In addition to work on investment behaviour in advanced economies, he has also provided a neoclassical explanation of the development of 'dualism' in underdeveloped countries, rejecting W.A. Lewis's (q.v.) influential theory of 'economic growth with unlimited supplies of labour'. This Jorgenson paper, 'Testing Alternative Theories of the Development of a Dual Economy', in I. Adelman and E. Thorbecke (ed), *Theory and Design of Economic Development* (Johns Hopkins University Press, 1966), has quickly become a classic in its own right in the literature on economic development. 'Transcendental Logarithmic Production Frontiers', *Review of Economics and Statistics*, August 1973, with L.R. Christensen and L.J. Lau, is another of Jorgensen's influential papers. A book on *Productivity and US Economic Growth* (Harvard University Press, 1987), with F.M. Gollop and B.M. Fraumeni, summed up more than two decades of Jorgensen's research on capital investment and economic growth.

Jorgenson was born in 1933 in Boseman, Montana. He received his BA from Reed College in 1955, and his MA and PhD from Harvard University in 1957 and 1959 respectively. He began teaching at the University of California, Berkeley in 1959, becoming a Professor of Economics at Berkeley in 1967. In 1969 he moved to a professorship at Harvard University, where he still resides.

He received the John Bates Clark Medal of the American Economic Association in 1971 for his work on the econometric modelling of investment, and was elected President of the Econometric Society in 1987.

# Kaldor, Nicholas (1908–86)

Nicholas Kaldor is a combination unusual in economics of a first-rate theorist who was taken seriously by all the leading theoreticians of the day and a first-rate policy-adviser who had the ear of governments throughout the world. His contributions to theory ranged from welfare economics to capital theory, business cycle theory and the theory of economic growth; his contributions to applied economics ranged from tariff policy to taxation policy, monetary policy and international commodity stabilisation, centring on his proposal of a comprehensive 'expenditure tax' to replace the existing system of taxation. A prominent British defender and expounder of Keynesian economics in the 1930s, he moved after the war towards a theory of economic growth founded on the spirit rather than the letter of Keynes, independently of but along the same lines as his colleague at the University of Cambridge, Joan Robinson (q.v.).

Kaldor gradually took up a stand in diametrical opposition to American-style mainstream economics, that is, competitive price theory based on marginal productivity principles and a theory of income determination based on the IS–LM apparatus (see Hicks, J.R.). In later years, he consistently pressed the view that slow growth and stagflation in Britain and elsewhere were due to the failure of governments to maintain the level of aggregate demand for the output of the manufacturing sector, which he regarded as the engine-house of economic growth under capitalism. The argument applied to any economy like the British one in which growth is export-led; exports depended basically on the level of real wages and the pace of productivity improvements, but productivity improvements in turn depended on buoyant markets for export goods. Thus, Kaldor argued, if demand for exports is somehow kept high for a period of time, the growth of productivity causes costs and prices of exports to fall, which then justifies the initial stimulus and makes it self-sustaining. His book *The Scourge of Monetarism* (Oxford University Press, 1982) left no doubt of his scathing rejection of the deflationary policies of the Thatcher government. His own alternative economic strategy for Britain was a budgetary stimulus accompanied by import controls (or else a dual exchange rate system discriminating in favour of manufactured goods) and a strict prices-and-incomes policy.

Kaldor was born in Budapest, Hungary, in 1908, the son of a Jewish barrister. As a boy, he attended the 'Model Gymnasium' in Budapest, a private school which has produced an almost endless stream of famous Hungarians. After a year at the University of Berlin, he moved to Britain in 1927 to study at the London School of Economics, from which he graduated in 1930. Two years later, he was appointed an assistant lecturer at the LSE, becoming a Reader in 1942. He left the LSE in 1947 to become Director of the Research and Planning Division of the Economic Commission for Europe, serving eventually as one of a small group of experts to write the influential UN report, *National and International Measures for Full Employment* (United Nations, 1949). He returned to academic life as a Fellow at King's College, Cambridge, in 1949, becoming a Reader in 1952 and a Professor of Economics in 1966. He retired from academic life in 1975.

Throughout this latter period at Cambridge, he also served as a tax adviser to the governments of India, Sri Lanka, Mexico, British Guiana, Turkey, Iran, Venezuela, and Ghana, capped by his appointment as Special Adviser to the Chancellor of the Exchequer of two British Labour governments during the years 1964–8 and 1974–6. Among his potent contributions to the economic policies of the Labour government was the Selective Employment Tax, a payroll tax designed to discriminate in favour of the manufacturing sector of the British economy. In gratitude for his services to the state, he was given a life peerage in 1974.

Kaldor has written no books besides *An Expenditure Tax* (Allen & Unwin, 1955; 2nd edn, 1965) and *The Scourge of Monetarism*, but his output of papers, reports, and memoranda is enormous and his *Collected Economic Essays* (Duckworth, 1960, 1964, 1978, 1979, 1980, 1989) runs to nine volumes. They include a number of classics, such as 'A Model of Economic Growth', *Economic Journal*, December 1957, and 'What is Wrong with Economic Theory?', *Quarterly Journal of Economics*, August 1975, but every one of them displays outstanding qualities of clarity and incisiveness. There must be few economists who have written so many good essays in their lives. One of Kaldor's distinct and lasting contributions was the 'Keynesian' theory of steady-state growth in which two rates of savings, those of workers and those of capitalists, determine the distribution of income between wages and profits as well as the rate of growth of income and employment of the economy. Although much criticised, this theory has become one of the cornerstones of so-called 'post-Keynesian economics' (see Pasinetti, L.L.).

Kaldor is a living example of an old-fashioned 'political economist' in the best sense of the word. A collection of his speeches to the House of Lords, published under the title of *The Economic Consequences of Mrs Thatcher* (Duckworth, 1983) reveals his abilities as a debater with a political audience of non-economists.

*Primary Literature*
N. Kaldor, 'Recollections of an Economist', in J.A. Kregel (ed.), *Recollections of Eminent Economists*, vol. 2 (Macmillan, 1988).

*Secondary Literature*
L.L. Pasinetti, 'Kaldor, Nicholas', in D.L. Sills (ed.), *International Encyclopaedia of the Social Sciences*, vol. 18 (Free Press, 1979); A. Wood, 'Kaldor, Nicholas', in J. Eatwell, M. Millgate and P. Newman (eds), *The New Palgrave: A Dictionary of Economics*, vol. 3 (Macmillan, 1987); A.P. Thirlwall, *Nicholas Kaldor: Economist and Adviser* (Wheatsheaf, 1987); F. Targetti, 'Kaldor, Nicholas', in P. Arestis and M. Sawyer (eds), *A Biographical Dictionary of Dissenting Economists* (Edward Elgar, 1992); M.S. Turner, *Nicholas Kaldor and the Real World* (M.E. Sharpe, 1993).

# Kalecki,
# Michal
# (1899–1970)

If you want to make an impact on contemporary economics, you must be in the right place at the right time and also you must publish in the right language. Michal Kalecki violated all three conditions: he discovered many of the basic elements of the Keynesian system three years before Keynes published his *General Theory* (1936), and he went beyond Keynes in embedding those elements in a model that incorporated the phenomena of imperfect competition, but he published these ideas in Polish while sitting in Warsaw. In 1935, when he finally published simultaneously in French and English, his ideas were expressed in abstruse algebra and were therefore ignored for a new reason. By the time of the appearance of his first books in English, *Essays in the Theory of Economic Fluctuations* (Allen & Unwin, Russell, 1939) and *Studies in Economic Dynamics* (Allen & Unwin, 1943), the Keynesian steamroller was in full swing and Kalecki was misunderstood as saying more or less the same thing as Keynes. It is only in recent years that the full measure of his economic ideas has been appreciated. Some post-Keynesians, such as Joan Robinson (q.v.), have even gone so far as to rank Kalecki above Keynes as a point of departure for the reconstruction of macroeconomics in the 1980s. This is a minority view. Nevertheless, Kalecki's reputation has continued to wax even as that of Keynes has waned.

Kalecki was born in 1889 in Lodz, Poland. He studied engineering at Warsaw Polytechnic and at Gdansk Polytechnic but never took his degree. In his twenties, he worked as a freelance economic journalist and from 1929 to 1937 as an analyst at the Polish Research Institute for Business Cycles and Prices. In 1940, having visited Britain several times in the preceding years, he joined the Oxford Institute of Statistics to work on wartime rationing schemes and to pursue his theoretical work on business cycles. In 1954 he published *Theory of Economics Dynamics* (Allen & Unwin, 1954; 2nd edn, 1965), followed in 1966 by the English translation of his first Polish book, *Studies in the Theory of Business Cycles, 1933–1939* (Basil Blackwell, 1966) and in 1969 by the translation of another Polish book, *Introduction to the Theory of Growth in a Socialist Economy* (Basil Blackwell, 1969). He returned to Poland in 1955 to serve as economic adviser to the Polish government and later as Polish representative to the United Nations; he was a leading contributor to the Polish Planning Commission's Perspective Plan, 1961–75, which however was made obsolete as soon as it appeared by Gomulka's fall from power. He died in 1970. Four posthumous collections of papers, *Selected Essays on the Dynamics of the Capitalist Economy, 1933–1970* (Cambridge University Press, 1971), *Selected Essays on the Economic Growth of the Socialist and the Mixed Economy* (Cambridge University Press, 1972), *Essays on Developing Economies* (Harvester, 1976) and *Selected Essays on Economic Planning*, ed. J. Toporewski (Cambridge University Press, 1976) are testaments to his productive life.

Perhaps the most interesting feature of Kalecki's economics is the way in which he starts from Marx and works out a Keynesian model of a long-run equilibrium growth by attributing all savings to capitalists, savings being simply a proportion of profits, and by assuming that firms set prices by marking-up average costs, the level of the mark-up being determined by the strength of their monopoly power. In so doing, he integrated business cycles and economic growth into one framework, even providing along the way a coherent argument for believing that capitalist governments would never in fact be able to sustain full employment levels of income for any length of time. Early versions of this theory were set out in equations and were often criticised for being tautological, that is, true by the definition of terms. Later, however, Kalecki put flesh on the mathematical skeleton by various theoretical arguments, supplemented by empirical results. The fact remains, however, that the model is available in four or five successive versions and much depends, therefore, on which version a friend or critic is discussing. This fact, in addition to all the other reason previously mentioned, has reduced the impact which Kalecki might otherwise have had. Nevertheless, the continued influence of Kalecki, particularly on post-Keynesian writers at the University of Cambridge in England, is amply demonstrated by J. Robinson and J. Eatwell's textbook, *Introduction to Modern Economics* (McGraw-Hill, 1973), large parts of which are pure Kalecki.

*Secondary Literature*
G.R. Feiwel, *The Intellectual Capital of Michal Kalecki* (University of Tennessee Press, 1975); J. Poschl and G. Locksley, 'Michal Kalecki: A Comprehensive Challenge to Orthodoxy', in J.R. Shackleton and G. Locksley (eds), *Twelve Contemporary Economists* (Macmillan, 1981; Wiley, Halsted Press, 1981); K. Laski, 'Kalecki, Michal', in J. Eatwell, M. Milgate and P. Newman (eds), *The New Palgrave: A Dictionary of Economics*, vol. 3 (Macmillan, 1987); M.C. Sawyer, 'Kalecki, Michal', in P. Arestis and M. Sawyer (eds), *A Biographical Dictionary of Dissenting Economists* (Edward Elgar, 1992).

# Kindleberger, Charles P. (1910– )

Charles Kindleberger is the author of the most successful introductory textbook in *International Economics* (Richard D. Irwin, 1953; 6th edn, 1978), with P. Linder, in the post-war era; the book has been endlessly translated and with new co-authors (E. Despress and W.S. Salant) is now in its sixth edition. Kindleberger's first book, *International Short Term Capital Movements* (Columbia University Press, 1937), was a monograph in international economics and a recent work, *International Money: A Collection of Essays* (Allen & Unwin, 1981), collects together widely scattered essays and articles which trace the development of his thinking in international finance over the last thirty years. A leading theme of his work has been the notion that the world financial system is, like the financial system of an individual country, a hierarchical structure in which some leading country must act as a 'lender of last resort' if global financial stability is to be ensured. Throughout the 1950s and '60s, the USA acted as such a central banker, providing the world with liquidity. In the 1970s, however, a variety of circumstances threatened to bring America's last-resort lending to an end; from this springs all the global instability of the last decade.

International economics and international finance have not been the only subject of Kindleberger's interest. He has also made distinguished contributions to economic history. The titles of *Economic*

*Growth in France and Britain, 1851–1950* (Harvard University Press, 1964), *The World in Depression, 1929–1939* (Allen Lane, 1973; 2nd edn, University of California Press, 1986), *Economic Response: Comparative Study in Trade, Finance and Growth* (Harvard University Press, 1978), and *Manias, Panics and Crashes: A History of Financial Crises* (Macmillan, Basic Books, 1978) speak for themselves. In one of his most influential historical works, *Europe's Postwar Growth: The Role of Labor Supply* (Harvard University Press, 1967), he applied W.A. Lewis's (q.v.) model of 'economic growth with unlimited supplies of labour' to the explosive growth of Western Europe in the years after World War II, arguing that the German and French 'economic miracles' would have been impossible without the importation of foreign labour from East Germany, Turkey, Yugoslavia, Spain, and Algeria. The latest summing up of his theme is his *Financial History of Western Europe* (Allen & Unwin, 1994). His many journal articles are collected in *Keynesianism vs Monetarism and Other Essays in Financial History.* (Allen & Unwin, 1985), *The International Economic Order: Essays on Financial Crisis and International Public Goods* (MIT Press, 1988), and *Historical Economics: Art or Science?* (University of California Press, 1990). His writings have great style, verve and charm – as does his conversation.

He was born in 1910 in New York City. He received his BA from the University of Pennsylvania in 1932, and his MA and PhD from Columbia University in 1934 and 1937. After working as a research economist at the Federal Reserve Bank of New York, the Bank for International Settlements at Basle, and the Board of Governors of the Federal Reserve System in Washington, and on completion of his wartime service, he began teaching at the Massachusetts Institute of Technology in 1948, becoming a Professor in 1951 and remaining there until his retirement in 1976. Since then he has been a Visiting Professor at Middlebury College, Vermont.

He was Vice-President of the American Economic Association in 1966, a Distinguished Fellow of the Association in 1980, and was recently elected as President of the Association in 1985. He received the Harms Prize of the Institut für Weltwirtschaft, Kiel, Germany, 1978 and honorary degrees from several European universities.

*Primary Literature*
C. Kindleberger, 'The Life of an Economist', in J.A. Kregel (ed.), *Recollections of Eminent Economists*, vol. 1 (Macmillan, 1989); C.

Kindleberger, *Life of an Economist: An Autobiography* (Blackwell, 1991); C. Kindleberger, 'My Working Philosophy', in M. Szenberg (ed.), *Eminent Economists* (Cambridge University Press, 1992).

*Secondary Literature*
D.N. McCloskey, 'Kindleberger, Charles', in J. Eatwell, M. Milgate and P. Newman (eds), *The New Palgrave: A Dictionary of Economics*, vol. 3 (Macmillan, 1987).

# Klein,
# Lawrence R.
# (1920–   )

The computer revolution of the 1960s ushered in a golden age of econometric model-building, particularly the big econometric models with hundreds of equations describing the workings of different sectors of economic activity and the flows of consumer expenditure, business and government saving, private and public investment, transfer payments, the money supply, exports, imports, capital flows, etc., all of which were estimated simultaneously and used to forecast the performance of the economy. The days of such large multi-equation econometric models are perhaps over but there can be little doubt that the experience of large-scale model-building did much to improve the standards of econometric research. Lawrence Klein was constantly in the forefront of this development, being particularly associated with the so-called 'Brookings Econometric Model Project', the largest econometric model that has ever been constructed for any economy. He was awarded the Nobel Prize in Economics in 1980 for this and other contributions to applied econometrics. Honours of this kind have been showered on him ever since the late 1950s: he was awarded the John Bates Clark Medal of the American Economic Association in 1959 and was President of the Econometric Society in 1960, the Environmental Economics Association in 1975, and the American Economic Association in 1977.

Klein was born in Omaha, Nebraska, in 1920. He received his Bachelor's degree from the University of California, Berkeley, in 1942 and his PhD from the Massachusetts Institute of Technology in 1944. He became a research associate at the Cowles Commission at the University of Chicago (1944–7), then at the National Bureau of Economic Research in New York (1948–51) and finally at the Survey Research Center of the University of Michigan (1949–54), where he taught from 1950. In 1954 he left the USA, in protest against the activities of the McCarthy Committee, for a readership at the Oxford University Institute of Statistics. In 1958, he returned to America to take up a professorship at the University of Pennsylvania, where he remained until his retirement from teaching in 1990. In 1947, he published his first book, *The Keynesian Revolution* (Macmillan, 1947; 2nd edn, 1966), an early study of the process whereby Keynes had moved from the arid formulas of his *Treatise* (1930) to the more promising line of advance in his *General Theory* (1936); this is a subject which has recently been re-examined with the aid of new evidence from Keynes' *Collected Writings* (see Patinkin, D.). This was followed a few years later by a major piece of macroeconomic model-building, *Economic Fluctuations in the United States, 1921–1941* (Wiley, 1950), which in turn gave way to a still more ambitious *Econometric Model of the United States, 1929–52* (Wiley, 1955), co-authored with A.S. Goldberger, followed by a complementary *Econometric Model of the United Kingdom*, with R.J. Ball and others (Basil Blackwell, 1961). *The Brookings Model* (Wiley, 1975), co-authored with G. Fromm, and *Econometric Model Performance*, (University of Pennsylvania Press, 1976), co-authored with E Burmeister, reviews some of the findings of this and other large-scale American econometric models and tests their comparative performance during the preceding ten years. He summed up his lifetime effort at macroeconomic modelling in a recent *History of Macroeconomic Model-building*, co-authored with R.G. Bodkin and K. Marwah (Edward Elgar, 1991).

Klein has long been concerned with improving the teaching of econometrics and his *Textbook of Econometrics* (Row, Peterson, 1953) and *An Introduction to Econometrics* (Row, Peterson, 1962) have continued to hold their own in a field that has recently seen as explosion of competing material; see also his *Lectures in Econometrics* (North-Holland, 1983). A recent book, *The Economics of Supply and Demand* (Johns Hopkins University Press, 1983), marks a break in his work: it takes a new critical look at the Keynesian ideas that

Klein has adhered to all his life and attempts to take account of the new supply-side economics of the Reagan administration.

*Primary Literature*
L.R. Klein, 'My Evolution as an Economist', in W. Breit and R.W. Spencer, *Lives of the Laureates* (MIT Press, 1986); L.R. Klein, 'My Professional Life Philosophy', in M. Szenberg (ed.), *Eminent Economists* (Cambridge University Press, 1992).

*Secondary Literature*
R.V. Ball, 'Lawrence Klein's Contributions to Economics', in H.W. Spiegel and W.J. Samuels (eds), *Contemporary Economists in Perspective*, vol. 1 (JAI Press, 1984).

# Knight, Frank H. (1885–1972)

Knight's reputation as an economist extended far beyond his one undisputed achievement, *Risk, Uncertainty and Profit* (London School of Economics, 1921; Kelley, 1957; Harper, 1965): his teaching at Chicago University in the interwar years inspired generations of students and many famous economists have testified to the stimulus they received in their youth from Knight's sceptical, rambling, and discursive lectures.

*Risk, Uncertainty and Profit* was Knight's first book and its status as a classic cannot disguise the fact that its message was never fully assimilated into mainstream theory. The problem he attacked was how to account for profits under perfect competition when received theory clearly suggested that the existence of profits is incompatible with competitive equilibrium. Knight's answer was to relate profits to the phenomenon of 'uncertainty' generated by rapid economic change. Many economic risks are like the risk of dying at a certain age: their objective probability can be calculated and hence shifted via insurance to the shoulders of others. There are risks, however, which can never be reduced to objective measurement because they are unprecedented. It is the existence of this kind of 'uncertainty' which allows entrepreneurs to earn positive profits as a windfall difference between the expected and realised returns of an enterprise, despite perfect competition and despite long-run, static equilibrium. Profit would only disappear in a stationary economy in which all future events can be perfectly foreseen. It follows that profits correspond to the performance of a specific function, and yet this function cannot be hired in the market place because it is, by definition, a non-contractual residual left over after all other inputs have been rewarded at their contractual prices.

Knight's masterpiece has withstood the test of time remarkably well. Unfortunately, it failed to persuade orthodox economics that the uncertainty theory of profits was anything but a footnote to mainstream analysis, tying together some loose ends that had been left lying around ever since Adam Smith. Economics was now provided with a satisfactory explanation of profits but the main focus of analysis continued to be the pricing of factors of production in accordance with marginal productivity principles under stationary conditions, that is, conditions in which profits are zero.

Frank Knight was born on a farm in McLean County, Illinois, in 1885. He received a BA from Milligan College, Tennessee, in 1911, an MA from the University of Tennessee in 1913, and a PhD from Cornell University in 1916, the subject of his dissertation being *Risk, Uncertainty and Profit*. He started teaching at Cornell in 1918, moved to Chicago and Iowa in the early 1920s, finally returning to Chicago in 1927, where he remained for the rest of his academic life. He retired in 1955. He served as President of the American Economic Association in 1950 and was awarded the Association's Francis Walker Medal in 1957.

Knight's *Economic Organization* (University of Chicago Press, 1933; Kelley, 1951; Harper, 1966), a set of lecture notes prepared at Iowa University in the early 1920s, gradually took on the status of a minor classic in its own right. Some of its features, such as the diagram of the 'wheel of wealth' or circular flow model of the economy, the modern statement of the law of variable proportions, and the emphasis on the equalisation of returns at the margins as the central principle of economics have become standard ingredients of virtually every introductory textbook of economics. His many complex and sometimes puzzling essays on the social philosophy implied by economic investigations are to be found in a series of volumes: *The Ethics of Competition, and Other Essays* (University of Chicago Press, 1935; Kelley, 1951), *On the History and Method of Economics: Selected Essays* (University of Chicago Press, 1956), and

*Freedom and Reform: Essays in Economics and Social Philosophy* (Harper, 1947; Liberty Press, 1982).

In the 1930s he launched a veritable campaign against the Austrian theory of capital, publishing a long series of papers designed to show that capital cannot be measured in terms of a definite 'period of production', as the Austrians had thought, and that the rate of return on capital is in no sense a return to 'waiting' for a time-delayed output. Although his views aroused some opposition, he succeeded by the end of the decade in virtually killing off whatever respect remained for the Austrian theory of capital (see Hayek, F.A.). Its disappearance from mainstream economics may, indeed, be credited almost entirely to Knight's vehement crusade against it.

In a remarkable article, 'Some Fallacies in the Interpretation of Social Cost', *Quarterly Journal of Economics*, August 1924, Knight discovered a serious flaw in Pigou's *Economics of Welfare* (1920), namely, when Pigou suggested that road congestion justified government intervention in the form of road taxation. Knight showed instead that privatisation of road ownership would lead to toll charges, thus automatically inhibiting congestion. In short, Knight pointed to what was later to become the First Commandment of the theory of property rights: markets are only efficient if property rights in scarce resources are clearly defined (see Demsetz, H.). Knight's last book, *Intelligence and Democratic Action* (Harvard University Press, 1960), containing lectures delivered at the University of Virginia, returned to one of his favourite themes: the extremely limited possibilities of rational 'social engineering' and the fallacies involved in viewing social science in general and economics in particular as a body of knowledge designed to solve practical problems. If these are depressing conclusions, the fact remains that many of Knight's mature views on economics are depressing: in his view, the study of economics led to 'understanding' but not to genuine 'explanation' and certainly not to the accurate prediction of economic events.

*Secondary Literature*
J.M. Buchan, 'Knight, Frank H.', in D.L. Sills (ed.), *International Encyclopaedia of the Social Sciences*, vol. 8 (The Free Press, 1968); W. Breit and R.L. Ransom, 'Frank H. Knight: Philosopher of the Counterrevolution in Economics', in *Academic Scribblers: American Economists in Collision*, 2nd edn (Dryden Press, 1982); G.J. Stigler,

'Knight, Frank Hyneman', in J. Eatwell, M. Milgate and P. Newman (eds), *The New Palgrave: A Dictionary of Economics*, vol. 3 (Macmillan, 1987).

# Koopmans, Tjalling C. (1910–85)

Tjalling Koopmans won the Nobel Prize in Economics in 1975 for his work on 'linear programming' or 'activity analysis', sharing the prize with Leonid V. Kantorovich, a Soviet mathematician-economist, who had independently discovered the same method several years before the outbreak of the World War II. In the orthodox, neoclassical theory of production, we usually start off by supposing the existence of a 'production function', namely, a relationship between maximum output on the one hand and all possible combinations of inputs on the other, on the assumption that engineers have eliminated all those input combinations that yield less than the maximum output. But this procedure sweeps too much under the carpet: in the short run, a firm cannot adopt all possible input combinations because it has only limited amounts of inputs at its disposal; moreover, it is usually impossible to combine even those limited inputs in all possible combinations, smoothly substituting a little more of one for a little less of another, because the existing techniques are only available in definite mixes, or not at all. In all such cases where the substitution between inputs is subject to jumps and discontinuities, and where the firm faces bottlenecks in the capacity to produce, the appropriate technique of analysis is linear programming, which is essentially a computational method for solving problems that are somehow consigned to engineers in conventional production theory. This technique was largely developed during World War II by American mathematicians and was then rapidly imported after the war into economics, principally by Koopmans, at which time it was discovered that the technique was already known to Soviet planners, who had not however recognised its connections with the long history of marginal analysis in Western production theory.

In a path-breaking essay, 'Analysis of Production as an Efficient Combination of "Activities"', published in a book which he edited with others, *Activity Analysis of Production and Allocation* (Yale University Press, 1951), Koopmans explored the economic implications of activity analysis, illustrating its use in the solution of many traditional problems in transportation economics. In *Three Essays on the State of Economic Science* (McGraw-Hill, 1957), he related it in the first essay to recent developments in general equilibrium theory, demonstrating that many of the results of standard economics could be restated with advantage in the language of activity analysis. Since then he has gone on to apply activity analysis to the problem of allocating resources over time, seeking to improve our criteria for evaluating investment projects. A number of papers on this subject are reprinted in *The Scientific Papers of Tjalling C. Koopmans* (Springer-Verlag, 1970) and *The Scientific Papers of Tjalling C. Koopmans*, vol. 2 (MIT Press, 1985).

Koopmans was born in the Netherlands in 1910 and received his BA and MA in physics and mathematics from the University of Utrecht in 1932 and 1933. He went on to complete a PhD, again in physics and mathematics, at the University of Leiden in 1936, but his interest had already turned towards economics and particularly econometrics. From 1936 to 1940, he worked at the League of Nations in Geneva, during which period he published *Linear Regression Analysis of Economic Time Series* (Netherlands Economic Institute, 1937) and *Tanker Freight Rates and Tankership Building* (Netherlands Economic Institute, 1939). He emigrated to America in 1940 and spent the war years as Statistician at the Combined Shipping Adjustment Board in Washington. In 1944 he joined an impressive team of young econometricians at the Cowles Commission attached to the University of Chicago (see Marschak, J.). In 1948, he co-edited *Statistical Inference in Dynamics Economic Models* (Yale University Press, 1950), an important milestone in econometric theory, which popularised the use of simultaneous-equation estimates (see

Marschak, J.). In 1955, when the Cowles Foundation moved to Yale University, he became a Professor of Economics at Yale, a post from which he retired only in 1981.

He was President of the Econometric Society in 1950 and of the American Economic Association in 1978. He received honorary degrees from several Dutch, Belgian and American universities. He was an accomplished musician and composer, music being his lifetime hobby. He died in New Haven in 1985.

*Secondary Literature*
L. Werin and K.G. Jungenfelt, 'Tjalling Koopmans's Contributions to Economics', in H.W. Spiegel and W.J. Samuels (eds), *Contemporary Economists in Perspective*, vol. 1 (JAI Press, 1984); C.F. Christ and L. Hurwicz, 'Koopmans, Tjalling Charles', in J. Eatwell, M. Milgate and P. Newman (eds), *The New Palgrave: A Dictionary of Economics*, vol. 3 (Macmillan, 1987).

# Kornai,
# János
# (1928–   )

Kornai is one of the few economists of the Eastern bloc whose work has kept in touch with economic theory in the West and whose writings are regularly translated and read with interest by Western economists. He was among the first economists in the communist world to argue for more decentralisation and for greater use of market forces. He was also one of the prime movers in a pioneer post-war project to introduce mathematical programming into Hungarian planning. *Overcentralisation in Economic Administration* (Oxford University Press, 1959) and *Mathematical Planning of Structural Decisions* (North-Holland, 1967; 2nd edn, 1975) are representative examples of his preoccupation with mathematical modelling of the planning process.

In *Anti-equilibrium* (North-Holland, 1971; 2nd edn, 1975), he took up the cudgel against Walrasian general equilibrium theory which, he argues, dominates Western economics and prevents it from dealing with practical economic problems (see Hahn, F.): he proceeded in the closing chapters of the book to sketch an alternative framework for a non-Walrasian type of economics, blending elements of organisation theory, information theory, management science and the new disequilibrium economics (see Clower, R.W.). The book attracted considerable discussion and so did his next: *The Economics of Shortage* (North-Holland, 1980, 2 vols), an impressive attempt to elaborate a general theory of an economy like those of Eastern Europe in which all goods are continually and deliberately kept in short supply, and in which demand and supply are therefore brought into balance by quantity and not by price adjustments.

This theory was designed to constitute a framework for a more general study of the economics of communist bloc countries, which appeared a few years later.: *Growth, Shortage and Efficiency: A Microdynamic Model of the Socialist Economy* (Basil Blackwell, 1982). In Kornai's view, the economics of communist countries is not as different from the economics of capitalist countries as first appears: in the East, unemployment and underutilisation of resources is disguised and appears as long queues for consumer goods in short supply; in the West, there is likewise underutilisation and excess capacity but it shows up directly in factor and not in product markets; in both economic systems, however, there is little price flexibility and markets are cleared by adjusting quantities and not prices. Economists in communist countries have therefore something to learn from economists in capitalist countries but the reverse is also true. The argument is summed up in his accessible survey paper, 'The Hungarian Reform Process: Visions, Hopes and Reality', *Journal of Economic Literature*, December 1986. More recent works along the same lines are *The Road to a Free Economy: Shifting from a Socialist System. The Example of Hungary* (W.W. Norton, 1990), and *The Socialist System: The Political Economy of Communism* (Princeton University Press, 1992).

Kornai was born in 1928 in Budapest, Hungary. He took his first degree in history and philosophy from the Hungarian Academy of Sciences in 1956 and then switched to economics, receiving a doctorate in 1961 from the Karl Marx University of Economics, Budapest. In 1966 he acquired a second doctorate in economic science, again from the Hungarian Academy of Sciences. In 1967, he became Professor of Economics in the Institute of Economics of the Hungarian Academy. In 1986 he was named Professor of Economics at Harvard University.

Kornai was President of the Econometric Society in 1978, the European Economic Association in 1987, and was elected an Honorary Member of the American Academy of Arts and Sciences (1972), the American Economic Association (1976), and the Royal Swedish Academy (1980). He was Vice-Chairman of the UN Committee on Development Planning from 1972 to 1977 and has received honorary degrees from the universities of Paris (1978) and Poznan, Poland (1978). In 1982, he was awarded the Frank E. Seidman Distinguished Award in Political Economy.

*Secondary Literature*
B. Csikós-Nagy, 'János Kornai', in W.J. Samuels (ed.), *New Horizons in Economic Thought* (Edward Elgar, 1992).

# Kuznets, Simon (1901–85)

Simon Kuznets' Nobel Prize in Economics in 1971 was clearly designed to underline the importance for a subject like economics of the patient gathering and measurement of statistical data. Kuznets' pre-war efforts in reconstructing the national income and product accounts of the United States back to 1919, and eventually back to 1869, in such books as *National Income, 1929–1932* (National Bureau of Economic Research, 1934), *National Income and Capital Formation, 1919–1935* (National Bureau of Economic Research, 1941) and *National Product since 1869* (National Bureau of Economic Research, 1946), co-authored with E. Jenks and L. Epstein, made it possible to put empirical flesh on the Keynesian skeleton, which played a crucial role in the rapid acceptance of Keynesian economics during and after World War II. Similarly, the then young science of econometrics leaned heavily on Kuznets' data and would have been virtually still-born without it.

Kuznets broadened his research in the 1960s, extending it to a comparative study of the economic growth patterns of different countries. Much of what we now know about economic growth is due to his work, embodied in such books as *Economic Growth and Structure: Selected Essays* (W.W. Norton, 1965), *Modern Economic Growth: Rate, Structure and Spread* (Yale University Press, 1966) and *Economic Growth of Nations: Total Output and Production Structure*

(Belknap, 1971). In the 1970s, his focus shifted once again to the field of population growth and this theme is combined with that of economic growth and income distribution in some of his later works, such as *Population, Capital, and Growth: Selected Essays* (W.W. Norton, 1973) *and Growth, Population and Income Distribution: Selected Essays* (W.W. Norton, 1979).

Kuznets was born in Kharkov, Russia, in 1901 and rose at an early age to become head of a statistical office in the Ukraine under the Bolsheviks. In 1922 he emigrated to the United States and entered Columbia University, receiving his BSc in 1923, his MA in 1924 and his PhD in economics in 1926 with a dissertation on cyclical fluctuations in retail and wholesale trade. Joining the National Bureau of Economic Research, headed by his PhD supervisor Wesley Mitchell, he launched upon a study of national income. In 1930 he took up a teaching post at the University of Pennsylvania, where he remained as professor until 1954, interrupted only by two years as Associate Director of the Bureau of Planning and Statistics of the US War Production Board during World War II. In 1954 he moved to Johns Hopkins University as Professor of Political Economy, moving again in 1960 to Harvard University, where he remained until his retirement in 1971. He was President of the American Statistical Association in 1949, and of the American Economic Association in 1954, the Falk Programme for Economic Research in Israel (1953–63), and received the Francis A. Walker Medal of the American Economic Association in 1977. He died in 1985 at the age of eighty-four.

In an early work, *Secular Movements in Production and Prices* (Houghton Mifflin, 1930), Kuznets identified fluctuations of 15–20 years' duration in a number of economic time series for the United States. He returned to this subject several times in his later writings, and these 'Kuznets Cycles' as they are called, although still somewhat controversial, are now a common feature of the business-cycle literature. Another key finding associated with his name is the inverse-U relationship between national income per head of population and the degree of inequality in the distribution of income as measured by the Gini coefficient, such that in poor countries inequality rises as income levels rise, while in rich countries inequality falls as income increases. Kuznets has analysed this relationship between economic development and income inequalities at the level of countries and sectors of economic activity within countries, distinguishing between self-employed income, income from employment and property income, and in so doing has sparked off an empirical literature on income distribution that grew from almost nothing in the 1950s to a veritable flood in the 1970s. Needless to say, however, it is in the field of national income accounting that Kuznets' influence has left the deepest mark. For years he was closely associated with the US Department of Commerce responsible for the official estimates of GNP in the USA. In the late 1940s, however, he became increasingly critical of its methods, in particular the failure to include estimates of the value of unpaid housework. His standpoint was that the measurement of national income is not just a practical exercise in social accounting but rather an attempt to depict changes in economic welfare. However, this was one fight which he lost. He went on to create the International Association for Research in Income and Wealth to spread the GNP gospel around the world.

*Secondary Literature*
R.A. Easterlin, 'Kuznets, Simon', in D.L. Sills (ed.), *International Encyclopaedia of the Social Sciences*, vol. 18 (The Free Press, 1979); E. Lundberg, 'Simon Kuznets's Contributions to Economics', in H.W. Spiegel and W.J. Samuels (eds), *Contemporary Economists in Perspective*, vol. 2 (JAI Press, 1984); R.A. Easterlin, 'Kuznets, Simon', in J. Eatwell, M. Milgate and P. Newman (eds), *The New Palgrave: A Dictionary of Economics*, vol. 3 (Macmillan, 1987).

# Lancaster
# Kelvin J.
# (1924– )

Kelvin Lancaster is the inventor of a new theory of consumer demand, first announced in 'A New Approach to Consumer Theory',
*Journal of Political Economy*, April 1966, and then elaborated in a
book, *Consumer Demand: A New Approach* (Columbia University Press,
1971). Lancaster's theory is known as the 'characteristics' theory of
consumer behaviour because it assumes that consumers are motivated, not by the direct utility of individual goods, but by the utility
of the services that are indirectly provided by a whole class of
similar but not identical goods. In short, the consumer has a demand for a car with certain 'characteristics' (size, performance, extra features, etc.) and not a demand for a Buick or an Oldsmobile.
Stated as such, this idea is trivial and probably unproductive of
new insights. However, Lancaster goes on to make the daring assumption that the 'characteristics' of goods can be objectively measured in physical terms, and the even more daring assumption that
each separate good represents a bundle of these objectively measured characteristics combined in fixed proportions. It is this latter
assumption which allows Lancaster to apply to consumption 'activity analysis' previously only applied to production (see Koopmans,
T.C.): each consumer chooses his own preferred combination of
consumer 'activities', made up of a fixed vector of objectively measured 'characteristics', which are in turn embodied in a particular

149

bundle of goods. The result is a theory which is just as rigorous as the traditional indifference theory of consumer behaviour (see Hicks, J.R.) but which has all sorts of unfamiliar implications, for example, that individual purchases of goods may be completely unaffected by price changes throughout a considerable range, or that new goods may be entirely displaced from the market by a change in price or the introduction of new goods. Furthermore, in the Lancasterian theory, product variety and product differentiation, which are usually taken to be manifestations of departures from perfect competition, are regarded as essential to the very notion of consumer demand even under perfect competition. Despite the elegance with which the new theory is expounded, fellow economists have not been wholly converted to Lancaster's alternative approach. Thus, the characteristics theory has not so far been incorporated in elementary textbooks other than in Lancaster's own *Introduction to Modern Microeconomics* (Rand McNally, 1969). In a later book, *Variety, Equity and Efficiency* (Columbia University Press, 1979), Lancaster attempts to display the power of the new theory in dealing with many of the observed features of retail markets, as well as labour markets and money markets. There is little doubt that the years to come will see more work in this area and perhaps the gradual acceptance of the characteristics theory by mainstream economics.

Lancaster is also the joint author with R.G. Lipsey (q.v.) of a famous paper on 'The General Theory of Second Best' which has left a permanent mark on applied welfare economics. In addition, he has generalised the 'qualitative calculus', an invention of Paul Samuelson's (q.v.), which amounts to a precise technique of evaluating the empirical content of economic models. In his *Foundations of Economic Analysis*, Samuelson had argued that the comparative statics method of economics, comparing the change between an initial and subsequent state of equilibrium, must at least yield a 'qualitative calculus' allowing one to infer the *direction* of change of the relevant economic variables, even though it may not be sufficient to infer the exact quantitative *magnitude* of that change. Lancaster's *Mathematical Economics* (Macmillan, 1968), an intermediate textbook, contains a detailed discussion of this method of appraising the qualitative implications of different economic models.

Lancaster was born in 1924 in Sydney, Australia. He received his BSc in 1948, his BA in 1949 and his MA in 1952, all from the University of Sydney. In 1953, he left Australia and came to the University of London to study for his doctorate. Obtaining his PhD in 1958, he began teaching at the University of London in 1959. In 1962, he emigrated to America to become a professor at Johns Hopkins University. Four years later, he moved to Columbia University, where he is teaching today.

# Leibenstein, Harvey (1922–93)

Harvey Leibenstein was an off-beat economist whose specialty seemed to be the invention of thorns to prick the flesh of orthodox economists. In a frequently cited essay, 'Allocative Efficiency vs. "X-Efficiency"', *American Economic Review*, June 1966, he put forward the view that most business firms fail to minimise costs per unit of output either because some of the inputs they employ are not marketed or because the production function – the technical relationship between inputs and output – cannot be completely specified or fully known; more generally, 'X-efficiency', or rather the non-allocative aspects of *in*efficiency, is due to inertia, a conservative desire for manoeuvring room, and imperfections in markets for knowledge. Employing this concept, Leibenstein was able to account for a large number of frequently observed features of business life, all of which involve 'slack' – the possibility of getting something for nothing – which are difficult to explain with the orthodox theory of profit maximisation. Subsequently, in *Beyond Economic Man: A New Foundation for Microeconomics* (Harvard University Press, 1976; 2nd edn, 1980), *General X-Efficiency Theory and Economic Development* (Oxford University Press, 1978), *Inflation, Income Distribution and X-Efficiency Theory* (Barnes & Noble 1980), and *Inside the Firm: The Inefficiencies of Hierarchy* (Harvard University Press, 1987), he broadened the original statement of the theory into a more comprehensive type of analysis, according to which economic agents are typically non-maximisers but gradually adopt maximising behaviour as external pressure on them increases.

X-efficiency theory does not provide a systematic framework for predicting when and how business enterprises will fail to minimise costs and the evidence offered by Leibenstein in favour of the existence of 'slack' in firms was admittedly casual. No wonder then that the concept of X-efficiency has been frequently attacked on the grounds that the phenomena to which Leibenstein drew attention can be explained in terms of the orthodox theory of the firm when that theory is suitably 'modernised' by considerations of transaction costs, informational uncertainty, and unspecified property rights (see Alchian, A.A.; Coase, R.H.; Demsetz, H.). Be that as it may, Leibenstein's theory shows how difficult it is to pin down precisely what is meant by 'efficiency' – if people enjoy slack, are they necessarily being inefficient? – and it has been instrumental in stimulating further inquiries into the process of decision-making within business firms. In this way, X-efficiency theory joins hands with the Carnegie School (see Simon, H.A), a connection which Leibenstein underlined in one of his best papers, 'A Branch of Economics is Missing: Micro-micro Theory', *Journal of Economic Literature*, June 1979.

Apart from work on business behaviour, Leibenstein also made use of X-efficiency theory to throw light on the macroeconomics of human fertility. His first book, *Economic Backwardness and Economic Growth* (Wiley, 1957), analysed population growth in developing countries and, indeed, demography was a constant theme throughout his career. In 'An Interpretation of the Economic Theory of Fertility: Promising Path or Blind Alley?', *Journal of Economic Literature*, June 1974, he contrasted his own approach with that of the Chicago School (see Becker, G.S.). This and other brilliant papers over the years were brought together in a three-volume edition of his *Collected Essays*, ed. K.J. Button (Edward Elgar, 1989).

Leibenstein was born in Russia in 1922 but arrived in Canada at the age of three with his parents. He received his BSc in 1945 and his MA in 1946, both from Northwestern University, followed by a PhD from Princeton University in 1951. His first post was that of a Social Affairs Officer with the Population Division of the United Nations in 1949. His first teaching job was in 1951 at the University of California, Berkeley, which he combined with a consultancy at the Rand Corporation. In 1960 he became Professor of Economics at Berkeley, a post which he left in 1967 to become Professor of the Economics of Population at Harvard University. In 1978–9 he took leave to spend a year at the Institute of Advanced Study, Princeton University. A severe car accident ended his career in 1987. He died in Cambridge, Massachusetts, in 1993.

*Secondary Literature*
M. Perlman, 'Harvey Leibenstein', in W.J. Samuels (ed.), *New Horizons in Economic Thought* (Edward Elgar, 1992).

# Leijonhufvud, Axel (1933– )

Leijonhufvud is Swedish for 'lion-head' and although it is virtually unpronounceable in English, the name has the great advantage that, having once learned how to spell it, it remains indelibly imprinted on the mind. Leijonhufvud published a long, provocative book in 1968, entitled *On Keynesian Economics and the Economics of Keynes: A Study in Monetary Economics* (Oxford University Press, 1968), conveniently summarised in his own pamphlet, *Keynes and the Classics* (Institute of Economic Affairs, 1970), which reopened the old what-Keynes-really-meant question, a problem which most economists thought had been more or less resolved. What Leijonhufvud argued was that the standard Hicks–Hansen IS–LM diagram, which students are still taught as a simplified version of what Keynes meant to say in *The General Theory* (see Hicks, J.R.), does justice neither to the letter nor to the spirit of Keynes.

More specifically, Leijonhufvud claimed that (1) Keynes' economics is not equilibrium economics; (2) Keynes assumed a world of less than perfect information, as a result of which markets adjust to disturbances by first altering quantities (output, employment, etc.) and only later by altering prices; (3) Keynes did not assume that money wages are inflexible but rather that all prices, including wages, change only slowly; and (4) the basic cause of unemployment in Keynes is that 'relative prices are wrong': interest rates are too high, and long-term bond prices are too low, to generate full employment. These claims were supported by hundreds of quotations from Keynes but doubts about Leijonhufvud's interpretation nevertheless remain even after all this documentation.

Leijonhufvud's unorthodox interpretation of Keynes was deeply indebted to earlier work by his colleague, Robert Clower (q.v.) which he nevertheless amplified and extended in new directions. Like Clower, Leijonhufvud also went beyond the discussion of Keynes' own intentions to argue that Keynesian concepts are more fruitfully interpreted as a first, hesitant step towards Disequilibrium Economics, the analysis of the behaviour of markets when demand is not matched by supply and when economic agents are off, not on, their demand and supply curves. As a contribution to disequilibrium economics, Leijonhufvud's book was a resounding success and disequilibrium analysis has ever since become an accepted feature of modern macroeconomics.

Leijonhufvud is also the author of a number of sparkling essays on various aspects of macroeconomics. *Information and Co-ordination: Essays in Macroeconomic Theory* (Oxford University Press, 1981) presents a sample of these, including the delightful spoof-essay 'Among the Econ.' (1973), the findings of an anthropological field-trip to that strange tribe, the economists.

Leijonhufvud was born in 1933 in Stockholm, Sweden, and was educated in Sweden at the University of Lund, receiving his doctor's degree in 1960. Emigrating to America, he then obtained an MA from the University of Pittsburgh in 1961 and another PhD from Northeastern University in 1967. He became an Associate Professor at the University of California, Los Angeles, in 1964 and a full Professor in 1971, a post which he still holds. He has been a visiting Professor at various European universities in the 1960s and '70s. He is a member of the Board of the Economic Institute at Boulder, Colorado.

# Leontief,
# Wassily W.
# (1906– )

Leontief's work is one of the best examples in economics of the advantages of intellectual specialisation: his entire life has been devoted to the development and refinement of a single technical tool, input–output analysis, which he conceived in his early youth and which he carried from Russia to America and from America to almost every country in the world. His efforts on behalf of input–output analysis have won him the French Legion of Honour in 1968, the Presidency of the American Economic Association in 1970, the Nobel Prize in Economics in 1973, Presidency of Section F of the British Academy for the Advancement of Science in 1976, a place in the Russian-American Hall of Fame in 1980, and innumerable honorary degrees from both American and European universities. Throughout the 1930s, 1940s and 1950s he was at Harvard University. Today, at the age of ninety, he is still directing research on input–output analysis at New York University.

He was born in St Petersburg, Russia, in 1906, the son of a Professor of Labour Economics at the University of St Petersburg. He entered his father's university at the age of fifteen and received his MA four years later in 1925. He left Russia in the same year to take a PhD at the University of Berlin. He brought with him a paper, which appeared first in German and then in Russian, in which he argued that the purely abstract equilibrium system of Léon Walras (see Arrow, K.J.) could be simplified and filled in with actual numbers derived from observed technology in different industries. In input–output analysis, the economy is broken into industries or sectors and the flow of goods and services among industries or sectors is recorded systematically in rows and columns to indicate their interrelationships. These interrelationships are called input–output vectors because they tell us what inputs of one industry are required to produce the output of another, which in turn become the inputs of still other industries. Leontief's original proposal provided some practical examples but he lacked the resources at that time to construct an actual input–output table for even one industry. From Berlin, Leontief went to the Institut für Weltwirtschaft in Kiel and then to Nanking as economic adviser to the government of China. In 1931 he went to America as a research worker at the National Bureau of Economic Research, leaving the following year for Harvard.

In 1936 he announced his intention to construct an actual input–output table for the American economy but it was five more years before *The Structure of the American Economy, 1919–1939* (Oxford University Press, 1941; 2nd edn, 1951; International Arts and Sciences Press, 1976) appeared. In those days, all the tedious calculations required to construct an input–output table had to be carried out by hand with the aid of desk calculators: it was only with the coming of electronic computers in the 1950s that input–output analysis became a feasible tool for governments around the world.

*The Structure of the American Economy* was followed by *Studies in the Structure of the American Economy* (Oxford University Press, 1953; International Arts and Sciences Press, 1976), *Input–Output Economics* (Oxford University Press, 1966; 2nd edn, 1986), *The Future of the World Economy* (Oxford University Press, 1977), and a two-volume collection of Leontief's classic *Essays in Economics* (Oxford University Press, 1966, 1977; Basil Blackwell, 1977). Input–output analysis, or as it is sometimes called 'interindustry analysis', has been put to numerous uses: to calculate the resource costs of conversion to peacetime production in 1945; to calculate the flow of trade between regions in a country; to analyse the pollutants generated by different industries in a country; and to spell out relative factor-intensities of exports and imports; see *The Future of the World Economy* (Oxford University Press, 1977), co-authored with A.P. Carter and P. Petri, and *Military Spending: Facts and Figures: Worldwide Implications and*

*Future Outlook* (Oxford University Press, 1983), co-authored with F. Duchin.

In one of his most famous articles, 'Domestic Production and Foreign Trade: the American Capital Position Re-examined', *Economia Internazionale*, February 1954, Leontief discovered that American exports are labour-intensive, while American imports are capital-intensive, which contradicts the so-called 'Heckscher–Ohlin theorum' of modern international trade theory (see Ohlin, B.), according to which countries like the United States plentifully endowed with capital compared to labour would tend to export goods made with high capital–labour ratios and to import goods made with low capital–labour ratios. This finding has been labelled the 'Leontief Paradox' and it generated a great deal of fruitful theoretical and empirical work designed to explain it. Indeed, such consequences of input–output analysis have proved to be of even greater importance than the actual tables which Leontief and his associates have constructed: a whole branch of advanced economic theory known as 'linear production theory' owes its inspiration to input–output analysis (see Koopmans, T.C.). Because input–output analysis deals essentially with large sets of linear equations, it lends itself naturally to the use of matrix algebra, and the widespread use of matrix algebra in modern economics is simply another one of the major influences of Leontief's work.

Input–output analysis has sometimes met with resistance, especially in America. It is a kind of 'priceless economics' in the sense that it operates entirely with physical quantities, and some have even expressed the fear that input–output analysis provides a kind of blueprint for centralised economic planning of the economy. Moreover, it has proved difficult to take account in input–output tables of the general tendency to substitute cheaper inputs for expensive ones in response to changes in their prices, not to mention dynamic changes in the entire technology of an industry. Leontief, however, has worked hard to dynamise input–output analysis and to widen its practical applicability by taking account of price changes, excess capacity and technical progress. In recent years, he has shown an increasing interest in using input–output analysis to construct and evaluate development plans in Third World countries.

A recurrent note in all of Leontief's writings is the insistence that economists must 'get their hands dirty' by working directly with raw data. He remains adamant in old age that much of modern economics is hopelessly impractical and anti-empirical, assigning greater prestige to hypothetical model-building expressed in mathematics than to painstaking efforts to marshall statistical data and to employ it in the analysis of real-world problems. His presidential address to the American Economic Association, 'Theoretical Assumptions and Nonobserved Facts', *American Economic Review*, June 1971, summed up his lifetime indictment of the sterility of much contemporary economics.

*Secondary Literature*
L. Silk, *The Economists* (Basic Books, 1974), ch. 4; M. Cave, 'Wassily Leontief: Input–Output and Economic Planning', in J.R. Shackleton and G. Locksley (eds), *Twelve Contemporary Economists* (Macmillan Press, 1981; Wiley, Halsted Press, 1981); R. Dorfman, 'Leontief, Wassily', in J. Eatwell, M. Milgate and P. Newman (eds), *The New Palgrave: A Dictionary of Economics*, vol. 3 (Macmillan, 1987).

# Lerner, Abba P. (1903–82)

Abba P. Lerner was one of the many talented young economists – others were Roy Allen, John Hicks, Nicholas Kaldor, Arthur Lewis, George Shackle, Tibor Scitovsky, and Brinley Thomas – who taught at the London School of Economics in the 1930s in a department presided over by Lionel Robbins (q.v.). Lerner was born in Bessarabia, Russia, in 1903 but came to Britain with his parents at an early age. After a series of false starts as a Hebrew teacher and businessman, he arrived as a student at the London School of Economics in 1929 and within a year began to win a whole series of essay prizes, including the much-coveted Tooke Scholarship in 1930. His first paper on the geometry of international trade, pioneering the use of social indifference curves to illustrate a two-country equilibrium, was published as early as 1932, and this was followed two years later by a seminal paper, 'The Concept of Monopoly and the Measurement of Monopoly Power', *Review of Economic Studies*, June 1934, which laid the foundation for the marginal-cost-pricing rule that was soon to emerge in applied welfare economics. These and other of Lerner's classic articles were reissued as *Selected Economic Writings of Abba P. Lerner*, ed. D.C. Colander (Columbia University Press, 1983).

In 1933, he helped to found the new *Review of Economic Studies*, which he continued to co-edit until 1937. In 1935, he began teaching at the London School of Economics and also spent a term at Cambridge University, which converted him to Keynesian economics. More fellowships followed and so did articles applying diagrammatic techniques to international economics (see his *Essays in Economic Analysis*, Macmillan, 1953). He became involved in the great debates about the economics of socialism between Ludwig Mises (q.v.) and Oskar Lange and published an important contribution to the discussion. In 1939 he left Britain for the United States where he spent the next forty years in a bewildering number of universities, rarely staying more than a few years at a time: Columbia, Virginia, Kansas City, Amherst, The New School for Social Research, Roosevelt, Johns Hopkins, Michigan State, the University of California, Berkeley, Queen's College of the City of New York, and the State University of Florida, from which he finally retired from teaching at the age of seventy-seven.

In 1944 he published his most famous book, *The Economics of Control* (Macmillan, 1944), which had earned him a doctorate the year before from the University of London. The book had begun as a contribution to the economics of socialism but had soon grown into a statement of a completely general set of principles, based on the equation of marginal costs and marginal benefits, which could be applied by policy-makers to improve the performance of any economy, socialist or capitalist. In one sense, it was a reworking of Pigou's *Economics of Welfare* (1920) with the aid of 'general' rather than 'partial' equilibrium analysis but it paid much less attention to the institutional context of economic activity than Pigou's treatise. It was, in fact, a working out of the 'new' welfare economics of the 1930s in which the only guide to practical policy was the maxim of Pareto: an economic change is an improvement in economic welfare if and only if it makes at least one person better off without making so much as one other person worse off; if it does make someone worse off, it still counts as a potential improvement in welfare if the gainer has more than sufficient gains to compensate the loser for his losses. In this way, one can talk about economic welfare without ever directly comparing the 'utility' or satisfactions of individuals; it is the individuals themselves who decide when they are better or worse off, and not the economist as superarbiter of the social interest, and that is why it was called the 'new' welfare economics (see Bergson, A.).

*The Economics of Control* contained two further features that attracted much attention: a utilitarian argument in favour of perfect equality in the distribution of income and a neo-Keynesian exposition of the principles of 'functional finance', according to which the size of deficits and surpluses in the government budget are to be judged solely with reference to the levels of employment and prices in the economy – the public debt is in no sense an economic burden on future generations. *The Economics of Employment* (McGraw-Hill, 1951) amplified this particular interpretation of Keynes' message while expressing misgivings about the problem of containing prices at high levels of employment. This theme of inflationary pressures at high levels of employment emerges boldly in Lerner's *Flation: Not Inflation of Prices, Not Deflation of Jobs* (Quadrangle, 1972; Penguin, 1973) and his *MAP – A Market Anti-inflation Plan* (Harcourt Brace Jovanovich, 1980), co-authored with D.C. Colander, which proposes an ingenious scheme for controlling inflation by the state issue of 'permits' for wages and price increases, which any business firm can buy and which are tradable on the market like stocks and shares; the total supply of such 'permits', however, is only allowed to grow at the same rate as real GNP. This is not to be confused with similar but different proposals for taxing business firms that raise wages or prices (see Weintraub, S.).

Lerner acted as adviser to the Government of Israel in the 1950s and published a major work, with H. Ben-Shahar, on *The Economics of Efficiency and Growth: Lessons from Israel and the West Bank* (Ballinger, 1975). He became a Distinguished Fellow of the American Economic Association in 1966. In 1980, at the tender age of seventy-seven, he served as President of the Atlantic Economic Society, adding himself to the long list of septuagenarians in economics. He continued to sculpt and to construct wire mobiles, a hobby he kept up for over forty years, until the day of his death in 1982.

*Secondary Literature*
D. Laidler, 'Lerner, Abba P.', in D.L. Sills (ed.), *International Encyclopedia of the Social Sciences*, vol. 18 (The Free Press, 1979); W. Breit and R.L. Ramson, 'Abba P. Lerner: The Artist as Economist', *The Academic Scribblers: American Economists in Collision*, 2nd edn (Dryden Press, 1982); I. Sobel, 'Lerner', in H.W. Spiegel and W.J. Samuels (eds), *Contemporary Economists in Perspective* (JAI Press, 1984), T. Scitovsky, 'Lerner, Abba Ptachya', in J. Eatwell, M. Milgate and P. Newman (eds), *The New Palgrave: A Dictionary of Economics*, vol. 3 (Macmillan, 1987).

# Lewis,
# W. Arthur
# (1915–91)

Arthur Lewis shared the Nobel Prize in Economics with Theodore Schultz in 1979 for a lifetime of effort in the field of development economics. His *Theory of Economic Growth* (Allen & Unwin, 1955) – which should have been called 'Theory of Economic Development' to avoid confusion with the totally different field of steady-state growth theory (see Harrod, R.F.; Domar, E.D.) – was one of the first text books in the post-war era to explore the development problems of the Third World. A year earlier, he published a paper, 'Economic Development with Unlimited Supplies of Labour', *The Manchester School*, May 1954, which has since become one of the most frequently cited publications by any modern economist: it spawned a whole literature on 'dual economies' – small, urban, industrialised sectors of economic activity surrounded by a large, rural, traditional sector, like minute islands set in a vast ocean – and put its stamp on the character of development economics for decades to come. The Lewis model has not lacked critics (see Jorgenson, D.W.). Nevertheless, even today, large parts of development economics can be described as elaborations of Lewis' classic article of 1954.

A central theme of that article was that labour in dual economies is available to the urban, industrialised sector at a constant wage determined by minimum levels of existence in traditional family farming: because of 'disguised unemployment' in agriculture, there is a practically unlimited supply of labour available for purposes of industrialisation, at least in the early stages of development. At some later point in the history of dual economies, the supply of surplus labour is exhausted and then only a rising wage rate will draw more labour out of agriculture. The Lewis model was almost immediately interpreted throughout the Third World as justifying an import-competing, industrialisation growth strategy (see Chenery, H.B.) and must therefore be given some of the blame, through no fault of the author, for the neglect of rural development in the countries of Africa, Asia and Latin America, which has been singled out as the great scandal of development in the 1970s.

Lewis was born in St Lucia, West Indies, in 1915. After attending high school in St Lucia, he entered the London School of Economics in 1934, graduating in 1937. In 1938 he began teaching at the LSE where he remained until 1948, except for wartime service with the British government at the Board of Trade and the Colonial Office. He received his MA from the University of Manchester and his doctorate from the University of London, both in the early 1940s. In 1948, he became a Professor of Economics at the University of Manchester, where he spent an extremely productive decade, publishing *Economic Survey, 1918–1939* (Allen & Unwin, 1949), *Overhead Costs* (Allen & Unwin, 1949), *The Principles of Economic Planning* (Allen & Unwin, 1950; 3rd edn, 1969), and *The Theory of Economic Growth*, referred to above, while still finding time to serve as a member of the UN Group of Experts on Underdeveloped Countries, a consultant to the government of the Gold Coast (1953) and Western Nigeria (1955), and an Economic Adviser to the Prime Minister of Ghana (1957–8). He left Manchester in 1958 to become Principal of University College of the West Indies, when it was enlarged into the University of the West Indies in 1962, he became its first Vice-Chancellor. In 1963, Lewis was knighted by the British government and moved to the USA to take up a professorship at Princeton University. He left America in 1970 to take up the presidency of the Caribbean Development Bank but returned to Princeton in 1973, where he still remains as a Professor of Economics. He died in Princeton, New Jersey in 1991.

His literary output has gradually shifted over the years from development planning to comparative economic history. Books like *Development Planning: The Essentials of Economic Planning* (Allen & Unwin, 1966), *Reflections on the Economic Growth of Nigeria* (OECD,

1967), and *Some Aspects of Economic Development* (Ghana University, 1969) have given way to *Tropical Development, 1880–1913* (Allen & Unwin, 1971), *The Evolution of the International Economic Order* (Allen & Unwin, 1977) and a major study of *Growth and Fluctuations, 1870–1913* (Allen & Unwin, 1978). *Selected Economic Writings of W. Arthur Lewis*, ed. M. Gersovitz (Columbia University Press, 1980) reprints his significant papers on development, trade, and foreign aid. He has received honorary degrees from twenty universities in America, Europe and Africa, and served as Chancellor of the University of Ghana during 1966–73, itself an honorary appointment. He became an Honorary Fellow of the Weitzmann Institute of Israel in 1969 and President of the American Economic Association in 1982. In short, Lewis is an amazingly prolific economist who has somehow managed to combine two lives in one, that of a detached academic intellectual and that of an active man of affairs.

*Secondary Literature*
R. Findlay, 'Sir Arthur Lewis's Contributions to Economics', in H.W. Spiegel and W.J. Samuels (eds), *Contemporary Economists in Perspective*, vol. 1 (JAI Press, 1984); R. Findlay, 'Lewis, W. Arthur', in J. Eatwell, M. Milgate and P. Newman (eds), *The New Palgrave: A Dictionary of Economics*, vol. 3 (Macmillan, 1987).

# Lipsey, Richard G. (1928– )

Richard Lipsey is the author of one of the most successful introductory textbooks of recent years. *An Introduction to Positive Economics* (Weidenfeld & Nicolson, 1963; 7th edn, 1989), known in America as *Economics* (Harper & Row, 1966; 7th edn, 1983), co-authored with G. Purvis, J. Sparks and P.O. Steiner. The book has been widely translated and repeatedly reprinted because its qualities are unique: no other introductory text book places so much emphasis on the need to submit economic theories to empirical tests and no other first text is so frank about those theories where convincing empirical evidence is so far lacking.

It is probably true to say that no introductory text book ever succeeds unless the author has previously established his professional credentials by the publication of articles in one of the major journals: students may not care but their teachers do, and it is teachers who assign textbooks. It is not surprising, therefore, to learn that Lipsey is also the author, with Lancaster, of a classic paper on 'The General Theory of Second Best', *Review of Economic Studies*, June 1956, which established the theorem that economic policies designed to turn a second-best into a first-best situation may instead succeed only in bringing about a third-best situation. The basic idea of the second-best theorem is very simple: imagine trying to get a good sound mix in a chorus when some of the sopranos are ill; making the tenors sing louder, or everyone else softer, or reducing the number of all other voices proportionately does not necessarily work. Lipsey and Lancaster showed that this basic idea could be expressed in general terms to demonstrate that, say, the elimination of a monopoly in an economy riddled with taxes – a second-best situation – may drive us further away instead of towards first-best, competitive equilibrium. Applied welfare economics has had to live ever since with the devastating implications of the Lipsey–Lancaster theorem.

Similarly, in another memorable paper on 'The Relation between Unemployment and the Rate of Change of Money Wage Rates in the United Kingdom, 1862–1975: A Further Analysis', *Economica*, February 1960, Lipsey managed to provide a microeconomic explanation for the macroeconomic relationship between unemployment and wage inflation which A.W. Phillips (q.v.) had earlier discovered, and in so doing was perhaps more responsible than anyone else in publicising the 'Phillips Curve'. In 'Understanding and Control of Inflation: Is There a Crisis in Macro-economics?', *Canadian Journal of Economics*, November 1981, he denied that refutations of the Phillips Curve had created a crisis in modern macroeconomics and vigorously defended the traditional Keynesian system as 'alive and well'.

Lipsey's work in the post-war period has ranged from monetary theory, international trade, and industrial organisation to location theory, the economics of spatial competition, and the cause of inflation. He has also written, with G.C. Archibald, an excellent introductory text as well as an intermediate text in mathematical economics: *An Introduction to Mathematical Treatment of Economics* (Weidenfeld & Nicolson, 1967; 2nd edn, 1977) and *Mathematical Economics: Methods and Applications* (Harper & Row, 1976). More recently, he has published a series of essays with C.B. Eaton, *On the Foundations of Monopolistic Competition and Economic Geography* (Edward Elgar, 1997). See also his two volumes of selected essays, *Macroeconomic Theory and Policy and Microeconomics, Growth and Political Economy* (Edward Elgar, 1997). *Collected Essays* in three volumes (Edward Elgar, 1997) has also just appeared.

Lipsey was born in Victoria, British Columbia, in 1928. He took his undergraduate studies at the University of British Columbia, receiving a BA in 1951, followed by an MA from the University of Toronto in 1953. Crossing the Atlantic, he studied for his doctorate at the London School of Economics. He obtained his PhD in 1957 with a doctoral dissertation on *The Theory of Customs Unions*, which eventually appeared as a book in 1973. He started teaching at the London School of Economics in 1958, became a professor at the School in 1961, but left in 1964 to head a new department of economics at the University of Essex. In 1969, he returned to Canada, first as a Visiting Professor at his old *alma mater*, the University of British Columbia, and then as a permanent Professor of Economics at Queen's University in Kingston, Ontario. Since 1989 he has been a professor at Simon Fraser University in Vancouver, British Columbia.

He edited the *Review of Economic Studies* from 1962–4, served on the governing council of a number of research institutes in Britain and Canada, received the Queen's Prize of Canada for Excellence in Research in 1980, and was Chairman of the Canadian Economic Association in 1980.

# Little,
# Ian M. David
# (1918–  )

Ian Little was well known in the 1950s for his *Critique of Welfare Economics* (Oxford University Press, 1950; 2nd edn, 1957), which threw cold water on the 'new' welfare economics (see Hicks, J.R.; Kaldor, N.; and Lerner, A.P.), in particular casting doubt on the sense in which perfect competition is characterised by welfare theorists as an 'optimal' solution. In effect, he denied that questions of 'efficiency' can be divorced in practical terms from questions of 'equity': every step towards efficiency involves changes in the distribution of income, which alters the efficiency state itself and, moreover, these income changes are liable to be far more significant for social welfare than the changes in efficiency. This was one of the first of what is now an almost standard criticism of modern welfare economics but it was Little more than anyone else who set this particular ball rolling.

In the 1960s, Little's interest turned towards foreign aid and the failures of the import-substitution, industrialisation policies of developing countries, which were then widely endorsed by development economists. *International Aid* (Basic Books, Allen & Unwin, 1965), with J.M. Clifford, and *Industry and Trade in Some Developing Countries* (Oxford University Press, 1970), with T. Scitovsky and M.F.G. Scott, were products of that decade in Little's output. And then in 1974 he joined with J. Mirrlees in the writing of *Project*

*Appraisal and Planning for Developing Countries* (Basic Books, Heinemann Educational, 1974), which instantly became a classic in development economics and a veritable handbook for administrators and policy-makers in developing countries.

In order to appraise a development project, it is necessary to express the inputs and outputs of the project in terms of some common yardstick. The usual rule is to use a 'shadow price' for foreign exchange, that is, the actual price of foreign exchange adjusted for the tariffs and other distortions which raise domestic prices above world prices in most developing countries. The central innovation of the Little–Mirrlees book is that they propose instead to base their yardstick on the actual exchange rate applied solely to the 'uncommitted income' of a project accruing to the government. In effect, resources accruing to government are given a higher value than the same resources committed to private use and, in addition, increases in the income of the rich resulting from a project are assigned a lower weight than increases in the income of the poor.

The book attracted a furious controversy. It contains remarkably lucid discussions of the economic principles underlying cost-benefit analysis, and the suggestion that weights ought to be attached to the income streams resulting from a project is a useful reminder that project appraisal involves questions of 'equity' as well as 'efficiency'. But the central proposal of the book, the Little–Mirrlees yardstick of measurement of the costs and benefits of a project, has met with steady objections, partly in terms of practical considerations – since the measure is convertible foreign exchange, what allowance is being made for overvalued exchange rate? – and partly in terms of 'ideology' – why are resources in government hands regarded as more valuable than resources in private hands? Even today, a decade later, the argument about the Little–Mirrlees yardstick is by no means at an end.

Little was born in Rugby, England, in 1918. He received a BA in 1947 and a DPhil in 1949, both from the University of Oxford. From 1952 to 1976, he was a teaching Fellow at Nuffield College, Oxford, interrupted by two years as Deputy Director of the Economic Section of the British Treasury (1953–5) and two years as Vice-President of the OECD Development Centre in Paris (1965–7). In 1972, he became a Professor of Economics at the University of Oxford but left in 1976 to become Economic Adviser to the World Bank in Washington. He retired in 1978.

He was a member of the UN Committee on Development Planning from 1972 to 1975 and has been a Fellow of the British Association since 1973.

# Lucas, Robert E., Jr (1937– )

Robert Lucas did not invent the theory of rational expectations but he has been its most vigorous advocate, insisting that, because the expectations of economic agents are 'rational', monetary and fiscal policy only affect physical output and employment in the extremely short run; for him, the 'new' classical macroeconomics based on the concept of rational expectations is irreconcilably opposed to Keynesian economics.

The theory of rational expectations was invented by J.F. Muth in an article on security and commodity markets, 'Rational Expectations and the Theory of Price Movements', *Econometrica*, July 1961. Muth's problem was to explain why no rule, formula, or model has ever been consistently successful in predicting prices in speculative markets, and his answer was, in effect, that all available information is already incorporated into current decisions by speculators, whose expectations are 'rational' in this precise sense.

Keynesian monetary and fiscal policies proved relatively ineffective in the early 1970s in solving the macroeconomic problems of the American economy and it occurred simultaneously to a number of economists, in particular Lucas and Thomas J. Sargent (q.v.), that the reason for this was the same as that advanced by Muth for the unpredictability of stock markets. Economic agents, instead of simply adapting their behaviour to the difference expected and realised events, which implies being constantly disappointed during periods of rising inflation, are conceived as forming their expectations on the basis of exactly the same information that is available to policy-makers. An expansionary fiscal policy or an easy monetary policy designed to reduce unemployment is correctly perceived to lead to higher prices; in consequence, private spending accelerates and the result is instant inflation without much effect on real variables like output and employment. To express it in the language of the Phillips Curve (see Phillips, A.W.), there is no trade-off between unemployment and inflation even in the short run. The only way a government can bring about deviations from the 'natural rate of unemployment' (see Friedman, M.) is by surprising people, but if people learn by experience, this will only work once or twice; sooner or later, people will learn to anticipate correctly any systematic government policy and, at that point, unemployment will never deviate, except momentarily, from its natural rate.

The empirical work that has been done to substantiate this policy-neutral conclusion of the 'new' classical macroeconomics is highly technical and involves, not the direct measurement of expectations, but the manipulation of estimated econometric models in which variables expressing people's expectations are replaced by lagged values of directly observable variables. Much depends, therefore, on the precise structure of these econometric models and, besides, the theory of rational expectations would appear to prove too much: unless we add special assumptions, it succeeds in explaining away even the phenomenon of business cycles. Suffice it to say that the 'new' classical macroeconomics had not lacked critics, including those who have their own quarrels with Keynesian or neo-Keynesian macroeconomic policies. A standard criticism is that the policy-neutral conclusion depends, not so much on the idea of rational expectations, as on the idea that all the markets are cleared instantaneously, which lies hidden beneath the arguments of the Rational Expectations School. Nevertheless, the New Macroeconomics had attracted a considerable following among younger 'conservative' American economists and is today at the crossroad of all the new developments in macroeconomic thinking.

Most of Lucas's path-breaking papers on rational expectations are reprinted in his *Studies in Business-cycle Theory* (MIT Press, 1981), a two-volume anthology, edited with T.J. Sargent, *Rational Expectations and Econometric Practice* (University of Minnesota Press, 1981;

Allen & Unwin, 1982), and *Econometric Practice: A Book of Reading*, 2 vols (University of Minnesota Press, 1981; Allen & Unwin, 1981). More recent examples of his work are *Models of the Business Cycle* (Basil Blackwell, 1987), and *Recursive Methods in Economic Dynamics* (Harvard University Press, 1989), with N.L. Stokey and E.C. Prescott.

Lucas was born in 1937 in Yakima, Washington, and received his BA in History in 1959 and his PhD in 1964, both from the University of Chicago. He became a Professor of Economics at Carnegie-Mellon University in 1970, followed by a professorship at the University of Chicago in 1974, a post which he still holds. He has been a co-editor of the *Journal of Political Economy* since 1978 and a member of the executive committee of the American Economic Association since 1979. He received the Nobel Prize in Economics in 1995.

# Machlup, Fritz (1902–83)

Fritz Machlup was a born teacher and all of his writings have the quality of being addressed to an audience of students, classifying terms, clarifying concepts, and explaining frequent misunderstandings. In a sense he never said anything new but he certainly placed a new perspective on what others had said before him. His lifelong interest in the philosophy of science and methodology of economics was part and parcel of this burning passion to teach the uninitiated.

He was born in 1902 just outside Vienna, Austria. In 1920, he enrolled at the University of Vienna, completing his doctoral dissertation on the gold standard in 1923 under the supervision of Ludwig von Mises. Following in his father's footsteps, he became a partner in a cardboard-manufacturing company but he continued to study economics as an active member of the Mises seminar (see Hayek, F.A. von). By 1931, he had published three books as well as many newspaper articles on international economics and was a recognised expert on foreign exchange. In 1933, he visited the USA on a Rockefeller Foundation Fellowship, spending time at several of the leading American universities. This led in 1933 to his first professorial appointment at the University of Buffalo, where he was to remain until 1947 when he moved to Johns Hopkins University, moving once again in 1960 to Princeton University. In 1971 he left

Princeton and took up a post-retirement professorship at New York University, which he held until his death in 1983.

In 1943, Machlup published a book on *International Trade and the National Income Multiplier* (Blakiston, 1943), which did much to popularise the Keynesian theory of the role of income variations in equilibrating the balance of payments. Three years later, in a famous article on 'Marginal Analysis and Empirical Research', *American Economic Review*, September 1946, he defended the orthodox profit-maximising theory of the firm against the empirical onslaughts of Richard Lester, a Princeton labour economist. Of course, Lester was right to argue, Machlup conceded, that businessmen frequently lack the knowledge to calculate marginal outlays and revenues and that, even possessing the knowledge, they sometimes maximise variables other than profits. But the purpose of the orthodox theory, Machlup argued, is not to account realistically for each and every firm but simply for the typical firm and, even then, not to account for all its actions but only for its reactions to given changes in demand, the prices of inputs, the rate of taxes, and the like. In other words, the orthodox concept of the firm is a modest abstraction compared to the actual firms that Lester had investigated.

Machlup amplified his arguments against Lester in two major treaties, *The Economics of Sellers' Competition* (Johns Hopkins University Press, 1952) and *The Political Economy of Monopoly* (Johns Hopkins University Press, 1952), and returned it again in his presidential address to the American Economic Association, 'Theories of the Firm: Marginalist, Behavioral, Managerial', *American Economic Review*, March 1967, elaborating but in no way qualifying his original reply to Lester: the orthodox theory of the firm had limitations but was perfectly valid on its own grounds. Another of his signal contributions to the theory of business behaviour was his masterful book on *The Basing-point System* (Blakiston, 1949), which is reputed to have influenced President Truman in vetoing a Congressional Bill to force cement producers to charge the same price irrespective of the location of customers.

Another of Machlup's favourite subjects was the economics of the patent system, an interest which resulted in a number of articles and a major study for a Congressional Committee, *An Economic Review of the Patent System* (Government Printing Office, 1958). The move in 1960 to Princeton University ushered in a decade in which he returned to the subject of his youth, international monetary reform. *Plans for Reform of the International Monetary System* (Princeton University Press, 1962; 2nd edn, 1964) was followed by an influential study of *International Monetary Arrangements: The Problem of Choice*, edited by Machlup and B.G. Malkiel (Princeton University Press, 1964), *Maintaining and Restoring Balance in International Payments* (Princeton University Press, 1966), *Remaking the International Monetary System* (Johns Hopkins University Press, 1968), and *A History of Thought on Economic Integration* (Columbia University Press, Macmillan, 1977). All in all, Machlup's work in international economics added up to seventeen books and nearly a hundred articles.

Another string to Machlup's bow was the philosophy of economics. A series of beautiful papers sorting out the meaning of central economic concepts was brought together in *Essays on Economic Semantics*, ed. M. Miller (New York University Press, 1963 2nd edn, Transaction Books, 1991) and *Methodology of Economics and Other Social Sciences* (Academic Press, 1978). *Selected Economic Writings of Fritz Machlup*, ed G. Bitros (New York University Press, 1976) provides further examples of this preoccupation with precision of language in economics.

Machlup did not lack honours: degrees from half a dozen universities, the presidency of the Southern Economics Association (1960), the American Association of University Professors (1962–4), the American Economic Association (1967), and the International Economic Association (1971–4). He was able in his later years to look back at a brilliant career, except that looking back was not something he was good at. In 1978, at the age of seventy-six, he calmly announced his intention to prepare a second edition of his classic book on *The Production and Distribution of Knowledge in the United States* (Princeton University Press, 1962) – in no less than eight volumes! The first three volumes of this second edition, entitled *Knowledge: Its Creation, Distribution, and Economic Significance*, vol. 1: *Knowledge and Knowledge Production* (1980), vol. 2: *The Branches of Learning* (1982), vol. 3: *The Economics of Information and Human Capital* (1984), all published by Princeton University Press, have already appeared; the remaining five volumes will, alas, never appear.

*Secondary Literature*
J.S. Dreyer, *Breadth and Depth in Economics. Fritz Machlup: The Man and his Ideas* (D.C. Heath, 1978); F. Machlup, 'My (Early) Work on International Monetary Problems', in J.A. Kregel (ed.), *Recollections*

*of Eminent Economists*, vol. 2 (Macmillan, 1989); J.S. Chipman, 'Machlup, Fritz', in J. Eatwell, M. Milgate and P. Newman (eds), *The New Palgrave: A Dictionary of Economics*, vol. 3 (Macmillan, 1987).

# Malinvaud, Edmond (1923– )

Edmond Malinvaud is a distinguished French econometrician and economic theorist whose works are read and admired on both sides of the Atlantic. Most French economists are virtually unknown outside their own country. But a few, of whom Malinvaud is an outstanding example, have managed to gain both an American as well as a French audience. Malinvaud's reputation was first secured by his *Statistical Methods of Economics* (North-Holland, 1966; 3rd edn, 1980), which quickly became a leading reference work in econometric theory. Next came *Lectures on Microeconomic Theory* (North-Holland, 1972) which, likewise, became standard reading in graduate courses on price theory, demanding as it does a high level of theoretical and mathematical sophistication. More recently, Malinvaud has ventured into macroeconomics with two slim but again rather difficult books, *The Theory of Unemployment Reconsidered* (Wiley, Blackwell, 1977) and *Profitability and Unemployment* (Cambridge University Press, 1980). A later book on *Mass Unemployment* (Blackwell, 1984) sums up his mature views on macroeconomic problems.

All of these works are concerned with the central problem of modern macroeconomics, which is how to model markets for labour and goods in which, despite unemployment and despite excess capacity, wages and prices never fall at all, or never fall rapidly enough, to bring the economy back to levels of full employment. In other words, what is it about markets today that makes them adjust to excess supply or deficient demand by its variations in quantities rather than prices? In the first of the two books, Malinvaud addresses the problem of simply assuming fixed nominal wage and price levels, but in the second book he complicates the picture by allowing prices to vary with the state of demand and by making investment depend on profitability and, hence, the level of real wages. In so doing, he produces a Keynesian result – a stable unemployment equilibrium for the economy as a whole – but with a microeconomic explanation that takes advantage of all the developments in disequilibrium economics since Keynes (see Clower, R.W.; Leijonhufvud, A.).

Malinvaud's reasoning does not critically depend on people's expectations and in that sense is different in style from the other strand in modern macroeconomics, which rests either on the idea of 'adaptive' expectations as embodied in the natural-rate hypothesis (see Friedman, M.) or on the concept of 'rational' expectations (see Lucas, R.E. Jr.). Finally, there is a third strand in modern macroeconomics, represented by the writings of R.G. Lipsey (q.v.) and J. Tobin (q.v.) in which we get a Keynesian 'unemployment equilibrium' because the labour market is a peculiar type of market: workers care about relative wages and are indifferent to inflation or deflation, provided it affects all wage rates equally.

Malinvaud was born in 1923 in Limoges, France. He attended *lycées* in Limoges and Paris and then went on to take a first degree in law at the *Ecole Polytechnique* in Paris. He started working as a statistician in 1948 at the *Institut National de la Staatistique et des Etudes Economiques* in Paris. In 1951, he spent a year on leave at the Cowles Foundation for research in economics, attached to the University of Chicago, and again in 1961 and 1967 he was Visiting Professor at the University of California, Berkeley. In 1957 he became Director of Studies at the *Ecole Pratique des Hautes Etudes* and in 1974 he also became Director General of the *Institut National de la Statistique*.

He was President of the *Société Internationale d'Econométrie* in 1963, President of the *Société de Statistique de Paris* in 1974, Director of Forecasting at the French Ministry of Economy and Finance (1972–4), President of the International Economic Association during 1974–7, Member of the General Council of the Bank of France since 1972, and Administrator of the National Bank of Paris since 1973. He is an honorary Member of the American Economic Association. He was awarded the Silver Medal of the *Centre National de la Recherche Scientifique* and the French Legion of Honour, the highest decoration a French person can achieve.

*Primary Literature*
E. Malinvaud, 'The Challenge of Macroeconomic Understanding', in J.A. Kregel (ed.), *Recollections of Eminent Economists*, vol. 2 (Macmillan, 1989).

# Marschak, Jacob (1898–1977)

Marschak's scholarly career straddled three countries – Germany, Britain, and the United States – and its essential outlines did not emerge until he finally emigrated to America in 1940. Even so, it was only when Marschak had passed the age of fifty that his writings began increasingly to focus on the problems of decision-making under uncertainty in complex organisations, where for the first time he commanded the field, having hitherto contributed deadly weapons to other people's battles. Nevertheless, he sat for long at the very centre of some of the most important advances in post-war economics and, when recognition of his work came in the 1970s, he rapidly acquired a large number of honorary fellowships and degrees, topped by the presidency of the American Economic Association in 1977. He died in the summer of that year and his presidential address was never delivered.

Marschak was born in Kiev, Russia, in 1898, the son of a professional Jewish family. At the age of seventeen, in the middle of World War I, he entered the Kiev School of Technology, joined the Menshevik faction as a Marxist, and was promptly arrested for agitating against the war. Released from prison when the Czar fell in February 1917, his parents left for the northern Caucasus where the young Marschak once more resumed his political activities as a Menshevik. Returning to Kiev after the triumph of the Bolsheviks in October 1917, he decided to leave for the University of Berlin to study economics and statistics. He obtained his doctorate from the University of Heidelberg in 1922, after which he worked as an economics reporter for the *Frankfurter Zeitung* and a research assistant in several German research centres. In 1930 he found his first teaching post at the University of Heidelberg, which led to a number of articles and a book on the empirical measurement of the elasticity of demand. With the rise to power of Hitler in 1933, he left Germany to take up a lectureship at All Souls' College, Oxford. Two years later, when the Oxford Institute of Statistics was created to promote systematic empirical work in economics, Marschak was appointed Director, a post he held all through the 1930s. Working with Helen Makower and H.W. Robinson, he published a number of articles on the causes of labour mobility in Britain and the demand for money as an element in the wealth holdings of individuals.

In 1940, shortly before the outbreak of World War II, he crossed the Atlantic to take up a position as professor at the New School for Social Research in New York City. Three years later he was appointed Director of the Cowles Commission for Research in Economics at the University of Chicago, which carried with it a professorship at the University. It was during Marschak's directorship of the Cowles Commission (1943-8) that the foundations of what is now elementary econometric theory were laid, replacing the old classical least squares method of estimating single equations, say, the relationship between the price of butter and quantity of butter sold, with a new method of estimating the underlying set of simultaneous 'structural equations', say, the demand for and supply of butter, which would then be capable of 'identifying' the 'reduced form' single equation. Kenneth Arrow, Trygve Haavelmo, Lawrence Klein, Don Patinkin, and Tjalling Koopmans were only some of the brilliant young economists whom Marschak gathered under his wing at the Commission in the early 1940s to work on this and other problems relating to the foundations of econometrics.

Stimulated by Neumann and Morgenstern's *Theory of Games and Economic Behaviour* (see Morgenstern, O.), Marschak began working with Roy Radner on a new approach to the study of organisational decision-making as a problem in the 'theory of teams', a simplification of the theory of games. This led eventually to a book with Radner on the *Economic Theory of Teams* (Yale University Press, 1972), an important landmark in the growing understanding of the problem of informational decentralisation, which in turn is vital to the old debate on the merit or demerits of centralised planning.

In 1955, he left Chicago for Yale University along with the rest of the Cowles Commission, now renamed the Cowles Foundation for Research in Economics. In 1960 he moved to the University of California, Los Angeles, as Professor of Economics and Director of the Western Management Science Institute. He was made a Distinguished Fellow of the American Economic Association in 1967 and was elected President of the Association in 1977, the year of his death.

His many papers on statistical inference, decision rules, and the evaluation of information are collected together in three volumes under the title *Economic Information, Decision and Prediction* (Reidel, 1977).

*Secondary Literature*
K.J. Arrow, 'Marschak, Jacob', in D.L. Sills (ed.), *International Encyclopaedia of the Social Sciences*, vol. 18 (The Free Press, 1979); R. Radner, 'Marschak', in H.W. Spiegel and W.J. Samuels (eds), *Contemporary Economists in Perspective*, vol. 2 (JAI Press, 1984); R. Radner, 'Marschak, Jacob', in J. Eatwell, M. Milgate and P. Newman (eds), *The New Palgrave: A Dictionary of Economics*, vol. 3 (Macmillan, 1987).

# McCloskey, Deirdre (1942– )

Deirdre McCloskey was born Donald McCloskey and has been a prominent spokesperson for the 'new' quantitative economic history, also known as cliometrics, but whereas most members of that school have concentrated their efforts on the American economy (see Fogel, R.W.; North, D.C.), McCloskey has done her best work with reference to the British economy. Sine the New Economic History has never caught on in Britain in the way that it has in the USA, McCloskey's contributions have stood out like a mountain in a plain. Her range has been enormous but certain topics, like the economics of enclosures creating the English open-fields system of agriculture, the slowing-down of British growth during the late Victorian period, and the workings of the international gold standard during the nineteenth century, have loomed large in her output. Papers like 'English Open Fields as Behavior Towards Risk', in P. Uselding (ed.), *Research in Economic History* (JAI Press, 1976) and 'How the Gold Standard Worked, 1880–1914', in J.A. Frenkel and H.G. Johnson (eds), *The Monetary Approach to the Balance of Payments* (Allen & Unwin, 1976), co-authored with J.R. Zecher, and books like *Economic Maturity and Entrepreneurial Decline: British Iron and Steel, 1870–1913* (Harvard University Press, 1973), *Enterprise and Trade in Victorian Britain: Essays in Historical Economics* (Allen & Unwin, 1981), and *The Economic History of Britain, 1700–Present*, 2 vols (Cambridge

University Press, 1982; 2nd edn, 1994), edited with R. Floud, convey the high quality of her work. For an overview of two decades of cliometrics, see her *Econometric History* (Macmillan, 1987).

Her writings share many of the characteristics of the New Economic History: the appeal to standard price theory, the imaginative use of available statistical data, the constant attention to the specification of property rights, and the emphasis on information and transaction costs, and yet they depart less radically from traditional economic history than do those of many other 'new' economic historians. In a splendid paper, 'Does the Past Have Useful Economics?', *Journal of Economic Literature*, June 1976, McCloskey berated her fellow economists for neglecting the study of economic history and showed the difference that historical insights can make to the understanding of present economic phenomena.

McCloskey is also the author of an unusual intermediate textbook on price theory, *The Applied Theory of Price* (Macmillan, 1982). More recently, her interests have turned to 'The Rhetoric of Economics', *Journal of Economic Literature*, June 1983, meaning the language in which economists express themselves so as to persuade their peers and members of the public to believe them; in short, she appears to have turned away from economic history to the philosophy of economics. The 1983 paper was expanded two years later into a book, *The Rhetoric of Economics* (University of Wisconsin Press, Wheatsheaf, 1985) and defended in two later works, *If You're So Smart: The Narrative of Economic Expertise* (University of Chicago Press, 1990) and *Knowledge and Persuasion in Economics* (Cambridge University Press, 1993). The argument seems to be that economics, and indeed all social and physical sciences, is first and foremost a language which uses all the rhetorical devices of daily conversation and therefore must be judged by the aesthetic and literary standards and not the so-called 'modernist' criteria of mathematical rigour backed up by empirical evidence. I say 'seems' because the McCloskey message, while vividly expressed in sparkling prose, is by no means unambiguous and has in fact met with bitter opposition.

McCloskey was born in Ann Arbor, Michigan, in 1942. She received her BA in 1964, MA in 1967, and PhD in 1970, all from Harvard University. She began teaching at the University of Chicago in 1968 but left in 1980 to become Professor of Economics and History at the University of Iowa, where she remains today. She has been a Visiting Professor at Stanford University (1972), Birkbeck College and the London School of Economics (1975–6), and the Australian National University (1981). She has served as a Member of the Editorial Boards of the *Journal of Economic History, Explorations in Economic History,* and the *Economic History Review,* and has co-edited the *Journal of Economic History* since 1980. In 1995, McCloskey startled all her readers by announcing a sex change, signing herself henceforward as Deirdre McCloskey.

# Meade, James Edward (1907–96)

James Meade shared the Nobel Prize in Economics in 1977 with Bertil Ohlin for his work on international trade as represented by the two volumes of his *Theory of International Economic Policy* (Oxford University Press, 1951, 1955), which together have become the bible of every trade economist. But his early studies of national income accounting and his liberal-radical writings on policy questions might have served equally well as deserving of special praise. Moreover, in the great disputes that surround the rise of Keynesian economics before and after World War II, his amiable and courteous defence of Keynes helped to smooth the troubled waters of British economics.

He was born in 1907, educated privately at Malvern College, and entered Cambridge University in 1925, graduating in 1928. Switching fields, he went to Oxford University where he obtained a second Bachelor's degree in 1930. Taking up a teaching post at Hertford College, Oxford, in 1930, he was nevertheless deeply involved in the Cambridge 'circus' around Keynes and was one of the first to embody the Keynesian framework in a text book, *An Introduction to Economic Analysis and Policy* (Oxford University Press, 1936; 2nd edn, 1938), which appeared only a few months after Keynes' *General Theory* (1936).

In 1938 he left academic life for the League of Nations in Geneva, moving back to Britain in 1940 to serve as Director to the Economic

Section of the British Cabinet Office. At the Cabinet Office, he worked with Richard Stone on the first Keynesian-style national income accounts for Britain, an effort that led to their *National Income and Expenditure* (Bowes, 1944; 3rd edn, 1952). In 1947, he returned to academic life as Professor of Commerce at the London School of Economics. In *The Balance of Payments* (1951), the first volume of *The Theory of International Economic Policy*, he systematically explored the relationship between a country's internal and external balance in a general equilibrium framework that incorporated both the price effects of pre-Keynesian and the income-effects of Keynesian economics. Many early readers were put off by the book's taxonomic style, endlessly classifying the various theoretical possibilities, which failed to highlight the author's original contributions. Nevertheless, its central message filtered through other writers in the field and gradually lifted international economics on to a new plane of increased sophistication in the analysis of policy questions. *Trade and Welfare* (1955), the companion-piece to *The Balance of Payments*, reexamined the arguments for trade controls and in so doing discovered the 'theory of second best', an important addition to the armoury of welfare economists (see Lipsey, R.G.). *A Geometry of International Trade* (Allen & Unwin, 1952; Kelley, 1969) and *The Theory of Customs Unions* (North-Holland, 1955; 3rd edn, 1968) rounded off Meade's contributions to international economics.

In 1957 Meade became Professor of Political Economy at the University of Cambridge, where he remained for over ten years. Threatening to become embroiled in the great 'Cambridge controversies' between Robinson and Kaldor on one side of the Atlantic and Samuelson and Solow on the other (see Pasinetti, L.L.; Robinson, J.), he attempted unsuccessfully to resolve the debate in *A Neo-classical Theory of Economic Growth* (Allen & Unwin, 1961; 2nd edn, Oxford University Press, 1962). His continuous concern with problems of income distribution and his deeply held belief that capital is too unequally distributed in Britain and the USA, are reflected in a long series of works in applied economics, such as *Efficiency, Equality and the Ownership of Property* (Harvard University Press, 1964), *The Inheritance of Inequalities* (Oxford University Press, 1974), *The Intelligent Radical's Guide to Economic Policy* (Allen & Unwin, 1975), one of the best short statements of Meade's creed, and the last two volumes of his massive *Principles of Political Economy* (Allen & Unwin, 1965–76) in four volumes. Finally, Meade chaired an influential

British committee of inquiry into *The Structure and Reform of Direct Taxation* (Allen & Unwin, 1978), whose recommendations bear the unmistakable stamp of his characteristic approach to issues of policy. A recent work, *Stagflation*, 2 vols (Allen & Unwin, 1981, 1983), co-authored with D. Vines and J. Maciejowski, sets out Meade's analysis of the causes and cures of the current malaise of industrialised economies. His cure includes a prices-and-incomes policy: without assuming that the recent bouts of inflation and unemployment are entirely cost-push phenomena, he is nevertheless convinced that modern economies have become so inflation-prone that anything approaching full employment is impossible without wage and price controls or else a business tax on wage increases (see Lerner, A.P.; Weintraub, S.). Profit-sharing schemes, producer co-operatives and labour-managed enterprises represent another of Meade's policy concerns as expressed in two more recent works: *Alternative Forms of Business Organisation and Workers' Remuneration* (Allen & Unwin, 1985) and *Different Forms of Share Economy* (Public Policy Centre, 1986). His many journal articles were brought together in a four-volume edition of his *Collected Papers* (Allen & Unwin, 1988–9).

President of Section F of the British Association for the Advancement of Science in 1957, Honorary Member of the American Economic Association in 1962, President of the Royal Economic Society in 1964–6, and the recipient of many honorary degrees, Meade himself has described his lifetime's work as that of a 'tool-setter' rather than a tool-maker or even a tool-user. In other words, he takes the view that economics is well endowed with intellectual tools to achieve almost any set of policy objectives; the problem is to find an appropriate, practical combination of those tools to solve prevailing economic problems.

*Secondary Literature*
W.M. Corden and A.B. Atkinson, 'Meade, James E.', in D.L. Sills (ed.), *International Encyclopaedia of the Social Sciences*, vol. 18 (The Free Press, 1979); H.G. Johnson, 'James Meade's Contributions to Economics', in H.W. Spiegel and W.J. Samuels (eds), *Contemporary Economists in Perspective*, vol. 1 (JAI Press, 1984); D. Vines, 'Meade, James Edward', in J. Eatwell, M. Milgate and P. Newman (eds), *The New Palgrave: A Dictionary of Economics*, vol. 3 (Macmillan, 1987).

# Mincer,
# Jacob
# (1922–   )

Jacob Mincer 'discovered' the theory of human capital even before Theodore Schultz and Gary Becker, both of whom are frequently credited with its invention. Mincer's 1958 paper on 'Investment in Human Capital and Personal Income Distribution', *Journal of Political Economy*, August 1958, was in fact the first attempt to develop a model in which the characteristic features of the personal distribution of income are explained entirely by differences between individuals in the amount of labour training they have received. Subsequently, in another path-breaking paper, 'On-the-Job Training: Costs, Returns and Some Implications', *Journal of Political Economy*, Supplement, October 1962, he used the observed earnings differentials between individuals to estimate both the total amount of US investment in on-the-job training and the private rates of return earned on such investments. Later, he was one of the first to formulate a so-called 'earnings function', which accounts for variations in individual earnings solely by differences in the length of schooling received and years of work experience acquired.

Mincer's work on earnings function over more than a decade is summed up in his difficult but rewarding book, *Schooling, Experience and Earnings* (Columbia University Press, 1974). One of the most original contributions of this book is the concept of the 'overtaking' period. Some entrants to the labour market choose jobs at the highest pay they can get; others choose jobs which pay less now for the promise of more pay later; in addition, young workers change jobs frequently. The result is that an earnings function can explain only a small proportion of the variance in earnings of men and women in their teens and twenties. However, after 7–8 years of work experience, those in low-paying jobs 'overtake' those in high-paying ones, in consequence of which the explanatory power of an earnings function rises sharply. Indeed, Mincer shows that it is possible to explain more than half of all the variation of earnings of men and women aged around thirty by means of an earnings function consisting of only two explanatory variables.

Another of Mincer's breakthrough contributions was his essay on the 'Labour Force Participation of Married Women', in H.G. Lewis (ed.), *Aspects of Labor Economics* (Princeton University Press, 1962), which was the first to place the theory of labour supply in the context of family decision-making, combining non-market household behaviour with market behaviour. He has since employed the same apparatus to throw light on 'Family Investment in Human Capital: Earnings of Women', *Journal of Political Economy*, March/April 1974, a paper co-authored by S. Polachek. Mincer and Polachek argue essentially that the lower earnings of women in labour markets are not due to discriminatory hiring practices but rather to the interrupted careers of most women, which reduce their years of work experience compared to men. More recently, Mincer has applied the 'new' economics of the family (see Becker, G.S.) to the explanation of fertility changes and household migration decisions. His major papers have recently appeared in a two-volume edition: *Studies in Human Capital* and *Studies in Labour Supply* (Edward Elgar, 1993).

Mincer was born in 1922 in Tomaszow, Poland. He came to the United States as an adolescent and received his BA from Emory University, Atlanta, in 1950 and his PhD from Columbia University in 1957. After two years as a post-doctoral fellow at the University of Chicago, he joined the research staff of the National Bureau of Economic Research in New York. He taught at the City College of New York from 1954 to 1959 and at Columbia University from 1959. In 1962 he became a Professor of Economics at Columbia University, where he has remained ever since, except for spells as a Visiting Professor at the University of Chicago, Hebrew University in Jerusalem, and the Stockholm School of Economics.

He was voted a Fellow of the American Statistical Association in 1967 and the Econometric Society in 1975. He served as a Member of the American Economic Association's Advisory Committee on the US Census from 1972 to 1976. He has also been an Associate Editor of the *Review of Economics and Statistics* since 1977 and of the *Economics of Education Review* since 1979.

# Mises,
# Ludwig E. von
# (1881–1973)

Ludwig von Mises was one of the last representatives of the Austrian School of economics, which began with the writings of Carl Menger in the 1870s and was elaborated by his disciples, Friedrich Wieser and Eugen von Böhm-Bawerk, finally merging with the mainstream of neoclassical economics and in that sense disappearing in the 1930s. The Austrians shared many common views with other economists of their times but placed greater emphasis on the necessity to study all economic phenomena from the subjective viewpoint of individual economic agents. In addition, they attached supreme significance to the role of time in economic processes and insisted on applying the subjectivist-marginalist approach, not just to price formation, but also to the study of business cycles and monetary disturbances.

The Austrian School showed every sign of having melted away in the 1930s but in recent years, particularly since the early 1970s, it has enjoyed a remarkable recovery. A new generation of modern Austrians has sprung up in the United States whose 'patron saint' is Ludwig von Mises. In consequence, virtually all of Mises' works have been translated and reprinted and are now being read by an entirely new audience. Inspired by Mises, the new Austrians reject general equilibrium theory, mathematical economics, econometrics, and economic forecasting for purposes of managing the economy. Moreover, they also reject the orthodox emphasis on equilibrium analysis, being much more concerned with analysing the process of competition, leading to an equilibrium than with the properties of the final equilibrium state, and this element in their thinking perhaps owes more to Mises' student, Friedrich Hayek (q.v.) than to Mises himself. A striking example of the work of this New Austrian School is I.M. Kirzner's *Competition and Entrepreneurship* (University of Chicago Press, 1973), in which the concept of the entrepreneur as business tycoon is generalised to mean any economic agent who seizes a profit-making opportunity, whether by trading, producing, or merchandising, without which competition would never lead to equilibrium.

To return to Mises: the books for which he was best known in his own lifetime were *The Theory of Money and Credit* (1912; Liberty Classics, 1981), an attempt to show that the demand for money can be derived from utility theory like the demand for any commodity and that business cycles are essentially the result of the uncontrolled expansion of bank credit, and *Socialism: An Economic and Sociological Analysis* (1922; Yale University Press, 1951), the demonstration that socialist societies can never achieve a rational allocation of resources because they necessarily lack a true price system. As the Austrian School went into eclipse under the impact of the Keynesian Revolution, Mises' interests turned increasingly towards philosophical questions. In books like *Epistemological Problems of Economics* (1933; New York University Press, 1981), *Human Action: A Treatise on Economics* (1940; Henry Regnery, 3rd edn, 1966), and *The Ultimate Foundation of Economic Science: An Essay on Method* (Van Nostrand, 1962; Sheed Andrews & McNeel, 1978), he developed his own methodology of economics, known as 'praxeology', which argued that individual choices, being essentially purposive, constituted the *a priori* foundation of all valid economic reasoning.

Mises was born in Lamberg in the Austro-Hungarian Empire in 1881. He received his doctorate from the University of Vienna in 1906 and taught as an unpaid *privatdozent* (junior lecturer) at the University of Vienna from 1913 to 1934. He also taught at the Graduate Institute of International Studies at Geneva from 1934 to 1940. In 1940 he emigrated to the USA and spent the war years teaching and writing as a freelancer. In 1945, he became a Professor of Economics at New York University, a post he held until his retirement in 1969, the year in which he became a Distinguished Fellow of the American Economic Association.

He was one of the founding members of the Mont Pèlerin Society, a post-war international association of free-market economists, and he continued until the day of his death to write and lecture on behalf of economic liberalism.

*Secondary Literature*
L.S. Moss (ed.), *The Economics of Ludwig von Mises* (Sheed & Ward, 1974); M. von Mises, *My Years with Ludwig von Mises* (Arlington House, 1976; 2nd edn, 1984); M.N. Rothbard, 'Mises, Ludwig Edler von', in J. Eatwell, M. Milgate and P. Newman (eds), *The New Palgrave: A Dictionary of Economics*, vol. 3 (Macmillan, 1987).

# Modigliani, Franco (1918– )

Franco Modigliani was an important contributor in the 1940s to the codification of the Keynesian system in terms of IS–LM curves (see Hicks, J.R.). In the early 1950s, he originated the 'lifecycle hypothesis' of consumption, which finally provided a microeconomic foundation in individual behaviour for the observed patterns of national saving. According to Keynes, the average propensity to save – the ratio of savings to income – increases as household income increases and yet historical evidence shows no tendency for the saving rate to rise as all households become richer. Milton Friedman's 'permanent income hypothesis' – saving is a function, not of current income, but of expected lifetime income – provides one way of reconciling cross-sectional data with time-series data on savings. Modigliani's lifecycle hypothesis – individuals save during their earning years and 'dissave' after retirement – provides another: although all household income is consumed over the lifecycle, a growing economy produces a positive amount of total saving because youthful savers are richer and more numerous than retired dissavers; given some assumptions about population growth and life expectancies, this argument yields a constant historical ratio between saving and income.

In the late 1950s and early 1960s, Modigliani established with Merton Miller the two basic 'Modigliani–Miller theorems' of the

Modern Theory of Finance: under perfect competition and abstracting from tax effects, both the market value of a firm and the cost of capital to the firm are independent of its debt–equity ratio – the ratio of issued bonds to outstanding stocks – as well as its dividend – payout ratio. Since both theorems are counter-intuitive (one would have thought that a firm with few debts would be worth more than one with heavy debts and could pay less to borrow funds; likewise for a firm that pays handsome dividends compared to one that ploughs back all its profits), the Modigliani–Miller theorems provoked endless controversy, thus creating what is now an entire subspeciality in economics, Financial Analysis. In addition, Modigliani has been a tireless critic of 'monetarism' (see Friedman, M.), insisting on the continued relevance of the Keynesian message of demand management. His book, *The Debate Over Stabilization Policy* (Cambridge University Press, 1986) amounts to a systematic critique not only of monetarism *à la* Friedman but also the new classical macroeconomics *à la* Lucas (see Lucas, R.). Although the co-author of a number of books on special topics, his best work (like that of so many modern economists) has taken the form of journal articles. The *Collected Papers of Franco Modigliani*, ed. A. Abel (MIT Press, 1980) spans three volumes. In the last fifteen years since the publication of his collected papers, he was published as many as twenty-five articles.

Modigliani was born in 1918 in Rome, Italy. He took his first degree from the University of Rome in 1939, but emigrated to the United States at the outbreak of World War II. In 1944 he received his doctorate from the New School of Social Research in New York City; the core of his doctoral dissertation became his first published article, which has since been frequently reprinted: 'Liquidity Preference and the Theory of Interest and Money', *Econometrica*, January 1944; it marked a milestone in the formal integration of money into the Keynesian system. He started teaching statistics at Barnard College, Columbia University, in 1942 and mathematical economics at the New School in 1943. In 1949, he joined the staff at the University of Illinois as Professor of Economics, leaving in 1952 to become Professor of Industrial Administration at the Carnegie Institute of Technology. In 1962 he moved to Northwestern University, moving again in 1962 to the Massachusetts Institute of Technology to become Professor of Economics and Finance. He remained at MIT until his retirement in 1988.

The move to MIT heralded a shift in Modigliani's interest from theory to empirical work. Joining forces with Albert Ando of the University of Pennsylvania, he designed a large computer model of the US economy, the MPS model (MPS: MIT–Penn–Social Science Research Council), expressly designed to trace the channels by which the supply of money influences output and income (see Klein, L.R.). MPS has since been widely employed, by Modigliani and others, to attack the pro-monetarist conclusions of Friedman and his disciples.

He has been a consultant to the Secretary to the Treasury of the United States from 1964 to 1972, to the board of Governors of the Federal Reserve System since 1966 and has been a Senior Adviser to the Brookings Panel on Economic Activity since 1971. He was President of the Econometric Society in 1962, the American Economic Association in 1976, the American Finance Association in 1981, and Vice-President of the International Economic Association 1976–81. He has received honorary degrees from several American and European universities and, to top them all, was awarded the Nobel Prize in Economics in 1985. He is a delightful speaker and superb teacher, combining the warmth of an Italian with the informality of an American. Although the bulk of his work has been concerned with the American economy, he has never lost interest in his native land and has written a number of articles (in Italian) on the Italian economy.

*Primary Literature*
F. Modigliani, 'My Evolution as an Economist', in W. Breit and R.W. Spencer (eds), *Lives of the Laureates: Ten Nobel Economists*, 2nd edn (MIT Press, 1990).

*Secondary Literature*
E. Schwartz, 'On Modigliani', in H.W. Spiegel and W.J. Samuels (eds), *Contemporary Economists in Perspective*, vol. 1 (JAI Press, 1984).

# Morgenstern, Oskar (1902–77)

Oskar Morgenstern is chiefly remembered for his joint authorship with John von Neumann of the *Theory of Games and Economic Behaviour* (Wiley, 1944; 3rd edn, 1964). Von Neumann, one of the greatest mathematicians of the twentieth century, had already conceived the structure of game theory when he first met Morgenstern at the Institute for Advanced Study, Princeton University, in 1939 but Morgenstern persuaded him of the potential applications of game theory to economics. Their book aroused enormous interest, and new applications to economics, political science, sociology, and law proliferated in the 1950s. Nevertheless, the initial impetus began to peter out in the 1960s and by the 1970s Morgenstern had more or less resigned himself to a long uphill struggle in gaining recognition for the game-theoretical approach in economics. Great advances in game theory have been made since the publication of the *Theory of Games* but the role of game theory in economics remains uncertain even now. Morgenstern himself, however, was basically concerned with the problem of prediction in economics and saw the formal mathematical models of games as only one helpful approach to solving that problem. His preoccupation with the predictability of economic phenomena is reflected in a searching book-length essay, *On the Accuracy of Economic Observations* (Princeton University Press, 1950; 2nd edn, 1963), and an influential study with C.W.J.

Granger of the *Predictability of Stock Market Prices* (Lexington Books, 1970), concluding essentially that stock prices vary randomly and hence cannot be predicted.

Game theory may be defined as the mathematical analysis of the principles of optimal decision-making in situations where there are two or more 'players' who act independently of each other and who have (at least partly) conflicting interests. The simplest example is a game of strategy like poker: every turn of play depends to some extent on the free decisions of the players, knowing the fixed rules of the game and the results of earlier turns of play; what some players win, other players lose – it is a zero-sum game; and the problem for each player at each turn of the game is independently to adopt the best strategy in order to win a hand. This simple type of two-person, 'non-co-operative' zero-sum game was the archetype of Neumann and Morgenstern's 'minimax' solution. They also asserted that almost any economic event could be viewed as the outcome of such a game of strategy but they were unable to offer determinate solutions for $n$ person, co-operative, non-zero-sum games involving a mixture of conflicting and coinciding interests and, of course, many economic problems are of the non-zero type (the value of output exceeds the sum of the values of the inputs) for which reason they do not involve totally opposing interests. It was this fact more than any other which caused economists to become increasingly sceptical of the potential uses of game theory in economics.

Game theory has marched forward since Neumann and Morgenstern. Solutions have now been found for a large class of $n$ person, non-zero-sum games – the so-called 'Nash non-co-operative equilibrium' solution – and these have been linked to an old idea of the 'core' of a pure-exchange economy. Every market may be regarded as having started off with a 'core' of traders bartering goods among each other and possibly forming co-operative coalitions with other traders if this served to improve their situation compared to trading alone; as the traders increase in number, a price system emerges, and under certain given circumstances this price system can be shown to produce results identical to those that would emerge from a situation of perfect, non-co-operative competition. The notion of the 'core' of an economy lends itself naturally to the application of game theory and it is here that game theory has joined hands in recent years with general equilibrium theory (see Arrow, K.J.; Debreu, G.; Hahn, F.) and welfare economics. Needless to say, this is forbidden territory for beginners in economics and, indeed, many graduate students of economics have difficulties with the ultra-mathematical sophistication of modern game theory.

Morgenstern was born in 1902 in Silesia, Germany, the son of a small businessman. He attended high school and university in Vienna, where he obtained his doctorate in 1925. He travelled throughout Europe and America during the next three years on a Rockefeller Foundation Fellowship and returned to Austria in 1929 to take up a lectureship at the University of Vienna, becoming a professor in 1935. As Director of the Austrian Institute for Business Cycle Research 1931–8, editor of the *Zeitschrift für Nationalokonomie*, adviser to the national bank of Austria, and member of the 'Vienna Circle' of philosophers and mathematicians, he was active throughout the 1930s in pure theory and applied research, publishing several articles and two major treatises on economic forecasting. He was on leave in America in 1938 when he was dismissed from the University of Vienna as a result of the Nazi occupation of Austria. In consequence, he took up a professorship at Princeton University to work with Neumann, where he remained until his retirement in 1970. He was made a Distinguished Fellow of the American Economic Association in 1976.

The economics of defence was a subject that came to preoccupy him in the 1960s. He published a book on *The Question of National Defense* (Vintage, 1959) and collaborated with K.P. Heiss and K. Knorr in works on the peaceful uses of underground nuclear explosions (1967), the space shuttle system (1972) and long-term military projections (1973). One of his last publications was a book with G.L. Thompson on the von Neumann growth model, entitled *Mathematical Theory of Expanding and Contracting Economies* (Lexington, 1976). His growing unhappiness about the state of modern economics is amply reflected in one of his great articles, 'Thirteen Critical Points in Contemporary Economic Theory', *Journal of Economic Literature*, December 1972, reprinted in A. Schotter (ed.), *Selected Economic Writings of Oskar Morgenstern* (New York University Press, 1976). He died in 1977.

*Secondary Literature*
A. Schotter, 'On Morgenstern', in H.W. Spiegel and W.J. Samuels (eds), *Contemporary Economists in Perspective*, vol. 1 (JAI Press, 1984);

M. Shubik, 'Morgenstern, Oskar', in J. Eatwell, M. Milgate and P. Newman (eds), *The New Palgrave: A Dictionary of Economics*, vol. 3 (Macmillan, 1987).

# Morishima, Michio (1923– )

Michio Morishima is a Japanese mathematical economist who has successfully bridged the communications gap between Japanese-speaking and English-speaking economists. His major work, *Theory of Economic Growth* (Oxford University Press, 1969), combining elements of general equilibrium theory, input–output analysis and economic dynamics, summed up two decades of work by him and others on multisectoral growth. Growth Theory, as invented by R.F. Harrod (q.v.) and E.D. Domar (q.v.), dealt entirely with aggregates, conceiving the economy as if it were made up of only one or at most two sectors producing capital goods and consumer goods respectively. But a more ambitious type of growth theory had been conceived in the 1930s by John von Neumann (see Morgenstern, O.), which incorporated both the requirements for steady-state growth of the economy and the associated requirements for the relationships between the indefinitely large number of individual sectors of the economy. It was this type of von Neumann growth theory which Morishima refined and extended in *Theory of Economic Growth*, and more recently in *Capital and Credit: A New Formulation of General Equilibrium Theory* (Cambridge University Press, 1992).

In *Marx's Economics: A Dual Theory of Value and Growth* (Cambridge University Press, 1973), supplemented by *Value, Exploitation and Growth* (McGraw-Hill, 1978), with G. Catephores, Morishima took a fresh look at Karl Marx from the standpoint of von Neumann growth theory, arguing that Marx's ideas can be rigorously reformulated to conform to the highest standards set by current 'dynamic general equilibrium theory'. Both books left the reader wondering whether the real Marx had been captured in the parade of mathematical formulas. Nevertheless, they were well received by Marxian economists and have played a major role in one of the phenomena of our times, the unexpected revival of Marxian economics and particularly Marxian mathematical economics.

In *Walras' Economics* (Cambridge University Press, 1977), Morishima attempted to do for Leon Walras, the founder of general equilibrium theory, what he had earlier done for Marx but not without some protest from historians of economic thought. His *Ricardo's Economics: A General Theory of Distribution and Growth* (Cambridge University Press, 1989) attempted similarly to dress Ricardo in a garb woven by von Neumann, again to howls of anguish from Ricardo scholars. Finally, Morishima's *Economic Theory of Modern Society* (Cambridge University Press, 1976), better described as 'The Modern Theory of Economic Society', is an elementary text book, which manages to present an amazing number of 'advanced' results in a way that makes them accessible without knowledge of mathematical concepts or sophisticated tools of economic analysis. More recently, his interests have turned away from technical economic growth theory to the social causes of rapid economic growth in Japan and slow economic growth in Britain: *Why Has Japan Succeeded: Western Technology and the Japanese Ethos* (Cambridge University Press, 1982).

Morishima was born in 1923 in Osaka, Japan, and educated at the University of Kyoto, where he received his BA in 1946. He started teaching at the University of Kyoto in 1950, moving to the University of Osaka in 1951. In 1956–8, he spent two years at the University of Oxford in England and Yale University in America as a Rockefeller Foundation Fellow. In 1963–4, he returned to Britain as Visiting Fellow at All Soul's College, Oxford. He finally emigrated to Britain in 1968, becoming first Professor of Economics at the University of Essex (1968–70), and then Professor of Economics and Chairman of the International Centre for Economics and Related Disciplines at the London School of Economics, a post which he held until his retirement in 1988.

He was President of the Econometric Society in 1965, Associate Editor of *Econometrica*, Editor of the *International Economic Review* in

1969–70, and Member of the Editorial Boards of *Economica* since 1974 and of the *Journal of Economic Literature* during 1975–80. He is an honorary Member of the American Academy of Arts and Sciences and the American Economic Association. In 1976 he was awarded the Cultural Order of Japan.

# Musgrave, Richard A. (1910– )

Richard Musgrave is the author of *The Theory of Public Finance* (McGraw-Hill, 1959), a masterful book which somehow manages to combine a survey of two centuries of economic analysis of the tax and spending policies of government with a modern textbook treatment of the relationship between public sector economics and economic theory as a whole; in short, it is at one and the same time a treatise and a text on public finance. The book is supposed to have taken Musgrave twenty years to write; today, more than twenty years later, it still stands unchallenged: anyone with a question in the theory of public finance can be told even now, 'it's all in Musgrave'. The secret of the book's success lies partly in its daring organising principle: the budget of the public sector is divided into three hypothetical branches concerned with questions of allocation, distribution and stabilisation, and the allocation branch is in turn divided between the twin functions of satisfying 'social wants' (wants reflecting individual preferences) and 'merit wants' (wants not reflecting individual preferences). Again and again Musgrave succeeds in showing that long-standing puzzles and confusions in the theory of public finance are dissolved once they are classified in accordance with this scheme. It is one of the best examples in economics of the merits of the method of isolation and abstraction: although in the real world everything happens at the same time and for all sorts of reasons, theoretical analysis consists of considering things one at a time.

In more recent years, Musgrave has twice provided supplements to *The Theory of Public Finance* with a greater emphasis on the institutional aspects of public sector activities around the world: *Fiscal Systems* (Yale University Press, 1969) and *Public Finance in Theory and Practice* (McGraw-Hill, 1973, 3rd edn, 1980) with P.B. Musgrave. He has also edited, with A.T. Peacock, a book of readings in *Classics in the Theory of Public Finance* (Macmillan, 1958), which has served to educate English-speaking economists in the Italian–Swedish 'voluntary exchange theory of public economy' (see Buchanan, J.M.). His many papers in refereed journals have been brought together in *Public Finance in a Democratic Society: Collected Papers of Richard A. Musgrave* (Wheatsheaf, 1986).

Musgrave was born in 1910 in Königstein, Germany. He received his first degree from the University of Heidelberg, Germany, in 1933. Emigrating to the United States in the same year, he took up doctoral studies at Harvard University, receiving his PhD in 1937. He began teaching at Harvard University in 1936 but left in 1948 to take up a professorship at the University of Michigan. In 1958, he moved to Johns Hopkins University, followed by three years at Princeton University (1962–5), after which he returned to Harvard. He retired from Harvard in 1981 to take up an Adjunct Professorship at the University of California at Santa Cruz.

He was Vice-President of the American Economic Association in 1962 and was made a Distinguished Fellow of the Association in 1978. He was also an Honorary Vice-President of the International Institute of Public Finance in 1978. During the years 1969–75, he served as editor of *The Quarterly Journal of Economics*.

*Secondary Literature*
P. Mieszkowski, 'Musgrave, Richard Abel', in J. Eatwell, M. Milgate and P. Newman (eds), *The New Palgrave: A Dictionary of Economics*, vol. 3 (Macmillan, 1987).

# Myrdal, Gunnar (1898–1987)

Gunnar Myrdal has enjoyed three careers in one lifetime: he has been in turn an economist, a sociologist, and a politician. *The Political Element in the Development of Economic Theory* (Routledge & Kegan Paul, Harvard University Press, 1953), originally published in Swedish in 1930, and *Monetary Equilibrium* (Hodge, 1939), originally published in German in 1933, are classics in the economic literature and would alone account for his Nobel Prize in Economics (shared with Friedrich Hayek) in 1974. *An American Dilemma: The Negro Problem and Modern Democracy* (Harper, 1944; McGraw-Hill, 1964) is a classic of sociology. *Asian Drama: An Inquiry into the Poverty of Nations* (Twentieth Century Fund, 1968) is a gigantic three-volume study combining economics, sociology and political science. In addition, however, he has twice been a Senator in the Swedish Parliament (1934–6, 1942–6), Swedish Ambassador to India (1939–42), a Minister for Trade and Commerce (1945–7), a Chairman of the Swedish Planning Commission (1945–7), and the Executive Secretary of the United Nations Economic Commission for Europe (1947–57). Honoured by degrees from thirty universities around the world and winner of many awards and prizes, Myrdal has nevertheless made as many enemies as friends, particularly in his own country; at every point in his career, he has been involved in furious political and intellectual battles.

Myrdal was born in 1898 in a farming community in Sweden, attended Stockholm University, where he studied economics under Knut Wicksell, Gustav Cassel, and Eli Heckscher, and took his PhD degree in 1927. After a few years of further study in the United States, he returned to Sweden, married Alva Myrdal (who received the Nobel Peace Prize in 1982), and threw himself into political activity. His *Political Element in the Development of Economic Theory* revealed a concern with the intrusion of value judgements into what appeared on the surface to be purely objective analysis, a theme that was to run through all his later writings. *Monetary Equilibrium* was almost the first book in economics to introduce a systematic discussion of expectations into the analysis of price formation and its contrast between *ex ante* and *ex post* or planned and realised values has since become a standard feature of macroeconomic theory. After a short spell at the University of Geneva in 1931–2, Myrdal was appointed to a professorship at the University of Stockholm in 1933.

In 1938, the Carnegie Corporation invited Myrdal to investigate the problem of black Americans, a project which resulted in *An American Dilemma* and a whole library of books by a team of American associates. Returning to Sweden in 1942, he entered Parliament for a second time and headed the committee that drafted the postwar programme of the Social Democratic Party. As Minister of Commerce in this period, he negotiated a controversial treaty with the Soviet Union. Leaving Stockholm for Geneva in 1947, he turned his attention towards the problems of the Third World. *An International Economy: Problems and Prospects* (Routledge & Kegan Paul, 1956), *Economic Theory and Under-Developed Regions* (Duckworth, Harper, 1957), *Beyond the Welfare State* (Yale University Press, 1960), and *Challenge to Affluence* (Vintage, 1962; 2nd edn, 1965) heralded ideas more fully explored in the three volumes of *Asian Drama*, a stark critique of the social and economic policies of Asian governments, touching upon almost every facet of Asian life and society. Having retired from the University of Stockholm in 1965, he turned back in *Objectivity in Social Research* (Pantheon, 1969) to his favourite topic of the impossibility of value-free social science. Next came *The Challenge of World Poverty: A World Anti-poverty Program in Outline* (Pantheon, 1970; Random House, 1971), which generalised the findings of *Asian Drama* into a positive programme of action. Many of his individual essays were gathered together in *Value in Social Theory: A*

*Selection of Essays in Methodology*, ed. P. Streeten (Routledge & Kegan Paul, 1958) and *Against the Stream: Critical Essays on Economics* (Pantheon, 1973; Random House, 1974); further essays were reprinted by M. Okada as *Essays and Lectures* (Keibunsha, 1973) and *Essays and Lectures after 1973* (Keibunsha, 1979).

Myrdal has been more successful in his long career in destroying ideas than in constructing them. He has been a consistent critic of conventional economic theory as applied to Third World countries on grounds of Eurocentricity, artificial isolation of economic from social and political forces and, above all, failure to recognise that many economic changes are cumulative, so that departures from equilibrium are more likely to lead the economy away from instead of towards equilibrium; the appropriate analogy for economic change, he would argue, is not the pendulum or the egg lying on its side but the snowball rolling down the hill. Thus, he did not expect the current gap between rich and poor countries to disappear spontaneously with time, as orthodox economics predicts, but instead to grow wider unless deliberately counteracted by public policy. On the other hand, he was not hopeful that governments in rich countries would channel effective foreign aid to poor countries, or that governments in poor countries would be capable of stimulating domestic economic growth. This left one wondering whether there is any room for a subject like development economics since the understanding of the development process seems to require every social science applied in tandem.

Similarly, Myrdal has been vehement in insisting that positive economics cannot be divorced from normative economics and that every economic proposition involves explicit or implicit value judgements. What then is the hope of something like a *science* of economics? If economists will carefully specify their underlying value premises, Myrdal has argued, economics can acquire quasi-objectivity. Many modern economists would agree, only to add that this is what they have been preaching all along; others would insist that there are – surely? – some economic propositions – the unemployment rate is 5 per cent – that do not involve value judgements. The real question is: are there many such propositions? It is the answer to this question that divides the sympathisers from the critics of Myrdal.

*Secondary Literature*
E. Lundberg and L.G. Reynolds, 'Gunnar Myrdal's Contributions to Economics', in H.W. Spiegel and W.J. Samuels (eds), *Contemporary Economists in Perspective*, vol. 2 (JAI Press, 1984); P. Streeten, 'Myrdal, Gunnar', in J. Eatwell, M. Milgate and P. Newman (eds), *The New Palgrave: A Dictionary of Economics*, vol. 3 (Macmillan, 1987); M.C. Sawyer, 'Myrdal, Gunnar', in P. Arestis and M. Sawyer (eds), *A Biographical Dictionary of Dissenting Economists* (Edward Elgar, 1992).

# North, Douglass C. (1920– )

Douglass North has been consistently in the forefront of the 'new wave' that has swept through economic history in recent years, which has involved the attempt to apply the standard tools of neo-classical economics and econometrics to outstanding problems of economic history (see Fogel, R.W.; McCloskey, D.). In his earlier work on ocean shipping and the American balance of payments, he stayed within the fold of the New Economic History, combining simple neoclassical production theory with the new methods of extracting data from historical records. Subsequently, he explored the implications of the theory of property rights (see Alchian, A.A.; Demsetz, H.) for the process of institutional change in American history and, still more recently, he has laid the foundations for a more general theory of the industrialisation of the Western world in the last two centuries, grounded once again on the theory of property rights. The earlier phases of his work are represented by *Economic Growth of the United States 1790 to 1860* (Prentice-Hall, 1961) and *Growth and Welfare in the American Past: A New Economic History* (Prentice-Hall, 1966). *Institutional Change and American Economic Growth* (Cambridge University Press, 1971), written jointly with L.E. Davis, marks the break to a wider perspective, announced by *The Rise of the Western World: A New Economic History* (Cambridge University Press, 1973), co-authored with R.P. Thomas.

*The Rise of the Western World* attracted much attention and a certain amount of criticism. North's reactions to these criticisms and some revisions of the original thesis are found in his latest book, *Structure and Change in Economic History* (W.W. Norton, 1981). In this work, North goes beyond his previous goal of explaining how economies change through time to asking how their 'structures' change, with the latter defined to include 'the political and economic institutions, technology, demography, and ideology of a society'. The analysis is based on attention to three variables: property rights, which create the incentives for economic action; the state, as the unit that specifies and enforces property rights; and ideology, the system of moral and ethical beliefs which influences how the perception of individuals are translated into actions.

To convey a little of the flavour of North's approach, consider the problem of labour dues under feudalism whereby serfs worked a certain number of days in the week for the lord of the manor. Marxists have always interpreted this phenomenon as a typical example of the naked attraction of surplus labour under pre-capitalist conditions, an extraction which persists under capitalism but is disguised by the contractual hire of labour in labour markets. North, on the other hand, interprets labour dues under feudalism as a tacit exchange of labour time for the protection of life and property in a period when law and order were at a premium and property rights were poorly defined. In consequence, the transition from feudalism to capitalism is marked, not by the forcible dispossession of serfs as in the Marxist scenario, but by the rise of the national state and the development of a legal framework to establish property rights in human and physical assets. The entire history of the Western world from 1660 to 1900 is thus viewed from a radically new perspective. This is only one of the many applications of his ideas in a book which present a panoramic survey of Western history from the paleolithic era to the present. The same theme is more fully explored in his *Institutions, Institutional Change and Economic Performance* (Cambridge University Press, 1990), the title of which is virtually a statement of North's research agenda.

North was born in Cambridge, Massachusetts, in 1920. His BA and PhD were obtained from the University of California, Berkeley, in 1942 and 1952 respectively and he began teaching at Berkeley in 1946. In 1950 he joined the University of Washington in Seattle, first as an assistant professor, then an associate professor, becoming a full professor in 1960, serving also as Director of the Institute of Economic Research at Washington after 1961. Spending a year at Rice University in 1979 and two years at the University of Cambridge, England; in 1981–2, he returned to the University of Washington in St Louis in 1983.

He was co-editor of the *Journal of Economic History* from 1960 to 1966, President of the Economic History Association in 1972 and the Western Economic Association in 1975, and Visiting Director of the *Centre de Recherche Historique* at the *Ecole Pratique des Hautes Etudes*, Paris, in 1973. He was awarded the Nobel Prize in Economics in 1993, jointly with Robert Fogel.

# Ohlin,
# Bertil G.
# (1899–1979)

Bertil Ohlin first made a name for himself in 1929 by disputing Keynes' treatment of the German transfer problem, that is, the problem of how Germany was to pay her World War I reparations. In effect, Ohlin argued the income-theory of the balance of payments, which Keynes later made his own, whereas Keynes oddly enough argued the old classical theory according to which price changes and not income change bring balance of payments into equilibrium. But Ohlin's reputation was only firmly secured by the publication of *Interregional and International Trade* (Harvard University Press, 1933; 2nd edn, 1967), a book which won him the Nobel Prize in Economics in 1977, shared jointly with James Meade. Starting from an article written in 1919 by his old teacher, Eli Heckscher, Ohlin developed the thesis that both interregional and international trade are devices for the spatial exchange of the goods and services produced by factors of production since these factors themselves are to a greater or lesser extent incapable of being moved in space – think of land as the classic case of an immovable factor – in consequence of which relative prices in different geographical locations depend on the relative scarcity of factor endowments in these locations.

To put in the language of modern trade theory: countries (or regions) will export commodities which are produced with their relatively abundant factors of production, and will import those which are produced with their relatively scarce factors, so that international trade tends towards an equalisation of factor prices between trading nations, which is not to say that they will be equalised in practice. This 'Heckscher–Ohlin Theorem', as it was soon to be called, entered almost immediately into the textbook literature, although not without a push from P.A. Samuelson in the 1940s (q.v.), and the stimulus of W.W. Leontief's (q.v.) apparent empirical refutation of the theorem in the 1950s. It is doubtful, however, whether any later textbook treatment improved on Ohlin's own masterful presentation: the theorem is laid out in the first two chapters; it is then modified and extended, dropping the assumptions that transport costs are zero, and there are no import duties, that economies of scale are absent, that the pattern of demand is identical everywhere, that capital as well as labour is immovable, and that exchange rates are freely flexible. By the end of the book, the entire range of international economic problems has been discussed and, moreover, the intimate connections between location theory, regional economics, and international trade have been brilliantly displayed.

Ohlin, however, has other claims to fame. In a number of publications, beginning with a 1927 pamphlet and ending with a report in 1934 to a Swedish government committee on unemployment, he developed an almost total anticipation of Keynes' theoretical schema in the *General Theory* (1936), including Keynes' policy recommendations. Nor was he the only Swedish economist to have scooped Keynes (see Myrdal, G.). Unfortunately, Ohlin's contributions were published in Swedish and remained untranslated. Thus, when he sought to remind the British Keynesians that they were not the only ones and not even the first ones in the field in 'Some Notes on the Stockholm Theory of Savings and Investment', *Economic Journal*, March, June 1937, they greeted his claims with incredulity. In recent years, however, the Stockholm School in general and Ohlin in particular have finally received proper recognition for their pioneering contributions to modern macroeconomics.

Ohlin was born in Klippan, Sweden, in 1899, the son of a lawyer and police superintendent. He entered the University of Lund at the age of sixteen, transferring to the Stockholm School of Economics and Business Administration two years later. Graduating in 1919, he began working for his doctorate under Gustav Cassel. He spent a few months at Cambridge University and a year at Harvard University before receiving his doctorate in 1924. From 1925 to 1930, he was a professor at the University of Copenhagen. In 1930 he returned to the Stockholm School of Economics to succeed Eli Heckscher, and remained there until his retirement in 1965. He was a member of the Swedish Parliament for thirty-two years from 1938 to 1970, and a leader of the Swedish Liberal Party during its twenty-three years of opposition from 1944 to 1967, serving as a Minister of Trade in the final years of World War II.

*Secondary Literature*
H. Dickson, 'Ohlin, Bertil', in D.L. Sills (ed.), *International Encyclopaedia of the Social Sciences*, vol. 18 (The Free Press, 1979); O. Steiger, H. Brems and D. Patinkin, 'A Bertil Ohlin Symposium', *History of Political Economy*, Fall 1978; H. Brems, 'Ohlin, Bertil', in J. Eatwell, M. Milgate and P. Newman (eds), *The New Palgrave: A Dictionary of Economics*, vol. 3 (Macmillan, 1987).

# Okun,
# Arthur M.
# (1928–80)

Arthur Okun died at the early age of 52 just after completing the first draft of a major book on macroeconomics. It was published posthumously under the title of *Prices and Quantities: A Macroeconomic Analysis* (Brookings Institution, 1981; Blackwell, 1982) and represents one of the most careful attempts to date to explain why product and factor markets in advanced economies tend increasingly to adjust to changes in demand and supply, not by altering prices, but by altering quantities; hence, unemployment does not lead to falling money wages and, similarly, excess capacity does not lead to lower prices. This is one neo-Keynesian answer to the contradiction-in-terms posed by Keynes: the existence of 'unemployment equilibrium' (see Clower, R.W.; Leijonhufvud, A.; Malinvaud, E.).

In his lifetime Okun was best known for the discovery of an empirical relationship in the American economy that has ever since been called 'Okun's Law'. In a famous paper, 'Potential GNP: Its Measurement and Significance' (1961), reprinted in a collection of his papers, *The Political Economy of Prosperity* (Brookings Institution, 1970), he analysed the real GNP of the USA in 1950 at the onset of the Korean war, when both unemployment and inflation were minimal, and extrapolated the national output of that year into the future by adding the long-run trend of productivity improvements.

This gave him a full-capacity, full-employment ceiling for the 1950s and 1960s. He then expressed the actual annual GNP observed after 1950 as a fraction of this potential annual GNP and compared the resulting ratio to the year-by-year changes in the observed unemployment rate. He noted that whenever the former changes by 3 per cent, the latter changes by 1 per cent in the opposite direction, which is to say that a rise in unemployment of 1 per cent corresponds roughly to a 3 per cent fall in the ratio of actual to potential real GNP; in other words, what might be called the Okun income elasticity of employment is three. This relationship has held up so well in the US economy throughout the 1960s, 1970s and early 1980s that it fully deserves to be called a 'law', always remembering however that it is only a useful rule-of-thumb, which may one day break down. Indeed, in recent years the Okun income elasticity for the USA has been estimated as 1.5.

Incidentally, when Okun's ratio of actual to potential GNP stands at unity, that is, when the American economy operates at feasible levels of full employment, as happened, for example, in the years 1964 and 1972, the observed unemployment rate in the USA is 5.2–5.6 per cent of the labour force. The difference between an economy's growth rate and its inflation rate – its real rate of economic growth – is often called the 'Okun index'. This is why an unemployment rate of something like 5.5 per cent is frequently described as the empirical value of Friedman's' 'natural rate of unemployment', meaning the level of unemployment which is compatible with a stable rate of wage and price inflation (see Friedman, M.).

Okun was born in Jersey City in 1928. He received his BA in 1949 and his PhD in 1956, both from Columbia University. He started teaching at Yale University in 1952, becoming Professor of Economics at Yale in 1963. From 1961 to 1962 he worked as a Staff Economist for President Kennedy's Council of Economic Advisers in Washington and two years later he was back at the Council under President Johnson, first as a Member (1964–8) and then as Chairman (1968–9). He joined the Brookings Institution as a Senior Fellow in 1969 and remained there until his death in 1980, publishing *The Political Economy of Prosperity* (Brookings Institutions, 1970) and *Equality and Efficiency: The Big Tradeoff* (Brookings Institution, 1975), and co-editing the *Brookings Papers on Economic Activity*, which quickly became a leading journal in macroeconomic policy. He received the Frank E. Seidman Distinguished Award for Political Economy in

1979. He died in 1980. Thirty-one of his papers have been reprinted under the title *The Economics of Policy-making*, ed. J.A. Pechman (MIT Press, 1983).

*Secondary Literature*
J. Tobin, 'Arthur M. Okun', in J. Eatwell, M. Milgate and P. Newman (eds), *The New Palgrave: A Dictionary of Economics*, vol. 3 (Macmillan, 1987).

# Pasinetti, Luigi L. (1930– )

Luigi Pasinetti is an important contributor to so-called 'post-Keynesian economics' and was a major participator in the furious battles about capital theory that were fought out between Cambridge, England, and Cambridge, USA, in the 1960s, which saw Kaldor and Robinson on one side of the Atlantic pitted against Samuelson and Solow on the other side (see Samuelson, P.A.; Solow, R.M.). What was at issue, at least at first, was the question of the 'switching' and 'reswitching' of techniques: is it possible for a capital-intensive technique to become profitable as the rate of interest falls, and then, as it continues to fall, to cease being profitable, possibly becoming profitable once again at still lower rates of interest?

Paul Samuelson published a famous paper, 'Parable and Realism in Capital Theory: The Surrogate Production Function', *Review of Economics Studies*, June 1962, implying that reswitching of the kind just described is not possible, whereupon Pasinetti joined another Italian economist, Piero Garegnani, in the pages of the *Quarterly Journal of Economics*, November 1966, to insist that it is indeed possible. Samuelson finally conceded that 'the nonswitching theorem is false'. What all this means is that different techniques for producing goods may be equally profitable at different interest rates, in consequence of which the relative value of goods may change although there has been no physical change in the technical methods of producing these goods. This creates problems for the measurement of capital and, strictly speaking, implies that it is impossible to draw a demand curve for capital as a simple function of the rate of interest. In other words, it is illegitimate to employ the value of capital as a variable to explain the determination of the rate of interest because the rate of interest has to be known to determine the value of capital. Having found what they thought was a major flaw in orthodox economics, the Cambridge UK faction, including Pasinetti, went on from the switching phenomenon to reject more or less the whole of orthodox microeconomics (see Kaldor, N., Robinson, J.).

Pasinetti's most original contribution to the ideas of the Cambridge School started from Kaldor's growth model in which Kaldor introduced the notion of two saving rates, one for the workers out of wages, and one for the capitalists, out of profits, the latter being higher than the former (see Kaldor, N.). In 'Rate of Profit and Income Distribution in Relation to the Rate of Economic Growth', *Review of Economic Studies*, October 1962, Pasinetti showed that the rate of profit in Kaldorian growth equilibrium is totally independent of the saving propensities of the working class, depending only on the saving rate of capitalists. This 'bootstrap' theorem, whereby capitalists appear to be capable of raising the profitability of their own capital simply by saving more, generated a great deal of discussion, which resulted, as so often happens in economics, in the conclusion that it all depends on a number of other circumstances, which may or may not prevail. This and other relevant papers by Pasinetti are reprinted in his *Growth and Income Distribution: Essays in Economic Theory* (Cambridge University Press, 1974).

In more recent years, he has turned his attention to linear production theory and input–output analysis, that is, the workings of an economic system in which production coefficients are fixed – there are no possibilities of substituting capital for labour – and in which new technology acts simply to reduce the production coefficients (see Leontief, W.W.). Convinced that marginalism is dead and that orthodox economics based on marginal techniques is simply a clever rationalisation for capitalism, Pasinetti has attempted to lay the foundations of a new, non-marginal economics in *Lectures on the Theory of Production* (Macmillan, Columbia University Press, 1977), *Structural Change and Economic Growth* (Cambridge University Press, 1981), and *Structural Economic Dynamics: A Theory of the Economic Consequences of Human Learning* (Cambridge University Press, 1993).

Pasinetti was born in 1930 in Bergamo, Italy. He received his first degree from the Catholic University of the Sacred Heart in Milan in 1954 and his PhD from the University of Cambridge in 1962. His first teaching assignment was at Nuffield College, Oxford, in 1959 but in 1961 he became a Fellow of King's College, Cambridge, where he remained until 1976. In 1971 and again in 1975, he was Visiting Research Professor at Columbia University, the Indian Statistical Institute in Calcutta, and the Delhi School of Economics. In 1977 he returned to Italy to become a Professor of Economics at his old *alma mater*, the Catholic University of the Sacred Heart in Milan.

He was awarded the St Vincent prize in economics in 1979 and has been a Member of the Executive Committee of the International Economic Association since 1980. He was President of the Italian Society of Economists from 1986 to 1989, of the Confederation of European Economic Associations from 1992 to 1993, and the European Society for the History of Economic Thought since 1995.

*Secondary Literature*
M. Baranzini, 'Luigi Lodovico Pasinetti', in P. Arestis and M. Sawyer (eds), *A Biographical Dictionary of Dissenting Economists* (Edward Elgar, 1992).

# Patinkin, Don (1922–95)

Patinkin's *Money, Interest, and Prices: An Integration of Monetary and Value Theory* (Row, Peterson, 1956; 2nd edn, Harper & Row, 1965; abridged edn, MIT Press, 1989) is one of the great books of post-war economics in which we can find the origins of almost all the developments of the 1960s and 1970s in monetary economics and macroeconomics. Here, for almost the first time, price theory and monetary theory were effectively integrated by means of the 'real balance effect', according to which demand functions in all markets are directly affected by the real value or purchasing power of the money holdings of individuals. Moreover, in a major contribution to the history of economic thought, Patinkin showed that this fact had never been adequately appreciated by the great monetary theorists of the nineteenth century, who in effect had 'dichotomised the pricing process' by divorcing the determination of the relative prices of commodities from the determination of the value of money, that is, the general level of prices. Although this theme was fully worked out in *Money, Interest, and Prices*, it was first stated in 1949 in a great paper on 'The Indeterminacy of Absolute Prices in Classical Economic Theory', *Econometrica*, January 1949.

The 'real balance effect' implies that a Keynesian 'unemployment equilibrium' is not an equilibrium in the usual sense of the word: the rise of unemployment and the growth of excess capacity causes wages and prices to fall, thus increasing the real value of people's money balances; having more money than they wish to hold, individuals will get rid of some of their money holdings by purchasing goods and services, in consequence of which aggregate demand increases and full employment is restored. In practice, Patinkin agreed, this process might require years and even decades, so that Keynes was perfectly justified in calling for fiscal measures to combat unemployment. Indeed, Keynes' theory of 'unemployment equilibrium' properly understood is a disequilibrium theory dressed up in equilibrium language, an insight which is undoubtedly the origin of the now standard interpretation of Keynesian economics as a theory of quantity rather than price adjustments (see Clower, R.W.; Leijonhufvud, A.; Malinvaud, E.; Okun, A.M.). *Money, Interest and Prices* provoked a keen debate among monetary economists and has been endlessly translated in various languages. Patinkin's comments on the debate and some of his later contributions to monetary theory are collected together in his *Studies in Monetary Economics* (Harper & Row, 1972).

In more recent years, Patinkin concentrated his efforts on tracing the precise steps by which Keynes arrived at his formulation in *The General Theory* (1936). In *Keynes' Monetary Thought: A Study of Its Development* (Duke University Press, 1976) and *Anticipations of the 'General Theory'* (University of Chicago Press, Basil Blackwell, 1982), beautifully summarised in his long entry on Keynes in *The New Palgrave: A Dictionary of Economics*, vol. 2 (Macmillan, 1987), he reexamined the history of the Keynesian Revolution, in particular the relationship between Keynes' thinking and certain forerunners, such as Kalecki (q.v.) and members of the Stockholm School (see Myrdal, G.; Ohlin, B.G.). According to Patinkin, the central element of Keynesian economics is not the consumption function, the multiplier, or the theory of liquidity preference, or even the notion of quantity rather than price adjustments, but rather the idea that key economic variables converge on equilibrium by means of changes in output or income rather than changes in prices. Patinkin finds no evidence of this idea in the writings of Kalecki, Myrdal and Ohlin, and he therefore denies that they anticipated the Keynesian system: Keynes was truly original.

Patinkin was born in Chicago in 1922 and took all his degrees from the University of Chicago: a BA in 1943, an MA in 1945 and a PhD in 1947. He was taught by such famous Chicagoans as Frank

Knight and Jacob Viner, an experience which coloured all of his earlier writings, as revealed in his tribute to Chicago, *Essays On and In the Chicago Tradition* (Duke University Press, 1981). After a few years of teaching at the University of Chicago, he emigrated to Israel to become Professor of Economics at the new Hebrew University in Jerusalem. In the years to come, he was largely if not solely responsible for putting Israel on the map as a country whose economists can stand next to the best in the world. He published a history of *The Israel Economy: The First Decade* (Maurice Falk Institute, 1959) and was President of the Israel Economic Society. He was Director of the Falk Institute for Economic Research in Israel from 1956 to 1972, President of the Israel Economic Association in 1976. He was also President of the Econometric Society in 1974 and was elected an Honorary Member of the American Economic Association in 1975.

Reading Patinkin is always a pleasure: his writings are marked by a firm commitment to analytic rigour, an acute sense of the practical relevance of economic theory, and a profound awareness of the historical evolution of economic ideas, all of which elements are held together by a limpid, easy-flowing literary style.

# Phelps,
# Edmund S.
# (1933–  )

Edmund Phelps independently invented the 'natural-rate' hypothesis in 1967, more or less at the same time that the idea occurred to Milton Friedman. The natural-rate hypothesis asserts that there is embedded in any economy a 'natural' or equilibrium rate of employment at which people's expectations of wage and price changes are fully realised by the actual rate of wage and price changes; any attempt by governments to lower the level of unemployment below that rate by expansionary fiscal and monetary policies generates expectations of rising wages and prices, which in turn induces behaviour that accelerates inflation, the entire process only coming to a halt when unemployment has risen once again back to the natural rate – at a permanently higher level of inflation (see Friedman, M.).

For Phelps, the natural-rate hypothesis was connected with the concept of job search as a major, although by no means the only, component of unemployment. In Keynesian economics, the unemployed are thought of as being involuntarily unemployed and actively seeking re-employment; Keynes, like everyone before him, recognised that there was also 'frictional' unemployment arising from special individual circumstances in addition to involuntary 'cyclical' unemployment; this was regarded as a minor element in the employment problem, however, accounting for at most 1–2 per cent of the unemployment rate. Somewhere in the 1960s, it occurred to a number of economists (see Alchian, A.A.) that unemployed workers do not necessarily accept the first job offered to them but search for the best job at the best pay, only lowering their aspirations gradually as the spell of unemployment lengthens. Moreover, since job searching is costly in time, they may even quit an existing job to search for a better one, and will search the longer, the more generous is the level of unemployment benefits. In *Microeconomic Foundations of Employment and Inflation Theory*) W.W. Norton, Macmillan, 1970), Phelps and others explored the implications of such job search models in the effort to account for the existing pattern of quits and layoffs in American labour markets and for the apparent rise in the natural rate of unemployment in the 1960s.

Job search theories of unemployment remain extremely controversial (see Feldstein, M.). Phelps himself has always combined the idea of search-unemployment on the supply side of labour markets with non-wage adjustments on the demand side, indeed extending the study of the phenomenon of adjusting quantities rather than prices to the behaviour of firms in product markets. *Inflation Policy and Unemployment Theory: A Cost-Benefit Approach to Monetary Planning* (W.W. Norton, 1972), a book which he edited with others, sums up much of Phelps' work on the problem of 'stagflation', the simultaneous occurrence, now so common, of inflation and unemployment. *The Slump in Europe: Open Theory Reconstructed* (Basil Blackwell, 1988), with J.-P. Fitoussi, and *Seven Schools of Macroeconomic Thought* (Clarendon Press, 1990) represent Phelps' continued effort to develop a unique approach to macroeconomic problems different from both monetarism and neo-Keynesianism.

Earlier in his career, Phelps wrote repeatedly on growth theory and in particular on 'golden rules' of economic growth, for example, the curious result that the rate of economic growth in certain abstract models converges on the rate of interest. In a famous article, his first published work, 'The Golden Rule of Accumulation: A Fable for Growthmen', *American Economic Review*, September 1961, he both expounded and ridiculed the principal 'golden rule'. His many sparkling and frequently amusing papers in growth theory and macroeconomics are conveniently reprinted in the two volumes of his *Studies in Macroeconomic Theory* (Academic Press, 1979, 1980). Another of his interests is the relationship between modern welfare economics and the older philosophical literature on distributive justice, as revealed by his book of readings on *Economic*

*Justice* (Penguin, 1973), and another book of readings, *Altruism, Morality and Economic Theory* (Basic Books, 1975). An introductory text, *Political Economy: An Introductory Text* (W.W. Norton, 1985), failed to catch on, perhaps because it was too innovative, violating the principle of minimum differentiation which seems to rule the market for first-year texts.

Phelps was born in 1933 in Evanston, Illinois. He took his BA from Amherst College in 1955 and his MA and PhD from Yale University in 1957 and 1959 respectively. After a year with the Rand Corporation, he spent a year at the Massachusetts Institute of Technology and three years at Yale University from 1963 to 1966 before moving to the University of Pennsylvania as Professor of Economics. After a year at New York University in 1978–9, he moved again to Columbia University, where he is still teaching. He is a Fellow of the American Academy of Arts and Sciences and the Econometric Society and was a Member of the Executive Committee of the American Economic Association 1976–8. He was also a consultant on social security to the US Senate in 1974.

# Phillips,
# A. William
# (1914–75)

The case of Bill Phillips demonstrates that it is possible to achieve immortal fame in economics with one paper. Phillips' 'The Relation between Unemployment and the Rate of Change of Money Wage Rates in the United Kingdom, 1861–1957', *Economica*, November 1958, gave birth to the 'Phillips Curve', at least after others had substituted the rate of change of prices for Phillips' rate of change of money wages (see Lipsey, R.G.). The Phillips Curve appeared to show that there is a stable trade-off between inflation and unemployment which governments can exploit: they can choose less unemployment and more inflation, or less inflation and more unemployment, but they cannot choose to have less of both unemployment and inflation.

Phillips' estimates for Britain showed that at a rate of unemployment of about 2.5 per cent, wages tended to rise at about 2 per cent per annum, which led to stable prices if productivity was also rising along its long-run trend line of 2 per cent. It was P.A. Samuelson and R.M. Solow, 'Analytical Aspects of Anti-inflation Policy', *American Economic Review*, May 1960, who popularised the idea of a Phillips Curve with prices, not wages, on the vertical axis; they found the American Phillips Curve to lie slightly to the right of the British one, such that it required an unemployment rate of almost 4 per cent to produce zero inflation in the USA. By the mid-1960s, the Phillips Curve had been estimated for many countries and was part and parcel of orthodox macroeconomics. It appeared as a fundamental relationship in the US President's *Economic Report to Congress* in 1969 and was incorporated into the eighth edition of Samuelson's popular textbook, *Economics* (1970). It was only later in the 1970s that doubts began to arise as new estimates revealed the Phillips Curve to be highly unstable and subject to outward shifts and twists. In the late 1960s, both Edmund Phelps and Milton Friedman began to distinguish a short-run and a long-run Phillips Curve, insisting that the long-run Phillips Curve is a vertical line at some 'natural' rate of unemployment (see Friedman, M.; Phelps, E.S.), meaning that unemployment cannot be permanently reduced without causing ever-accelerating inflation. The short-run Phillips Curve is indeed negatively inclined, as Phillips had believed, but arguments remain as to the length of this short run – possibly six months, possibly twelve months – and even the short-run Phillips Curve is nowadays regarded as too unstable to constitute a firm basis for government policy. In a mere twenty-five years, the Phillips Curve has travelled from being a key link in the structure of modern macroeconomics to being a minor and probably misleading element in current explanations of stagflation.

Phillips was born in Te Rehunga, New Zealand, in 1914 in a farming family and was educated in New Zealand. At the age of sixteen, he left school, started working in an Australian mining camp and began to study electrical engineering in the evenings. He arrived in London in 1937, passed the examinations of the Institution of Electrical Engineers in 1938, worked for the London Electricity Board, and then joined the Army, being taken prisoner of war in the Far East. It was only after World War II, at the age of thirty-two, that he enrolled at the London School of Economics as a sociology student. But his imagination was caught by the required course in economics, in particular by the concept of the circular flow and the notion of the economic system as a hydraulic machine. Together with William Newlyn, he built a mechanical Keynesian-type model of the economy using flows of coloured water, whose design and potential use was the subject of his first article, 'Mechanical Models in Economic Dynamics', *Economica*, August 1950. As a result, he was offered a teaching post at the London School of Economics. In 1952 he complete a doctoral dissertation and two years later he had risen through the ranks to become Professor of Statistics at the London School of Economics.

He published only six more papers in the remaining thirteen years at the London School of Economics, all of which were concerned in one way or the other with the problems of stabilising an economy whose responses exhibit lags of various lengths. In recent years, this branch of theory has come to be known as 'optimal control theory'. In the 1960s, however, there was little interest among economists in this problem. This may have been the reason that Phillips left Britain in 1967 to take a Chair at the Australian National University, hoping to take up the study of the economy of China. After suffering a severe stroke in 1970, however, he returned to his native New Zealand where he continued to teach part-time until his death in 1975 at the age of sixty-one.

*Secondary Literature*
K. Lancaster, 'Phillips, A. William', in D.L. Sills (ed.), *International Encyclopaedia of the Social Sciences*, vol. 18 (The Free Press, 1979); C.A. Blyth, 'Phillips Alban William Housego', in J. Eatwell, M. Milgate and P. Newman (eds), *The New Palgrave: A Dictionary of Economics*, vol. 3 (Macmillan, 1987).

# Posner,
# Richard A.
# (1939–   )

Richard Posner has been a prominent figure in the recent move-ment to introduce the study of economics in law schools and, in-deed, to provide an economic analysis of the legal system that would account both for its existence and for the way it functions. We have learned from the work of Ronald Coase (q.v.) that non-market methods of organising economic life spring up whenever transactions costs are too great to permit market exchange: like the business firm itself, the legal system substitutes for the market when market transactions are not feasible. However, when a voluntary market transaction takes place, it is likely that the result is a net increase in social efficiency because the transaction would not have taken place if it was not mutually beneficial to all parties. The question is whether a legally adjudicated transaction has similar properties.

The distinguishing characteristic of Posner's *Economic Analysis of Law* (Little, Brown, 1973; 2nd edn, 1977), *Antitrust Law: An Economic Perspective* (University of Chicago Press, 1976) and *The Economics of Justice* (Harvard University Press, 1981) is precisely the argument that common law and even criminal law works in favour of eco-nomic efficiency like the market mechanism itself. Posner analyses the operations of the legal system, not in terms of such traditional non-economic concepts as 'justice', but in terms of 'opportunity costs' or 'willingness to pay', concluding that most legal decisions achieve results that save resources compared to alternative bureaucratic methods for solving the problems that markets cannot handle. Alternatively expressed, Posner has redefined the standard definition of 'justice' so as to make it equivalent to the economist's definition of 'efficiency': the criterion for judging whether an act is 'just' or 'good' is whether it favours the pursuit of economic efficiency, as measured by an increase in national income.

Posner was born in 1939 and received his BA from Yale University in 1959. In 1962 he obtained his LLB from Harvard University. He started teaching at Stanford University, becoming a professor at the University of Chicago in 1969, and a professor at the University of Chicago Law School in 1981, where he remains today as a Professor of Law. He is a member of the American Bar Association and the American Law Institute and edited the *Journal of Legal Studies* from 1972 to 1981. He was recently appointed Judge in the US Court of Appeals for the Seventh Circuit.

# Robbins, Lionel (1898–1984)

Lionel Robbins spent almost the whole of his life at the London School of Economics: born of humble parents in 1898 and educated in a minor private school before the Great War, he entered the LSE as an undergraduate student in 1920: graduating in 1923, he was a research assistant from 1923 to 1924, a lecturer from 1925 to 1927, a Professor of Economics for thirty-two years from 1929 to 1961, a part-time professor for another five years, Professor Emeritus and honorary lecturer from 1967 to 1980, and Chairman of the Court of Governors from 1968 to 1974. Two short spells at Oxford University in the 1920s and wartime service as Director of the Economic Section of the United Kingdom Offices of the War Cabinet in the 1940s are the only exceptions to his continuous association with the LSE over a period of half a century. Indeed, there were years in the 1930s when he and Harold Laski *were* the LSE to the world at large.

Three masterful papers in the late 1920s – 'The Representative Firm', *Economic Journal*, September 1928; 'On the Elasticity of Demand for Income in Terms of Effort', *Economic Journal*, June 1930; and 'On a Certain Ambiguity in the Conception of Stationary Equilibrium', *Review of Economic and Statistics*, June 1930 – established the young Robbins as a powerful theorist. Then in 1932 he published a slim book, entitled *An Essay on the Nature and Significance of Economic Science* (Macmillan, 1932; 2nd edn, 1935; St Martins Press,

1969), the like of which had not been seen in English-speaking economics since the *Scope and Method of Political Economy* (1891) by Neville Keynes. The book was remarkable in the first instance in the extent to which it was indebted to Austrian economists, both living and dead, who had long been ignored by English writers. It was further remarkable in asserting the *a priori* certainty of fundamental economic postulates, based as they are on introspection and the logical meaning of terms, a style of argument which ran strongly against the stream of traditional empiricism in economics. The book aroused a furious controversy, centring on Robbins' famous definition of economics – 'Economics is the science which studies human behaviour as a relationship between given ends and scarce means which have alternative uses' – and on the associated proposition that the economist as economist is not concerned with ends but only with means. In effect, Robbins was saying, there is a watertight distinction between positive economics, involving statements of 'is', and normative economics, involving statements of 'ought'. Although this distinction is repeated in practically every second text book of economics, it has always been widely disputed then as now (see Myrdal, G.).

Joining a five-man committee of the newly formed Economic Advisory Council in 1930, Robbins found himself alone in opposing Keynes, Pigou, and others who advocated import restrictions and public works to remedy the Great Depression. Influenced as he was by the Austrian theory of business cycles, Robbins became a determined opponent of Keynes all through the 1930s, a view which he only abandoned in the 1940s when he worked for the British War Cabinet. *The Great Depression* (Macmillan, 1934) is typical of Robbins in his anti-Keynesian phase. *The Economic Problem in Peace and War* (Macmillan, 1947) announced his conversion to Keynesianism, the personal elements of which are movingly described in his fascinating *Autobiography of an Economist* (Macmillan, St Martins Press, 1971).

After the war, Robbins became increasingly active in the arts, his great loves being painting and opera. He became Trustee of London's National Gallery in 1952, Trustee of the Tate Gallery in 1953, and a Director of the Royal Opera House in 1962. In 1962 he added business management to his other activities, becoming Chairman of the *Financial Times*, the British equivalent of the *Wall Street Journal*. While thus engaged, his scholarly interests turned increasingly towards the history of economic thought. *The Theory of Economic Policy in English Classical Political Economy* (Macmillan, St Martins Press, 1952; 2nd edn, Porcupine, 1978) became a classic overnight but it was topped by his masterpiece, *Robert Torrens and the Evolution of Classical Economics* (Macmillan, St Martins Press, 1958), which established a vogue in viewing a whole period from the standpoint of a relatively minor economist of the day. Later works on the history of economic thought, which did not, however, live up to these earlier performances, are *The Theory of Economic Development in the History of Economic Thought* (Macmillan, St Martins Press, 1968), *The Evolution of Modern Economic Theory* (Aldine, 1970) and *Political Economy: Past and Present* (Macmillan, 1976).

In 1959 Robbins was given a life peerage. Two years later he was appointed Chairman of the official Committee on Higher Education. The *Report of the Committee* (1963), which bears the unmistakable stamp of Robbins' masterful eighteenth-century prose, recommended a massive expansion of higher education in Britain on the basis of student demand. The report, accompanied by five statistical appendices and seven volumes of oral and documentary evidence, was immediately endorsed and implemented by the Conservative government, thus producing an era of rapid growth in British higher education, which only came to an end in the late 1970s. All questions of higher education in Britain have ever since been characterised by repeated reference to 'the Robbins principle', the axiom that every student who is qualified must be admitted to effectively free higher education. Robbins' continued interest in questions of higher education is represented by his *University in the Modern World* (Macmillan, 1966) and *Higher Education Revisited* (Macmillan, 1980). Even in these last years, however, he returned occasionally to the macroeconomics themes of earlier years, as witnessed by *Politics and Economics* (Macmillan, 1963) and *Against Inflation* (Macmillan, 1979).

Lionel Robbins is one of the great teachers and prose artists of modern economics. He made no outstanding intellectual discoveries; he had no disciples and never formed a school of thought; but everything he did is marked by great style and elegance.

*Secondary Literature*
T.W. Hutchison, 'Robbins, Lionel', in D.L. Sills (ed.), *International Encyclopaedia of the Social Sciences*, vol. 18 (The Free Press, 1979); M. Peston, 'Lionel Robbins: Methodology, Policy and Modern Theory',

in J.R. Shackleton and G. Locksley (eds), *Twelve Contemporary Economists* (Macmillan, 1981; Wiley, Halsted Press, 1981); B.A. Corry, 'Robbins, Lionel Charles', in J. Eatwell, M. Milgate and P. Newman (eds), *The New Palgrave: A Dictionary of Economics*, vol. 4 (Macmillan, 1987); D.P. O'Brien, *Lionel Robbins* (Macmillan, 1988).

# Robinson, Joan (1903–83)

Joan Robinson is the only woman ever to have achieved outstanding eminence in economic theory (which, no doubt, tells us more about economic theory than about women). Her *Economics of Imperfect Competition* (Macmillan, 1933; 2nd edn, 1969) taught an entire generation of economists the microeconomics that now figures so heavily in elementary text books. A stalwart defender of Keynes and a leading populariser of Keynesian economics in the 1930s, she went on after the war to convert Keynesian short-period analysis into a Keynesian-type theory of economic growth, thus laying the foundation of a currently thriving school of post-Keynesian economics (see Kaldor, N.; Pasinetti, L.L; Weintraub, S.). Later she attacked the neoclassical theory of capital and the associated marginal productivity theory of distribution in a classic article, 'The Production Function and the Theory of Capital', *Review of Economic Studies*, 2, 1954, thereby launching the so-called 'Cambridge Controversies' – Cambridge, England, versus Cambridge, USA – one of the most acrimonious theoretical debates to have disfigured the face of modern economics (see Pasinetti, L.L.). Convinced that she had discovered a fatal flaw in standard economic theory – capital cannot be measured independently of the rate of interest and the rate of interest is not uniquely related to the marginal productivity of capital – she moved steadily away on almost all economic questions towards a unique heterodox position of her own. Her entire professional life seemed to refute the old adage that everyone becomes more conservative as they get older.

Joan Robinson was born in 1903 into a middle-class, academic English family, descended on her father's side from F.D. Maurice, the great nineteenth-century Christian Socialist. She graduated from Girton College, Cambridge, in 1925 and shortly thereafter married Austin Robinson, soon to become a Cambridge economist in his own right. After a spell in India the Robinsons returned to Cambridge where Joan joined the Cambridge faculty as an assistant lecturer in economics; she became a university lecturer in 1937, reader in 1949 and, finally, a full professor in 1965, retiring in 1971.

Her *Economics of Imperfect Competition* appeared in the same year as Edward Chamberlin's *Theory of Monopolistic Competition* (1933) and both authors independently explored the implications of advertising and product differentiation for the traditional theory of the competitive firm. The long debate about the subtle differences between Robinson's and Chamberlin's treatments occupied microeconomists for many years. Joan Robinson eventually repudiated her book as symptomatic of the kind of static equilibrium analysis she now deplored. Chamberlin, on the other hand, stuck to his guns and in the final analysis won the argument, in so far as there was any real argument. As a member alongside Harrod, Kahn, Meade, Austin Robinson, and Sraffa of the so-called 'Circus of Cambridge and Oxford economists who argued out Keynes's *Treatise* and helped him to formulate what was to become the *General Theory*, Joan Robinson played a key role in the story of the Keynesian Revolution. Her little book *Introduction to the Theory of Employment* (Macmillan, 1937; 2nd edn, 1969) was one of the most widely read pre-war introductions to the Keynesian system. A few years later, she performed the same function for Marx in *An Essay on Marxian Economics* (Macmillan, 1942; 2nd edn, 1966), a sparkling, heretical, no-nonsense attempt to give Marx his due as a sort of early Keynesian, which remains to this day one of the best books ever written on Marxian economics. *The Rate of Interest and Other Essays* (Macmillan, 1953), but particularly *The Accumulation of Capital* (Macmillan, Richard D. Irwin, 1956; 3rd edn, 1969), announced a new phase in her work, the attempt to dynamise Keynes and to establish a new analysis of long-run growth under capitalism.

*Exercises in Economic Analysis* (Macmillan, 1960), *Economic Philosophy* (Watts, 1962; Penguin, 1969), *Essays in the Theory of Economic*

*Growth* (Macmillan, 1962), *Economics: An Awkward Corner* (Allen & Unwin, 1966), and *Economic Heresies* (Macmillan, 1971) confirmed and extended her new departure into a wholesale rejection of the prevailing economic orthodoxy. Weaving together the ideas of such seemingly contradictory authors as Keynes, Kalecki, and Sraffa, she struggled hard in her later years to provide an alternative economics that would not depend, as orthodox economics clearly does, on the purely hypothetical comparison of two or more equilibrium positions: since historical time is irreversible, she argued, comparative static analysis is almost irrelevant. *An Introduction to Modern Economics* (McGraw-Hill, 1973), co-authored with J. Eatwell, was to be the fountainhead of this 'new' economics; however, the book was not well received and is generally judged to be a failure as an introductory text book for first-year students.

A glance at Joan Robinson's five volume of *Collected Papers* (Basil Blackwell, 1951, 1964, 1965, 1973, 1979) shows that she is one of the best counter-examples of the generalisation that all economists write badly: her style, marked by the frequent use of colloquialisms, rhetorical barbs, and a peculiar but intoxicating type of verbal algebra is a sheer delight to read. On the other hand, her admiration of Mao's China and Kim-Sung's North Korea was a continual embarrassment to her friends and foes alike. To read her *The Cultural Revolution in China* (Penguin, 1969) with the benefit of hindsight is to marvel at the utter political credulity of left-wing thinkers in the heady days of the 1960s. Be that as it may, the fact that she failed to win the Nobel Prize in Economics must be put down as one of the most extraordinary acts of academic vindictiveness – a revenge for her failure to acknowledge Swedish precedence for Keynesian economics – in recorded intellectual history.

*Secondary Literature*
G.C. Harcourt, 'Robinson, Joan', in D.L. Sills (ed.), *International Encyclopaedia of the Social Sciences*, vol. 18 (The Free Press, 1979); T. Skouras, 'The Economics of Joan Robinson', in J.R. Shackleton and G. Locksley (eds), *Twelve Contemporary Economists* (Macmillan, 1981; Wiley, Halsted Press, 1981); L.L. Pasinetti, 'Robinson, Joan Violet', in J. Eatwell, M. Milgate and P. Newman (eds), *The New Palgrave: A Dictionary of Economics*, vol. 4 (Macmillan, 1987); G.C. Harcourt, 'Robinson, Joan', in P. Arestis and M. Sawyer (eds), *A Biographical Dictionary of Dissenting Economists* (Edward Elgar, 1992).

# Rostow, Walt W. (1916– )

Walt Rostow's *Process of Economic Growth* (W.W. Norton, 1952; Oxford University Press, 1953; 2nd edn, 1960) and *The Stages of Economic Growth: A Non-Communist Manifesto* (Cambridge University Press, 1960; 2nd edn, 1971) were post-war best-sellers among non-fiction books. The Rostowian concepts of 'saving ratios' and 'capital–output ratios' reaching the critical levels required for 'take-off' to self-sustaining economic growth provided the vocabulary of the growth mania of the 1960s and for a few years it seemed as if literally every course in economics included *The Stages of Economic Growth* on its reading list. But steady criticism gradually eroded the enthusiasm which these works had earlier aroused and nowadays they are generally regarded as an embarrassing symptom of the hopelessly naive thinking about growth that characterised much economic thought in the early post-war period.

The Harrod–Domar model of economic growth (see Harrod, R.F.; Domar, E.D.) had demonstrated that any self-sustaining rate of growth of income in a country implies a definite relationship between the proportion of income saved, the saving ratio, and the productivity of new investment, the output–capital ratio. So, if one knew the value of one of these ratios, one could deduce the required value of the other one to produce steady economic growth. It appeared that the capital–output ratio is largely determined by the state of technology in a country and is, therefore, incapable of being quickly altered. However, the saving ratio depends entirely on voluntary decisions and is presumably capable of being manipulated by government policy. Rostow examined the historical record of the now industrialised countries and claimed to find definite phases in the two ratios, such that, given the prevailing capital–output ratio, saving rates gradually rose to reach the levels that permitted the 'take-off' to steady, exponential growth: Britain reached the take-off in the 1780s, the USA reached it in the 1820s, France and Germany reached it in the 1850s or 1860s, and so forth. Rostow also showed that most of the under-developed countries in Asia, Africa, and Latin America had not yet reached these critical levels in the two ratios but the underlying model permitted calculation of the saving rates required to achieve 'take-off'. In short, Rostow reinvented the old idea that there is a single global path to economic prosperity, marked off by definite stages or phases of development, such that the rich country of today shows a poor country of today where it will be tomorrow.

The argument was naive because the capital–output ratio in fact depends as much on economic incentives as on the brute facts of technology; similarly, the saving ratio depends on stable values and attitudes in a society as much as on economic incentives and, hence, may actually be more difficult to alter than the capital–output ratio. Moreover, the model is silent about the mechanism in a society for converting savings into investments. Finally, the historical record produces data about the *average* saving–income and capital–output ratios, whereas what matters for growth are the *marginal* saving–income and capital–output ratios and these may depart considerably from year to year from their average values.

Few economic historians today would give much credence to Rostow's claim that there are definite stages of economic growth, characterised by breaks in the time series of saving rates and capital–output ratios. Rostow himself, however, has never abandoned the ambition to produce a 'Non-Communist Manifesto' that could rival the Marxian system, and in *The World Economy: History and Prospect* (University of Texas Press, 1978) he attempted to recast his earlier theory into a new scenario of stages of economic growth. This work has not so far attracted much attention, no doubt because such ambitious efforts at world history have gone totally out of fashion. However, his contribution to G.M. Meier and D. Seers (eds),

*Pioneers in Development* (Oxford University Press, 1984) and his most recent *Theorists of Economic Growth from David Hume to the Present, with a Perspective on the Next Century* (Oxford University Press, 1990) show that the leopard has in no way changed his spots.

Rostow carried out distinguished work in British economic history both before and since *The Stages of Economic Growth. Essays on the British Economy of the Nineteenth Century* (Oxford University Press, 1948) was followed by two magnificent volumes on *The Growth and Fluctuation of the British Economy, 1790–1850* (Oxford University Press, 1953), with A.D. Gayer and A.J. Schwartz, a topic to which Rostow returned in *British Trade Fluctuations, 1868–1896: A Chronicle and a Commentary* (Arno Press, 1981).

Rostow was born in 1916 in New York City. He received his BA in 1936 from Yale University, his MA from Balliol College, Oxford, in 1938, and his PhD from Yale University in 1939. He began teaching at Harvard University in the 1940s and became Professor of Economic History at Harvard in 1952. In 1961 he left Harvard to become Deputy Special Assistant in National Security Affairs to President Kennedy. From 1961 to 1966 he was Chairman of the Policy Planning Council at the State Department and from 1964 to 1966 he was also US Member of the Inter-American Committee of the Alliance for Progress with the rank of Ambassador. Finally, from 1966 to 1969 he was Special Assistant in National Security Affairs to President Johnson. Rostow was deeply involved in President Johnson's discredited policies in Vietnam and he left government service in 1969, when the war in Vietnam was wound up, to take up a post at the University of Texas (Austin), from which he only recently retired.

*Primary Literature*
W.W. Rostow, 'Reflections on Political Economy: Past, Present and Future', in M. Szenberg (ed.), *Eminent Economists* (Cambridge University Press, 1992); W.W. Rostow, 'Reflections on the Drive to Technological Maturity', in J.A. Kregel (ed.), *Recollections of Eminent Economists*, vol. 2 (Macmillan, 1989).

# Samuelson,
# Paul Anthony
# (1915–   )

Paul Samuelson is in many ways the economists' economist: his output consists in large part of rigorous statements of fundamental concepts and theories in just about every branch in economics, international trade, production theory, capital theory, financial analysis, growth theory, macroeconomics, and the history of economic thought. There can be few graduate students of economics who have not read and re-read his classical essays, ranging from the statement of 'revealed preference theory', the interaction of the multiplier and accelerator, and the 'factor price equilisation theorem' to the modern definition of 'public goods'.

His very first paper, 'A Note on the Pure Theory of Consumers' Behaviour', *Economica*, February 1938, written at the age of twenty-three when he was still a graduate student, demonstrated that the famous demand curve of modern economics could be derived from the preferences 'revealed' by observable purchases in markets without invoking either marginal utility theory or indifference curves. A year later, 'Interactions between the Multiplier Analysis and the Principle of Acceleration', *Review of Economics and Statistics*, May 1939, showed that the addition of the 'accelerator' theory of investment (see Harrod, R.F.) to the Keynesian theory of income determination leads to a simple but powerful explanation of why modern economies suffer from business cycles. Then 'International Trade and the Equalisation of Factor Prices', *Economic Journal*, June 1948, provided an elegant proof of the stringent conditions required to carry free-trade arguments to the limit. Likewise, economists had long ago discovered that certain goods cannot be efficiently produced by a market mechanism because their benefits are equally available to everyone, so that no one is motivated to pay for them. However, Samuelson's 'The Pure Theory of Public Expenditure', *Review of Economics and Statistics*, November 1954, was the first rigorously to define the characteristics of such 'public goods'.

Samuelson's brilliant doctoral dissertation at Harvard University, *Foundations of Economic Analysis* (Harvard University Press, 1947; 2nd edn, 1982), completed in 1941 but not published until 1947, was a milestone in the conversion of modern economists to the view that all economic behaviour can be fruitfully studied as the solution to a maximisation problem explicitly or implicitly employing the mathematics of differential and integral calculus. In addition, his formulation of the 'correspondence principle' – static equilibrium analysis means nothing by itself without a 'corresponding' statement of the stability properties of the model, demonstrating that slight deviations of the variables from their equilibrium values are self-correcting – marked the beginning of the modern interest in economic dynamics, the study of price formation out of equilibrium.

As if all that were not enough, his elementary textbook, *Economics* (McGraw-Hill, 1948; 15th edn, 1995, with W.D. Nordhaus), containing his invention of the '45-degree Keynesian cross' diagram to depict the determination of national income, was a major factor in the Keynesian conquest of economics departments in the years after World War II. In the same way, *Linear Programming and Economic Activity* (McGraw-Hill, 1958), which he co-authored with Robert Dorfman and Robert Solow, played a significant role in disseminating the new wartime techniques of mathematical optimisation, which had grown up alongside Keynesian economics. Even that book was much more than a textbook in the field: it succeeded in integrating price theory, linear programming, and growth theory, subjects which had hitherto been regarded as existing in separate compartments.

Samuelson was born in Gary, Indiana, in 1915. He was admitted to the University of Chicago at the age of sixteen and took his master's degree at Harvard University before he was twenty. At the advanced age of twenty-six, he received his PhD for a thesis which promptly won him Harvard's David A. Wells Award, and became an instructor at the Massachusetts Institute of Technology. Six years later he was made a full professor at MIT where he has remained until his retirement in 1986. His many honours and prizes – the first John Bates Clark Award from the American Economic Association (for the most distinguished work by an economist under the age of forty) in 1947, President of the Econometric Society in 1953, the American Economic Association in 1961, and the International Economic Association from 1965 to 1968, the Albert Einstein Medal in 1970, etc. – were topped in 1970 by the award of the Nobel Prize in Economics. He has served as adviser to many government agencies, including the War Production Board, the Treasury, the Council of Economic Advisors, the Bureau of the Budget, and the Federal Reserve System. He also advised President Kennedy, and was the author of the 1961 Task Force Report to President Kennedy, *State of the American Economy*. For many years he was, like Milton Friedman, a regular contributor to *Newsweek*. His *Collected Scientific Papers*, ed. J.E. Stiglitz, R.C. Merton, H. Nagatomi and K. Crowley (MIT Press, 1966, 1972, 1977, 1983) runs to five fat volumes.

Samuelson's literary style is marked by abrasive humour and an utter disdain for lesser mortals; it is also marked, however, by a dedicated teacher's insistence on precision in the handling of ideas. One of the most prolific economists who ever lived – averaging almost one technical paper per month over a period of forty-five years – he is also one of the most successful in terms of royalties earned: *Economics*, now in its fifteenth edition, is used in over a dozen translations all over the world and its sales of more than four million copies have no equal in the entire history of the subject; it is even available in Russian, with many telling omissions and even a few unauthorised revisions. Economists had long been unhappy that there appeared to be little relationship between the old neoclassical microeconomics and the new Keynesian macroeconomics. Samuelson in *Economics*, however, claimed to have achieved 'the neoclassical synthesis' according to which the achievement of full employment requires Keynesian intervention with neoclassical theory coming to its own once full employment is reached. The immediate appeal of this claim had much to do with the almost instant success of *Economics*. One of the more remarkable features of this remarkable book (a beautiful example, incidentally, of the art of the modern typesetter and the first economic text book to use multiple colours in its diagrams) is the extent to which its successive editions have reflected the changing interests of the economics profession over the years: no sooner is the frontier explored in a new direction but the next edition of Samuelson's *Economics* contains a treatment of it.

Known for his 'liberal' political views (in the American sense of the word 'liberal'), Samuelson adheres to the golden mean on such central issues as markets versus bureaucracy, private versus public sector activities, and Keynesianism versus monetarism, avoiding extreme ideological positions. In short he is a perfect representative of the centrist political outlook of most economists, and this is one of the keys to his considerable personal influence. His enemies, and he has a few, dismiss him as an intellectual gymnast, a Paganini of economics, but his many admirers regard him as a major architect of modern mainstream economics and do not hesitate to describe the recent postwar era in economics as 'the age of Samuelson'.

*Primary Literature*
P.A. Samuelson, 'My Evolution as an Economist', in W. Breit and R.W. Spencer (eds), *Lives of the Laureates: Seven Nobel Economists* (MIT Press, 1986); P.A. Samuelson, 'My Evolution as an Economist', in M. Szenberg (ed.), *Eminent Economists* (Cambridge University Press, 1992).

*Secondary Literature*
L. Silk, *The Economists* (Basic Books, 1976), ch. 1; A. Gerschenkron, 'Samuelson in Soviet Russia: A Report', *Journal of Economic Literature*, June 1978; R. Sobel, *The Worldly Economists* (The Free Press, 1950), ch. 5; A. Kendry, 'Paul Samuelson and the Scientific Awakening of Economics', in J.R. Shackleton and G. Locksley (eds), *Twelve Contemporary Economists* (Macmillan, 1981; Wiley, Halsted Press, 1981); W.R. Breit and R.L. Ransom, 'Paul A. Samuelson: Economic *Wunderkind* as Policy Maker', in *The Academic Scribblers: American Economists in Collision*, 2nd edn (Dryden Press, 1982); S. Fischer, 'Samuelson, Paul Anthony', in J. Eatwell, M. Milgate and P. Newman (eds), *The New Palgrave: A Dictionary of Economics*, vol. 4 (Macmillan, 1987).

# Sargent,
# Thomas J.
# (1943–   )

Thomas Sargent is a co-founder of the 'new' classical macroeconomics based on the theory of rational expectations (see Lucas, R.E. Jr.). In a long series of papers, starting in the early 1970s, he has attempted a number of different empirical tests of the theory, all of which boil down to the proposition that (1) there is a 'natural rate of unemployment' in the economy, that is, an equilibrium level of unemployment to which the economy tends constantly to recur (see Friedman, M.), and (2) all departures from that natural rate are random, that is, not systematically related to any relevant economic variables, for the simple reason that economic agents are taking into account the policy rule the government is using – it is in this sense that expectations are said to be 'rational'. There is no problem in grasping the main arguments of the New Macroeconomics: it is obvious that if everyone correctly anticipates all future price changes, changes in government policy can only affect nominal and not real variables: The real problem is how to use observed behaviour to distinguish between partly specified, partly correct expectations and completely specified, totally correct 'rational' expectations, in particular as it hardly seems believable that all economic agents could correctly predict the consequences of every twist and turn of the government's monetary and fiscal policies. In other words, the New Macroeconomics stands or falls on econometric grounds. No wonder, then, that Sargent's work has aroused even more controversy than that of Lucas.

Most of Sargent's papers are too technical to be intelligible to undergraduate students of economics. But there is an essay by Lucas and Sargent, 'After Keynesian Macroeconomics' (1978), which is highly readable and which conveys much of the flavour of the Rational Expectations Revolution. It appears, together with all of Sargent's leading published papers, in the two-volume collection, *Rational Expectations and Econometric Practice*, eds. R.E. Lucas Jr and T.J. Sargent (University of Minnesota Press, 1981; Allen & Unwin, 1982). Sargent has also published an advanced textbook, *Macroeconomic Theory* (Academic Press, 1979), which contrasts the old Keynesian and the New Classical Macroeconomics. More recent books are *Rational Expectations and Inflation* (Harper & Row, 1986) and *Dynamic Macroeconomic Theory* (Harvard University Press, 1987).

Sargent was born in 1943 in Pasadena, California, received his BA from the University of California, Berkeley, in 1964 and his PhD from Harvard University in 1968. After a year as a research associate at the Carnegie Institute of Technology and another year serving in the US Army, he began teaching at the University of Pennsylvania in 1970, moving to the University of Minnesota in 1971, where he became Professor of Economics in 1975. Since 1987, he has been a Senior Fellow at the Hoover Institution of Stanford University.

# Schultz,
# Theodore W.
# (1902–95)

Theodore Schultz's many contributions to agricultural economics, and particularly his analysis of agricultural policies in developing countries, earned him the Nobel Prize in Economics in 1980 together with W. Arthur Lewis. But in addition to his own work in agriculture, he has been an effective populariser and disseminator of the ideas of others. Although he did not invent the theory of human capital (see Mincer, J.), his presidential address to the American Economic Association in 1960, 'Investment in Human Capital', *American Economic Review*, June 1961, did so much to draw attention to this field of research that he may be truly called the 'father' of human capital theory. He has done almost as much for the new 'economics of the family', associated, like human capital theory, with the name of Gary Becker (q.v.) and other fellow economists at the University of Chicago.

Schultz was born in Arlington, South Dakota, in 1902 in a German farming community and studied agricultural economics at South Dakota State College, receiving his bachelor's degree in 1926. Moving for postgraduate work to the University of Wisconsin, he completed a master's degree in 1928 and a doctorate in 1930. His first teaching post was at Iowa State College where he succeeded in attracting a large number of bright young economists into a department which combined agricultural economics and rural sociology.

In 1943, he became a professor at the University of Chicago and in the space of a decade published four critical books on American agricultural programmes, leading up to a major text book on agricultural economics, *The Economic Organization of Agriculture* (McGraw-Hill, 1953).

Another widely used text book in the economics of education, *The Economic Value of Education* (Columbia University Press, 1963), was succeeded by *Transforming Traditional Agriculture* (Yale University Press, 1964; Arno, 1976), his major work to date on the rural sector of the Third World. Traditional farmers, Schultz argued, are rational 'economic men'; their apparent unwillingness to innovate stems essentially from the uncertainty of the economic returns to farming, aggravated by the lack of agricultural extension services and the discriminatory price and tax policies of many Third World governments. *Economic Crises in World Agriculture* (University of Michigan Press, 1965), *Economic Growth and Agriculture* (McGraw-Hill, 1968) and *Distortions of Agricultural Incentives* (Indiana University Press, 1978), a volume which Schultz edited, demonstrated his continued interests in the agricultural problems of poor countries. A theme which runs through all these books is that rural poverty in the Third World is largely the result of the pro-urban bias of development planning in Asia, Africa, and Latin America: programmes of rapid industrialisation and import-substitution inevitably condemn the rural sector to subsistence production.

*Investment in Human Capital: The Role of Education and Research* (The Free Press, 1971) brought Schultz back to human capital theory, this time combined with the economic issues of pure and applied research. His flair for organising and presiding over academic conferences is conveyed by his editorship and enthusiastic contributions to such volumes as *Investment in Education: The Equity–Efficiency Quandary* (University of Chicago Press, 1973), *New Economic Approaches to Fertility* (University of Chicago Press, 1973), and *Economics of the Family: Marriage, Family, Human Capital and Fertility* (University of Chicago Press, 1974). More recent books are *Restoring Economic Equilibrium: Human Capital in the Modernizing Economy* (Basil Blackwell, 1990) and *Origins of Increasing Returns* (Basil Blackwell, 1993).

Schultz received many honorary degrees from universities in both North and South America. He was President of the American Economic Association in 1961, won the Francis A. Walker Medal of the

American Economic Association in 1972 and the Leonard Elmhirst Medal of the International Agricultural Economic Association in 1976, and was a member of innumerable academic bodies around the world. Although retired from the University of Chicago since 1974, he remained active as a consultant to UN specialised agencies and a number of private foundations until his death in 1995.

*Secondary Literature*
D.J. Johnson, 'Schultz, Theodore W.', in D.L. Sills (ed.), *International Encyclopaedia of the Social Sciences*, vol. 18 (The Free Press, 1979); M.J. Bowman, 'Theodore W. Schultz', in H.W. Spiegel and W.J. Samuels (eds), *Contemporary Economists in Perspective* (JAI Press, 1984).

# Scitovsky, Tibor (1910–   )

Tibor Scitovsky has worked on many topic in economics – the evaluation of income changes, the theory of capital, the theory of imperfect competition, the economics of advertising, the economics of culture, the theory of tariffs, international monetary reform, and macroeconomic policies – but running through all his writings is a central interest in welfare economics and the welfare meaning of economic 'progress'. The book that first established his reputation, *Welfare and Competition* (Richard D. Irwin, Allen & Unwin, 1951; 2nd edn, 1971), re-examined the standard arguments for the efficiency of competition and the inefficiency of monopoly with the tools of the 'new' welfare economics, understood, not as providing a perfect yardstick, but as furnishing benchmarks to which appropriate qualifications can be made. Its distinction between price-makers and price-takers introduced a necessary element of imperfection which, Scitovsky believed, characterised all competitive market structures. His next major book, *Economic Theory and Western European Integration* (Allen & Unwin, 1958), was an applied study in the theory of customs unions. *Papers on Welfare and Growth* (Stanford University Press, Allen & Unwin, 1964) brought together many of his classic articles over the years, including such influential papers as 'A Note on Welfare Propositions in Economics', *Review of Economic Studies*, November 1941, 'A Note on Profit Maximization and Its Implications', *Review of Economic Stud-*

*ies*, February 1943, 'Two Concepts of External Economies', *Journal of Political Economy*, April 1954, and 'What Price Economic Progress?', *Yale Review*, Autumn 1959. *Money and the Balance of Payments* (Rand McNally, 1969) addressed questions of international finance and balance of payments equilibrium. *Industry and Trade in Some Developing Countries* (Oxford University Press, 1970), with I.M.D. Little and M.F. Scott, was a fundamental contribution to development economics.

*The Joyless Economy* (Oxford University Press, 1976), with its revealing sub-title, *An Inquiry into Human Satisfaction and Consumer Dissatisfaction*, brought him back to the principle of consumer sovereignty, which had long troubled him: it compares and contrasts the economist's assumption of rational consumer behaviour with the evidence of behavioural psychology, suggesting that economists have something to learn from psychologists, an assertion which economists have always denied. Scitovsky argues that much observed consumer behaviour can only be explained by supposing that economic man has a craving for novelty and variety, which he is willing to pay for: he does not simply satisfy given wants but actively seeks the stimulus of novelty and sometimes sacrifices his comforts (and income) to obtain goods and services of which he has no previous experience. The implications of this theme are explored at length in this fascinating book in which Scitovsky emerges as a severe critic of the typical lifestyle of most Americans. This theme occurs again in his *Human Desire and Economic Satisfaction: Essays on the Frontiers of Economics* (Wheatsheaf, 1986).

Scitovsky was born in 1910 in Budapest, Hungary, a small country which has produced almost as many famous economists as Austria, Sweden, and the Netherlands. He received his first degree in Law from the University of Budapest in 1932 and went on to do a Master's degree at the London School of Economics in 1938. After teaching at the School for several years, he emigrated to the United States in 1939, served in the US Army 1943–6, worked at the US Department of Commerce in 1946, and began teaching at Stanford University in 1946. In 1958 he became Professor of Economics at the University of California, Berkeley. In 1966 he moved back to Europe to work at the OECD Development Centre in Paris. In 1968, he returned to America, spending two years at Yale University and a further six years at Stanford. In 1976 he capped his academic career by another two years at the London School of Economics. Today he is a Professor Emeritus at the University of California, Santa Cruz.

He was made a Distinguished Fellow of the American Economic Association in 1973.

*Primary Literature*
T. Scitovsky, 'My Search for Welfare', in M. Szenberg (ed.), *Eminent Economists* (Cambridge University Press, 1992).

*Secondary Literature*
I. Adelman, 'Scitovsky, Tibor', in J. Eatwell, M. Milgate and P. Newman (eds), *The New Palgrave: A Dictionary of Economics*, vol. 4 (Macmillan, 1987); P.E. Earl, 'Tibor Scitovsky', in W.J. Samuels (ed.), *New Horizons in Economic Thought* (Edward Elgar, 1992).

# Sen,
# Amartya K.
# (1933–  )

Amartya Sen's reputation is squarely based on two books, *Collective Choice and Social Welfare* (Holden-Day, 1971; 2nd edn, North-Holland, 1980) and *On Economic Inequality* (W.W. Norton, Oxford University Press, 1973), and one extremely influential article, 'The Impossibility of a Paretian Liberal', *Journal of Political Economy*, January/February 1970, reprinted in his collection of papers, *Choice, Measurement and Welfare* (Blackwell, 1982). *Collective Choice and Social Welfare* is a mathematically demanding book, only relieved by alternating chapters in prose, on the Arrow Problem: the question of whether it is possible to base some kind of rational social choice entirely on the preference orderings of individuals (see Arrow, K.J.). *On Economic Inequality* is almost equally demanding, although its subject matter is more easily grasped: in a slim book of just over a hundred pages, Sen examines and evaluates virtually every measure that has ever been proposed to quantify the degree of inequality of the distribution of income, showing that all of them involve hidden and sometimes surprising value judgements. 'The Impossibility of a Paretian Liberal', on the other hand, was one of the first papers to sow doubts about the premises underlying the concept of Pareto optimality – the notion that a market outcome is optimal if and only if a deviation from that outcome would make at least one person worse off. This concept of 'optimality' has always struck economists as perfectly reasonable, if not intuitively obvious, and what Sen shows in this paper is simply that it is much less reasonable than is usually believed.

Another of Sen's abiding interests has been development economics. His first book, *Choice of Techniques* (Blackwell, 1960; 3rd edn, 1968), the subject of his PhD dissertation, and a later study, *Employment, Technology and Development* (Oxford University Press, 1975), are concerned with the practical issues of investment criteria and the measurement of poverty and unemployment in developing countries. In a more recent major work, *Poverty and Famines: An Essay on Entitlement and Deprivation* (Oxford University Press, 1981), he attacks the doctrine that famines in the Third World are typically caused by droughts or floods: during most famines, there is in fact an adequate food supply in the country but people starve to death because they lack the 'entitlements' to food, that is, the purchasing power to enter the food market. He illustrates this argument by a careful examination of the circumstances surrounding some of the great Famines of recent years – this is indeed 'political economy' with a vengeance. This and closely related themes are further explored in *Commodities and Capabilities* (North-Holland, 1985), *The Standard of Living* (Cambridge University Press, 1987), and particularly *Hunger and Public Action* (Clarendon Press, 1989), with J. Dréze.

Sen was born in Santiniketan, Bengal, India, in 1933. He received his BA from the University of Calcutta in 1953 and then went to England to take another BA at the University of Cambridge in 1955, followed by a Cambridge PhD in 1959. He started teaching as Professor of Economics at Jadavpur University, Calcutta, in 1956 but soon returned to Britain to become a Fellow at Trinity College, Cambridge (1957–63). In 1963 he went back to India as Professor of Economics at Delhi University but this spell at home also ended in a return to Britain. After spending six years at the London School of Economics (1971–7), he became a Professor of Economics at the University of Oxford in 1977. In 1988, he moved to the United States to take up a professorship at Harvard, where he is teaching today.

He is a Fellow of the British Association and was Vice-President and then President of the Econometric Association in 1982, 1983 and 1984, the International Economic Association from 1986 to 1989, the Indian Economic Association in 1989, and the American Economic Association in 1994. He served as Chairman of the UN Expert Group on the Role of Advanced Skill and Technology in 1967 and as President of the Development Studies Association from 1980 to 1982. He won the Indian Mahalonobis Prize in 1976.

*Secondary Literature*
M. McPherson, 'Amartya Sen', in W.J. Samuels (ed.), *New Horizons in Economic Thought* (Edward Elgar, 1992); L. Putterman, 'Sen, Amartya', in P. Arestis and M. Sawyer (eds), *A Biographical Dictionary of Dissenting Economists* (Edward Elgar, 1992).

# Shackle,
# George L.S.
# (1903–92)

The name George Shackle immediately conjures up the words 'expectations' and 'uncertainty' because his entire career was tirelessly devoted to preaching the doctrine that economic activity is ruled by expectations of future events but that all future events are inherently uncertain and, therefore, more or less unpredictable. Stated like this, few economists would quarrel with the proposition: quarrelling only begins when we ask ourselves whether, in the light of this proposition, we can say anything about the formation of economic expectations; if future events are totally unpredictable, there is in fact little an economist can say about economic activity. Even Frank Knight (q.v.), who insisted long before Shackle that a great many economic events are 'uncertain' in the sense of being non-repeatable, made room for future events that are simply 'risky', in which case the probability of their occurrence is in fact calculable.

In his earlier books, *Expectations, Investment and Income* (Cambridge University Press, 1938; 2nd edn, 1968) and *Expectations in Economics* (Cambridge University Press, 1949; 2nd edn, 1952), Shackle avoided the extreme implications of his doctrine and offered a theory of 'the surprise function' as a way out of the dilemma of foresight in the presence of uncertainty: economic agents do have definite expectations about future events, at least in the negative sense of being 'surprised' by certain improbable outcomes, including the surprise of a totally unexpected event; 'the surprise function' is a special sort of non-probabilistic function of the expected values of future outcomes, and Shackle was able to formulate some general propositions about the shape of these surprise functions. However, Shackle's theory of surprise functions was not well received by the rest of the economics profession. Keynes had argued that investment is a volatile and unpredictable variable, precisely because of the unstable expectations of private investors, and this much was generally accepted by macroeconomists. But microeconomists nevertheless continued to operate with the working assumption that economic agents have perfect and hence correct foresight. In recent years, the theory of 'rational expectations' (see Lucas, R.E. Jr; Sargent, T.J.) has indeed addressed itself to the manner in which economic expectations are formed but with little attention to Shackle's earlier work in the area.

Shackle himself virtually abandoned his own technical contributions to the analysis of expectations and increasingly broadened his argument into a fundamental criticism of the whole of received economic theory for ignoring the problem of pervasive uncertainty. In books like *Decision, Order and Time in Human Affairs* (Cambridge University Press, 1961; 2nd edn, 1969), *Epistemics and Economics: A Critique of Economic Doctrines* (Cambridge University Press, 1972), *Keynesian Kaleidics: The Evolution of a General Political Economy* (Edinburgh University Press, 1974), and particularly *The Years of High Theory: Invention and Tradition in Economic Thought, 1926–1939* (Cambridge University Press, 1967), he traced the precise points at which the economics of the inter-war years went wrong, leaving little doubt that what is now needed is a total reconstruction of economic theory. The difficulty is to know how to set about this task and here Shackle was almost deliberately unhelpful. His vehement insistence that absolutely anything can happen tomorrow, and that economic expectation have literally no foundation on which to stand, was so destructive of all possibilities of economic theorising that his writings virtually amounted to the proposal to put a stop to the subject called 'economics'. His literary style, which has always read more like poetry than prose, in later years achieved an extraordinary rapturous intensity, better calculated to inflame the reader than to enlighten him. Nevertheless, his books leave an indelible impression and are a perfect antidote to the belief that there is absolutely nothing wrong with modern economics. His many papers are collected together in two volumes: *The Nature of Economic Thought: Selected Papers, 1955–64* (Cambridge University Press, 1966) and *Business, Time and Thought: Collected Essays, 1964–88*, ed. S. Frowen (Macmillan, 1989); a further volume is *Time, Expectations and Uncertainty in Economics: Selected Essays of G.L.S. Shackle*, ed. J.L. Ford (Edward Elgar, 1990).

Shackle was born in Cambridge, England, in 1903. He received his BA in 1931 and his PhD in 1937, both from the University of London. He began teaching at the London School of Economics in the 1930s and was deeply involved in the great debates of Keynesian Revolution, which divided the departments of economics at LSE as it divided economics departments all over the British Isles. During World War II, Shackle was a member of the wartime statistical committee assembled by Winston Churchill and, in the year after the war, a member of the Economic Section of the Cabinet Office. In 1950, he returned to academia as reader at the University of Leeds, leaving a year later to become Professor of Economics at the University of Liverpool, where he remained until his retirement in 1969. A Council Member of the Royal Economic Society from 1955 to 1969, President of Section F of the British Association for the Advancement of Science in 1966, and the recipient of several honorary degrees, Shackle was even more active in the years of his retirement from academic life than he was before: his output of books and articles showed a marked rise in the 1970s, continuing without let-up right until the day of his death in 1992.

*Primary Literature*
G.L.S. Shackle, 'A Student's Pilgrimage', in J.A. Kregel (ed.), *Recollections of Eminent Economists*, vol. 1 (Macmillan, 1988), G.L.S. Shackle, 'Shackle', in P. Arestis and M. Sawyer (eds), *A Biographical Dictionary of Dissenting Economists* (Edward Elgar, 1992).

*Secondary Literature*
G.C. Harcourt, 'Notes on an Economic Querist: G.L.S. Shackle', *Journal of Post-Keynesian Economics*, Fall 1981; M. Perlman, 'On Shackle, in H.W. Spiegel and W.J. Samuels (eds), *Contemporary Economists in Perspective*, vol. 2 (JAI Press, 1984); P. Earl, 'Shackle, George Lennox Sharman', in J. Eatwell, M. Milgate and P. Newman (eds), *The New Palgrave: A Dictionary of Economics*, vol. 4 (Macmillan, 1987); J.L. Ford, *G.L.S. Shackle: The Dissenting Economist's Economist* (Edward Elgar, 1994).

# Simon, Herbert A. (1916– )

Herbert Simon won the Nobel Prize in Economics in 1978 for a lifetime's study of administrative behaviour and decision-making in large organisations, not to mention the effort to persuade other economists that their picture of 'economic man' as a lightning calculator of costs and benefits is unrealistic. Economic action, argues Simon, is in fact 'bounded' by the costs of obtaining information about alternative opportunities and by sheer ignorance of the uncertain future; economic agents are unable to 'maximise' even if they wanted to; hence, they 'satisfice', that is, they do as well as possible to achieve certain aspiration levels and they gradually adjust these levels upwards or downwards, depending on whether outcomes exceed or fall short of the original target. The playing of chess is one of Simon's favourite examples: the problem of designing chess-playing computers is precisely the fact that almost every move in a game of chess involves millions of alternative possibilities and human beings do not decide on the next move by examining all these possibilities in turn but instead seize on promising patterns and lines of play. Likewise, rational economic conduct depends on information-saving rules of thumb. In dozens of essays – *Models of Man* (Wiley, 1956), *The Sciences of the Artificial* (MIT, 1969; 2nd edn, 1981), *Models of Discovery* (Reidel, 1977), *Models of Bounded Rationality and Other Topics in Economic Theory*, 2 vols (MIT, 1982), and *Economics, Bounded Rationality and the Cognitive Revolution* (Edward Elgar, 1992), with others – Simon has hammered away at the need to ground economics in a realistic rather than a fictional conception of human behaviour.

He and some of his associates at Carnegie-Mellon University, Pittsburg, have launched a new journal, The *Journal of Organizational Behavior*, to give expression to the feeling that economics lacks a 'micro-microeconomics': the study of how people actually make economic decisions in households, firms and government agencies. In addition to his methodological writings on 'bounded rationality', Simon has long taken a special interest in management science, the study of decision-making in hierarchically organised institutions with multiple objectives. His major book in the field, *Administrative Behavior* (Macmillan, 1947; 3rd edn, The Free Press, 1967), is a standard text in courses on business management and administration the world over. Other books of his in this area are *Public Administration* (Knopf, 1950), written with others; *Organizations* (Wiley, 1958; 2nd edn, 1966), written with J.G. March; *New Science of Management Decisions* (Harper, 1960; 2nd edn, 1977); and *The Shape of Automation for Men and Management* (Harper & Row, 1965).

Simon was born in 1916 in Milwaukee, Minnesota. He received his BA in 1936 and his PhD in 1943, both from the University of Chicago. His first post was that of a research assistant at the University of Chicago from 1936 to 1938. He then became a staff member of the International City Managers Association and Assistant Editor of the *Public Management and Municipal Year Book*. This was followed by a directorship of Administrative Measurement Studies at the Bureau of Public Administration of the University of California during the years 1939–42. He joined the teaching staff of the Illinois Institute of Technology in 1942, becoming Professor of Political Science in 1947. In 1949 he moved to Carnegie-Mellon University, first as Professor of Administration and Psychology (1949–55), and later as Professor of Computer Science and Psychology, a post which he held until retirement in 1988. He has also served as a consultant to the International City Managers Association (1942–9), the US Bureau of Budget (1946–9), the US Census Bureau (1947), the Cowles Commission for Research in Economics (1947–60), and other business and government organisations.

He was Chairman of the Board of Directors of the Social Science Research Council (1961–5), Member of the US President's Scientific

Advisory Committee (1968–71), Chairman of the Committee on Air Quality Control of the National Academy of Sciences (1974), Chairman of the Committee on Behavioral Sciences of the National Science Foundation (1975–6), winner of the Award for Distinguished Scientific Contributions of the American Psychological Association (1969), Distinguished Fellow of the American Economic Association (1976), and member of a large number of European professional associations. He has lectured at universities around the world and has received honorary degrees from nine of them.

Psychologists regard him as a psychologist; computer scientists regard him as a computer scientist; and economists regard him as an economist. To call him a 'social scientist' is no less than he deserves: he is a living denial of the proposition that there is no alternative to intellectual specialisation.

*Primary Literature*
H.A. Simon, *Models of My Life* (Basic Books, 1991); H.A. Simon, 'My Life Philosophy', in M. Szenberg (ed.), *Eminent Economists* (Cambridge University Press, 1992).

*Secondary Literature*
W.J. Baumol and A.K. Ando, 'Herbert Simon's Contributions to Economics', in H.W. Spiegel and W.J. Samuels, (eds), *Contemporary Economists in Perspective*, vol. 2 (JAI Press, 1984).

# Solow, Robert M. (1924–  )

Robert Solow is chiefly known for his path-breaking work on capital theory and growth theory in the 1950s and '60s but he also contributed in recent years, perhaps less definitively, to macroeconomic analysis and the economics of non-renewable resources. Two of his many papers, 'A Contribution to the Theory of Growth', *Quarterly Journal of Economics*, February 1956, and 'Technical Change and the Aggregate Production Function', *Review of Economics and Statistics*, August 1957, have become classics in the theory of economic growth, and his continued interest in growth theory is testified by his intermediate text book, *Growth Theory: an Exposition* (Oxford University Press, 1969). Earlier, he joined Dorfman and Samuelson in writing *Linear Programming and Economic Analysis* (McGraw-Hill, 1958), which did so much in the late 1950s to make the new post-war developments in growth theory accessible to young economists.

'A Contribution to the Theory of Growth' was the first 'neoclassical' version of the Harrod–Domar growth model (see Domar, E.D.; Harrod, R.F.) in the sense that, in Solow's model, capital and labour are substitutes for one another with the result that the long-run growth path of the economy is one of full employment. Similarly, 'Technical Change and the Aggregate Production Function' marked the origins of so-called 'sources-of-growth accounting (see Denison,

E.F.), which for a while produced an almost endless series of estimates of aggregate production functions (see Douglas, P.H.), attempting to separate the contributions to economic growth of
increases in the quantity of labour and capital from those of technical change. Solow went on in a number of other articles to create
'vintage models' of growth, that is, growth models in which capital
is measured, not simply in terms of size, but also in terms of its age
structure, new capital goods being counted as more capital than old
capital goods.

*Capital Theory and the Rate of Return* (North-Holland, 1963) was
another of Solow's brilliant performances in which many of the
age-old problems of capital theory were shown to be examples of
misplaced emphasis: the important question for capital theory is
not the measurement of capital, as is often argued (see Robinson, J.),
but rather how the rate of return on capital is determined, which
depends only on the nominal and not the real value of capital. In
addition, Solow has been a frequent and sparkling commentator on
the works of others, particularly those who deprecate the achieve-
ments of mainstream economics, and he was Samuelson's principal
ally in opposing the views of Robinson and Kaldor in the great
'Cambridge Controversies' (see Pasinetti, L.L.). A more recent work
is *The Labor Market as a Social Institution* (Basil Blackwell, 1990),
which revealed a somewhat surprising willingness to concede that
labour markets are unique markets, in the sense of adjusting little, if
at all, to ordinary economic pressures.

Solow was born in New York City in 1924. He obtained his BA in
1947, his MA in 1949 and his PhD in 1951, all from Harvard Univer-
sity. He started teaching at the Massachusetts Institute of Technology in 1950 and has remained there ever since as Professor of
Economics, except for a year at the University of Oxford (1968–9).
For five years he was a member and then Chairman of the Board of
Directors of the Federal Reserve Bank in Boston (1975–80). In 1961,
at the age of thirty-seven, he won the John Bates Clark Medal of the
American Economic Association. He served as President of the
Econometric Society in 1964 and the American Economic Association in 1979. He has received honorary degrees from several Ameri-
can and European universities. In 1987, he received the Nobel Prize
in Economics.

*Primary Literature*
R. Solow, 'My Evolution as an Economist', in W. Breit and R.W. Spencer (eds), *Lives of the Laureates: Ten Nobel Economists* (MIT Press, 1990); R. Solow, 'Notes on Coping', in M. Szenberg (ed.), *Eminent Economists* (Cambridge University Press, 1992).

# Spence,
# Michael A.
# (1943– )

Michael Spence's contributions fall neatly into two categories: an earlier and continued interest in the economics of information and a later interest in the dynamic aspects of competition, particularly the relationship between the competitive strategies of firms and their market performance. The earlier stage of his work is summed up in a brilliant and provocative book, *Market Signaling: Information Transfer in Hiring and Related Screening Processes* (Harvard University Press, 1974), a rewrite of his Harvard PhD dissertation. The problem that Spence examines is how employers and employees, insurance companies and insured clients, or indeed all buyers and sellers, select each other when their attributes matter but when information about these attributes is subject to uncertainty.

For example, since hiring and firing is expensive, employers would like to know in advance of hiring how productive their employees will turn out to be. There are two types of information they can use to judge job applicants: unalterable characteristics, such as age, race, and sex, and alterable characteristics, which applicants can improve by the investment of money or time. Spence calls the latter 'market signals'; since the costs of acquiring these signals in the form of, say, educational credentials is lower for the more able than for the less able, employers can safely use educational certificates to select more productive workers. Spence goes on to show that education may be unproductive in itself – the social rate of return on investment in schooling to society as a whole may be zero – and yet more education remains indispensable to individuals as a private signal, moreover, as educational expansion deflates the value of these signals, the pressure to acquire still more schooling increases, thus further reducing the social rate of return on educational investment. This theory of signalling as a feature of 'informational equilibrium' is not only extremely relevant to human capital theory (see Becker, G.S.; Mincer, J.) but also casts a new light on many other economic phenomena, including guarantees, tied sales, brand names, certifying agencies, and patterns of discrimination in labour markets.

Spence's more recent work on market structure and performance is represented by a long series of papers, such as 'Investment, Strategy and Growth in a New Market', *Bell Journal of Economics*, Spring 1979, and 'Notes on Advertising, Economies of Scale, and Entry Barriers', *Quarterly Journal of Economics*, November 1980. These may some day soon be drawn together in a book. In the meantime, he has co-authored an intermediate text on *Competition in the Open Economy* (Harvard University Press, 1980), with R.E. Caves and M.E. Porter, and is the author of a monograph on *Competitive Structure in Investment Banking* (Harvard University Press, 1983).

Spence was born in Montclair, New Jersey, in 1943. He received his BA from Princeton University in 1966, his MA from the University of Oxford in 1968, and his PhD from Harvard University in 1972. He started teaching at Harvard in 1971 but moved to Stanford University in 1973. In 1976 he returned to Harvard as Professor of Economics, becoming a Professor of Business Administration in 1979.

He was a Rhodes Scholar from 1966 to 1968, a Member of the Economics Advisory Panel of the National Science Foundation from 1977 to 1979, won the Galbraith Prize for Excellence in Teaching in 1978 and the John Bates Clark Medal of the American Economics Association in 1981, and has served as a Member of the Editorial Boards of various journals, such as the *Bell Journal of Economics*, *Journal of Economic Theory*, and *Public Policy*.

# Sraffa, Piero (1898–1983)

Piero Sraffa was born in Turin, Italy, in 1898, the son of a law professor. He attended the *lycée* and the University in Turin and was soon caught up in the wave of radicalism which swept through the industrial cities of Northern Italy after the Russian Revolution of 1917 and the end of the war in 1918. It was at this time that he formed a friendship with the now legendary Antonio Gramsci, the editor of the revolutionary weekly *L'Ordine Nuovo*: Sraffa began to contribute articles to Gramsci's journal and years later, when Gramsci was imprisoned by Mussolini, he maintained contact with him, fought unsuccessfully for his release, and played a vital part in preserving Gramsci's famous *Prison Notebooks*. Meanwhile, the young Sraffa also finished his undergraduate dissertation on Italian inflation, supervised by Luigi Einaudi, a famous Italian public finance expert, who later became President of Italy after World War II. In 1921 Sraffa visited England for the first time and met Keynes. His first article in economics in English appeared in 1922 in the *Economic Journal* and the *Manchester Guardian's Commercial Supplement for Europe*, both of which were edited by Keynes. In 1924 he became a university lecturer at Cagliari in Sardinia, and a professor at Perugia, followed by a professorship at Cagliari in 1926. In 1925, he translated Keynes' *Tract on Monetary Reform* (1923) into Italian and published a long article in the *Annali di Economia* on Marshall's theory of the firm, arguing that the theory logically required the assumption of constant returns of scale, which assumption was unlikely to be true under modern circumstances. The appearance of a shorter version of that paper in the *Economic Journal* in 1926 established Sraffa overnight as an important theoretical economist in the English-speaking world. In the following year he emigrated to Britain to become a Fellow of Trinity College, Cambridge, a post which he held until his death in 1983.

In Cambridge, Sraffa became one of the five or six members of the self-styled 'Circus', the inner circle of economists who met regularly with Keynes as he worked his way towards the ideas that were to surface in *The General Theory* (1936). In 1932, Sraffa was urged by Keynes to attack Hayek's *Prices and Production* (1931) and his *Economic Journal* critique of that book is generally credited with the demise of Hayek's theory of business cycles (see Hayek, F.A. von). Sraffa also began to collect and edit the *Works and Correspondence of David Ricardo* (Cambridge University Press, 1951–73), the economist whom he admired above all others. In his *Essays in Biography* (1933), Keynes announced the imminent publication of Sraffa's definitive edition of the complete works of Ricardo – in the event it took another forty years to complete. When it did appear in ten volumes in the years 1951–73, it proved to be worth waiting for; it included the discovery of at least one unpublished work by Ricardo and a considerable amount of hitherto unpublished correspondence; its editorial notes were marvels of exhaustive scholarship; and its introduction (co-authored with M.H. Dobb – q.v.) fundamentally revised the traditional interpretation of Ricardo's ideas.

By the 1950s, Sraffa's reputation had become that of a historian of economic thought rather than a contributor to current economic debates. But then in 1960, at the age of sixty-two, he published an extraordinary little book, whose title was almost as baffling as its content: *Production of Commodities by Means of Commodities: Prelude to a Critique of Economic Theory* (Cambridge University Press, 1960, 1975). The book contained no introduction or conclusion, no discussion of assumptions, no justification for its analysis and, apart from a passing reference to Marshall, it cited no writer later than Marx. What it seemed to be about was Ricardo's old problem of finding an invariable standard by which to measure prices, such that they will not depend on the level of wages and profits; Sraffa claimed to have solved this problem once and for all. Moreover, he claimed that, having solved it, he had destroyed the orthodox belief that factor prices and products prices are simultaneously determined. But what the book is really about has been the subject of a heated debate. A whole school of economists, who label themselves 'neo-Ricardians', has grown up to carry out that 'critique of economic theory' which Sraffa promised to provide but failed to deliver. Some economists, like Joan Robinson, insist that Sraffa has indeed laid the foundation for an alternative economics, while others, especially in the United States, have dismissed Sraffa's book as a heavy-handed exercise in linear production theory (see Leontief, W.W.; Pasinetti, L.L.), which was obsolete almost before it was published. Marxist economists, in particular, have bitterly divided themselves into Sraffians and anti-Sraffians, some contending that Sraffa makes it possible to modernise Marx, while others argue that Sraffa is simply irrelevant to Marx.

Throughout this controversy, Sraffa remained totally silent, adhering to a lifetime determination not to engage in controversy. His fame in old age capped what, surely, must be one of the most unpredictable success stories in the entire history of ideas.

*Secondary Literature*
L.L. Pasinetti, 'Sraffa, Piero', in D.L. Sills, *International Encyclopaedia of the Social Sciences*, vol. 18 (The Free Press, 1979); A. Roncaglia, 'Piero Sraffa's Contribution to Political Economy', in J.R. Shackleton and G. Locksley (eds), *Twelve Contemporary Economists* (Macmillan, 1981; Wiley, Halsted Press, 1981); J. Eatwell and C. Panico, 'Sraffa, Piero', in J. Eatwell, M. Milgate and P. Newman (eds), *The New Palgrave: A Dictionary of Economics*, vol. 4 (Macmillan, 1987); J.-P. Poitier, *Piero Sraffa: Unorthodox Economist (1898–1983. A Biographical Essay* (Routledge, 1991); G. Mongiovi, 'Sraffa, Piero', in P. Arestis and M. Sawyer (eds), *A Biographical Dictionary of Dissenting Economists* (Edward Elgar, 1992).

# Stigler, George J. (1911–91)

George Stigler won the Nobel Prize in Economics in 1982 for his work on the theory of economic regulation but if there were a Nobel Prize for beautiful, polished papers on economic theory, industrial organisation, and the history of economic thought, it should long ago have been given to him. One of his most original essays, 'Information in the Labor Market', *Journal of Political Economy*, Supplement, October 1962, is the starting point of all later work on 'search models' of unemployment, according to which unemployment is interpreted as a voluntary spell of searching for the best job at the best rate of pay (see Alchian, A.A.; Feldstein, M.; Phelps, E.S.). What Stigler demonstrated in that paper is that there is no such thing as single rate of pay for a job in a labour market; even when jobs are well-defined, they are in fact available at a whole spectrum of pay rates, so that the job-seeker has an information problem to solve.

Similarly, Stigler's empirical refutation of 'The Kinky Oligopoly Demand Curve and Rigid Prices', *Journal of Political Economy*, October 1947, the notion that industries containing few firms will rarely change prices has haunted the vast literature on this topic ever since. In 1971, another of his papers on 'The Theory of Economic Regulation', *Bell Journal of Economics and Management Science*, Spring 1976, suggested the simple hypothesis that government agencies set up supposedly to regulate the price and investment policies of public utilities in the interest of consumers are best understood as acting instead in the interests of producers, not out of malice but simply as a result of the logic of public regulation. Stigler and others have since gone on to explore the implications of this hypothesis for one US regulatory agency after another. Finally, and only 'finally' because space is lacking, Stigler's provocative essay on 'The Politics of Political Economists', *Quarterly Journal of Economics*, November 1959, arguing that the study of economics drives one inevitably towards economic conservatism, has been endlessly debated and serves as a perfect example of his inimitable style, made up of crystal-clear arguments, memorable summaries, the use of evidence from unexpected quarters, and a dry, teasing wit – his footnotes alone deserve to be reprinted in anthologies of American humour.

Stigler was born in Renton, Washington, in 1911. He took his Bachelors' degree from the University of Washington in 1931, his Master's degree from Northwestern University in 1932, and began to work in the following year on his doctoral dissertation under Frank Knight at the University of Chicago. The thesis was completed in 1938 and published in 1941 under the title *Production and Distribution Theories* (Macmillan, 1941). It represented the first serious attempt to trace the slow evolution of neo-classical production and distribution theory from 1870 onwards and was hailed immediately as a major landmark in the history of economic thought.

Stigler was invited by Theodore Schultz in 1936 to become an Assistant Professor at Iowa State University. He taught there for two years before moving to the University of Minnesota. After wartime service with the Office of Price Administration in Washington, he returned to Minnesota and published a slim but still useful intermediate text book on *The Theory of Price* (Macmillan, 1942; 3rd edn, 1966). In 1946 he became a professor at Brown University, leaving in 1947 to become a professor at Columbia University. In 1959 he moved back to the University of Chicago, where he has remained until his retirement in 1981. He served as President of the American Economic Association in 1964 and the History of Economics Society in 1977, besides receiving honorary degrees from five American and European universities. He edited the prestigious *Journals of Political Economy* from 1973 until his death in 1991. He was President of the Mont Pèlerin Society in 1977–8.

His outstanding articles on the history of economic thought are brought together in *Five Lectures on Economic Problems* (Macmillan,

1948), *The Intellectual and the Market Place and Other Essays* (Princeton University Press, 1963), and *Essays in the History of Economics* (University of Chicago Press, 1965). Similarly, *The Organization of Industry* (Richard D. Irwin, 1968), *The Citizen and the State: Essays on Regulation* (University of Chicago Press, 1975), and *The Economist as Preacher* (University of Chicago Press, Basil Blackwell, 1982) bring together his many essays on business behaviour and the theory of economic regulation. *Domestic Servants in the USA* (National Bureau of Economic Research, 1947), *Trends in Output and Employment* (National Bureau of Economic Research, 1947), *Trends in Employment in the Service Industries* (Princeton University Press, 1956), *Capital and Rates of Return in Manufacturing Industries* (Princeton University Press, 1963), *The Behaviour of Industrial Prices* (National Bureau of Economic Research, 1970), with J.K. Kindahl, and *Demand and Supply of Scientific Personnel* (National Bureau of Economic Research, 1975), with D. Blank, represent some of the empirical work which he carried out as a staff member of the National Bureau of Economic Research in the years 1943–59. An early pamphlet with M. Friedman, 'Roofs and Ceiling?' (Foundation for Economic Education, 1946), is still worth reading as one of the first attacks on rent control in the literature.

*Primary Literature*
G.J. Stigler, 'My Evolution as an Economist', in W. Breit and R.W. Spencer (eds), *Lives of the Laureates: Ten Nobel Economists* (MIT Press, 1990); G.J. Stigler, *Memoirs of an Unregulated Economist* (Basic Books, 1988).

*Secondary Literature*
T. Sowell and R. Schinalensee, 'Stigler, George Joseph', in J. Eatwell, M. Milgate and P. Newman (eds), *The New Palgrave: A Dictionary of Economics*, vol. 4 (Macmillan, 1987).

# Stiglitz,
# Joseph E.
# (1943–   )

Joseph Stiglitz's work in economics has ranged far and wide but it has always had a consistent focus on the role of imperfect and costly information in the competitive process. In a number of path-breaking papers, summed up in 'Information and Competitive Price Systems', *American Economic Review*, May 1976, written jointly with S.J. Grossman, he has demonstrated that the usual assumption that economic agents are well-informed about alternative market opportunities is not as innocent as it appears. Once this assumption is dropped, as it must be if we are being realistic, it is no longer possible to show that perfect competition maximises economic welfare; indeed, it is not even possible to show that perfect competition will necessarily lead to an equilibrium of demand and supply, and what is true of perfect competition is even more true of monopolistic competition and oligopoly. These papers are highly technical and typically generalise results achieved from the analysis of insurance markets. Their point of view has not yet trickled down to elementary text books– although his own *Economics* (W.W. Norton, 1993) was a first attempt to break the ice – but Stiglitz's findings on the economics of information is part of a wider trend, involving attention to transaction costs, property rights, incomplete contracts, and the analysis of decision-making under uncertainty, which has begun to affect undergraduate teaching: many of the simple truths that first-year students learn in courses on elementary economics now have to be unlearned in intermediate and advanced courses.

Stiglitz's output of journal articles has been large but he has only written five books: *Lectures in Public Economics* (McGraw-Hill, 1980), with A.B. Atkinson, an advanced text book in public finance, *The Theory of Commodity Price Stabilization* (Oxford University Press, 1981), with D.M.G. Newbery, *Economics of the Public Sector* (W.W. Norton, 1986), and *Whither Socialism?* (MIT Press, 1994), as well as the introductory text, *Economics*, mentioned above. He has also edited, with H. Uzawa, a book of *Readings in the Modern Theory of Economic Growth* (MIT Press, 1969).

Stiglitz was born in Gary, Indiana, in 1943 and received his BA from Amherst College in 1964. He received a PhD from the Massachusetts Institute of Technology in 1966 at the age of twenty-three, which is something of an all-time record. After receiving his doctorate, he started teaching at the Massachusetts Institute of Technology and then moved from university to university, rarely staying more than a few years: Yale University (1968–74), Stanford University (1974–6), St Catherine's College, University of Oxford (1976–9), Princeton University (1979–88) and, finally, once again to Stanford University (1988–94).

He received the John Bates Clark Medal of the American Economic Association in 1979. He has been an Editor and Associate Editor of a large number of professional journals, including the *Journal of Public Economics, Review of Economic Studies, American Economic Review, Journal of Economic Theory* and *Journal of Economic Perspectives*. He was named a member of President Clinton's Council of Economic Advisors in 1994, where he continues today.

# Tinbergen, Jan (1903–94)

Jan Tinbergen and Ragnar Frisch were the first recipients of the Nobel Prize in Economics in 1969. Four years later Tinbergen's younger brother, Nikolaas Tinbergen, shared the Nobel Prize in Biology for his work on animal behaviour. His youngest brother, Luuk Tinbergen, was a Professor of Zoology. These facts begin to suggest the gifted academic family into which Jan Tinbergen was born in 1903. After attending secondary school in The Hague, he studied physics at the University of Leiden from 1922 to 1926, receiving his doctorate in 1929 with a thesis on extremum problems in physics and economics. He then joined a new unit for business cycle research in the Dutch Central Bureau of Statistics, where he remained until 1945, apart from a two-year interlude in which he worked for the League of Nations in Geneva. He also became a part-time lecturer in statistics at the University of Amsterdam in 1931, becoming part-time professor at the Netherlands School of Economics (now Erasmus University) in Rotterdam in 1933.

Tinbergen threw himself into econometric research, attempting to test economic theories which were mathematically formulated, and soon found himself building econometric models of the entire economy. His first attempt to build such a model, containing twenty-four equations to describe the Dutch economy, was not published until 1936, ten years after it was first conceived. It foreshadowed elements of Keynes' *General Theory* (1936), the post-war notion of the Phillips Curve, and even the idea of rational expectations associated with modern macroeconomic theories. The pioneering significance of this Dutch publication attracted no attention outside or even inside the Netherlands. Nevertheless, it led to Tinbergen being invited to test the various business cycle theories which Gottfried Haberler (q.v.) had reviewed in his epoch-making book for the League, *Prosperity and Depression* (1937). The result was a two-volume work, *Statistical Testing of Business Cycle Theories* (League of Nations, 1939; Agatha Press, 1968), the first of which focused entirely on investment activity and the second on the macroeconomic modelling of business cycles in the United States. Keynes wrote a scathing review of the first volume in The *Economic Journal*, which drew a polite reply from Tinbergen complaining that Keynes had totally misunderstood his econometric methods. Even the more down-to-earth second volume was greeted with general scepticism. The fact is that model-building of this type had to wait until the 1950s before it was to become truly respectable. Tinbergen, however, was not discouraged from his aims and went on to duplicate his earlier American model for the British economy in *Business Cycles in the United Kingdom, 1870–1914* (North-Holland, 1951).

When the war ended in 1945, Tinbergen was appointed Director of the newly established Netherlands Central Planning Bureau and turned his attention to the problem of policy-making. *On the Theory of Economic Policy* (North-Holland, 1952) and *Centralization and Decentralization in Economic Policy* (North-Holland, 1954) were capped by *Economic Policy: Principles and Design* (North-Holland, 1956; 4th edn, Rand McNally, 1967), in which he advanced the thesis that a government cannot achieve a set of quantitative targets for specific economic variables (such as full employment, a stable price level, and balance of payments equilibrium) unless it employs an equal number of quantitative policy instruments (such as the level of government expenditure, the level of taxes, and the rate of growth of the money supply). The use of this framework was illustrated by a series of examples of actual problems facing the Dutch economy, which served to drive home its practical import. *Economic Policy* soon became one of Tinbergen's most widely read books and its message is now common parlance among policy-makers everywhere. It formed the basis for a number of Tinbergen's famous papers proclaiming the imminent convergence of the economic systems of communist and Western countries. This looked like wishful thinking in the 1950s, then like inspired guesswork in the 1960s, and, in the fulness of time, like another great prediction gone wrong.

In 1955 he left the Central Planning Bureau to become a full-time Professor of Development Planning at the Netherlands School of Economics, after which he concentrated his activities on the problems of the Third World. He became an adviser to many developing countries, a consultant to various UN agencies, a chairman of the UN Committee for Development Planning from 1966 to 1975, and travelled and lectured tirelessly around the world to persuade others of the need for an ambitious international development policy designed to close the gap between poor and rich nations. These activities are only imperfectly reflected in a series of books, such as *The Design of Development* (Johns Hopkins University Press, 1958), *Mathematical Models of Economic Growth* (McGraw-Hill, 1962), co-authored with H. Bos, *Econometric Models of Education* (OECD, 1965), again co-authored with H. Bos, *Development Planning* (McGraw-Hill, 1967), and *Reshaping the International Order* (Dutton, 1976), a report to the Club of Rome 'co-ordinated' by Tinbergen.

In 1973 he became Professor of International Co-operation at the University of Leiden, retiring in 1975 with the publication of *Income Distribution: Analysis and Policy* (North-Holland, American Elsevier, 1975), an ambitious work which attempted to provide in one framework both a positive explanation of the personal distribution of income and a normative statement of an equitable income distribution. On balance, this work was not well received and yet it marks an amazing achievement to round off an amazing career. Even this was not an end to his career. Further books on international peace and understanding appeared as late as 1990: *Production, Income and Welfare: The Search for an Optimal Social Order* (University of Nebraska Press, 1985) and *World Security and Equity* (Edward Elgar, 1990).

There are Tinbergen Institutes in both Amsterdam and Rotterdam, postgraduate research centres at which Dutch students and visiting scholars engage in economic study and research. Their foundation is just one of the ways in which Dutch economists have paid tribute to Tinbergen's international reputation. He was without doubt the greatest economist that the Netherlands ever produced.

*Primary Literature*
J. Tinbergen, 'Recollections of Professional Experience', in J.A. Kregel (ed.), *Recollections of Eminent Economists*, vol. 2 (Macmillan, 1988); J. Tinbergen, 'Solving the Most Urgent Problems First', in M. Szenberg (ed.), *Eminent Economists* (Cambridge University Press, 1992).

*Secondary Literature*
H.C. Bos, 'Tinbergen, Jan', in D.L. Sills (ed.), *International Encyclopaedia of the Social Sciences*, vol. 18 (The Free Press, 1979); S. Chakravarty, 'Tinbergen, Jan', in J. Eatwell, M. Milgate and P. Newman (eds), *The New Palgrave: A Dictionary of Economics*, vol. 4 (Macmillan, 1987).

# Tobin,
# James
# (1918–    )

James Tobin is America's most distinguished Keynesian economist, meaning not only that he has refused to climb on the bandwagon of 'monetarism' but also that he has consistently held the view that the original Keynesian theory of income determination is capable of being extended and refined to deal with the macroeconomic problems of the 1980s and 1990s. His path-breaking theoretical work of the interest-elasticity of the demand for money, his empirical studies of consumption and saving, his analysis of the effects of financial variables on spending decisions, his efforts to incorporate money and business cycles in models of economic growth, his trenchant criticism of Milton Friedman's (q.v.) theoretical framework for monetarism, and his defence of demand management against the negative conclusions of the 'new classical macroeconomics' (see Lucas, R.E. Jr; Sargent, T.J.) earned him the Nobel Prize in Economics in 1981. Many other honours have also come his way: the John Bates Clark Medal of the American Economic Association in 1955, President of the Econometric Society in 1958 and the American Economic Association in 1971, and honorary degrees from five American and European universities.

Tobin was born in 1919 in Champaign, Illinois, and received his Bachelor's, Master's and Doctor's degrees from Harvard University in 1939, 1940, and 1947 respectively. He began teaching at Harvard

University in 1945 but moved to Yale University in 1947 where he has remained ever since as Professor of Economics except for a year in Washington as member of President Kennedy's Council of Economic Advisers in 1961–2 and a year in Nairobi, Kenya, as Visiting Professor at the Nairobi Institute for Development Studies in 1972–3.

His years in Washington resulted in a set of lectures, *National Economic Policy* (Yale University Press, 1966). Apart from another more recent set of lectures, *Asset Accumulation and Economic Activity* (Basil Blackwell, 1980), his entire output has taken the form of articles in professional journals. They are collected together in his *Essays in Economics: Macroeconomics* (Markham, 1971; North-Holland, 1974), *The New Economics One Decade Older* (Princeton University Press, 1974), *Essays in Economics: Consumption and Econometrics* (North-Holland, 1975), *Essays in Economics: Theory and Policy* (MIT Press, 1982), and *Policies for Prosperity: Essays in a Keynesian Mode*, ed. P.M. Jackson (Wheatsheaf, 1987)

At the centre of Tobin's work has been the concept of asset-holding. Members of the public can hold money, bonds, or capital in the form of stocks and shares. In most macroeconomic models these three assets are reduced to two – say, money and bonds as in Keynes' *General Theory*, on the assumption that bonds and stocks are perfect substitutes in the portfolio of investors and hence can be treated as equivalent. Denying this assumption, Tobin was led to the conclusion that the effects of monetary policy on real output and income cannot be judged by looking only at the rate of interest: the ultimate gauge of monetary expansion or contraction is not the rate of interest but the rate of return that wealth-owners require in order to absorb the existing stock of bonds and shares into their portfolios. More generally, the ultimate measure of demand expansion or deflation is the relationship between the equities and debts of business enterprises as currently priced on the stock market, and the replacement cost of the assets of these enterprises at current prices; the ratio of these two global magnitudes he calls '$q$'. A change in $q$ may occur because of a change in the financial sector that changes the yield which investors require in order to hold equity capital but it may equally occur because of a change for any reason in investors' expectations. In 'A General Equilibrium Approach to Monetary Theory', *Journal of Money, Credit and Banking*, February 1969, an article which synthesised his earlier work on financial flows, he concluded that the principal way in which events in the financial sector affect aggregate demand is by changing $q$. Monetary policy can lead to such a change but so can a change in asset preferences for money, bonds, or equities. In this sense, monetary policy is only one of the elements which alter the rates of inflation and unemployment, and it is not necessarily the most important element. This, in essence, is his reply to 'monetarism'.

In a classic paper, 'Liquidity Preference as a Behavior Toward Risk', *Review of Economic Studies*, February 1958, Tobin suggested that investors trade off the mean against the variance of the returns on investment. Returns on financial assets depend on the interest rate and the capital gains or losses on the changing price of assets. These returns are, therefore, completely described in terms of mean returns, given by the interest rate, and the variance of these returns, given by the probability of capital gains and losses. Choice of an investment portfolio, made up of a mix of money, stocks and bonds, are hence made according to the preferences of investors for high mean/low variance versus low mean/high variance (money, of course, earns a zero mean and zero variance). Tobin's application of the concept of portfolio balance to the demand for money and assets in general in a whole series of papers since 1958 has figured heavily in the development of that branch of economics called the Theory of Finance (see Modigliani, F.).

Government debt and debt management, the economics of commercial banking, and active policies to stimulate economic growth have been Tobin's other areas of interest. Although an arch-opponent of Friedman's analysis of monetary problems, Tobin's studies of the poverty problem have led him to support Friedman's proposal for a guaranteed minimum annual income in the form of a negative income tax. He has also made a number of technical contributions to applied econometrics, originating a method known after him as TOBIT analysis for estimating statistical relationships involving explanations of dependent variables expressed in probabilistic terms, such as the probability of being unemployed, the probability of migrating, etc.

*Primary Literature*
J. Tobin, 'My Evolution as an Economist', in W. Breit and R.W. Spencer (eds), *Lives of the Laureates: Ten Nobel Economists* (MIT Press, 1990).

*Secondary Literature*
D.D. Purvis, 'James Tobin's Contributions to Economics', in H.W. Spiegel and W.J. Samuels (eds), *Contemporary Economists in Perspective*, vol. 1 (JAI Press, 1984).

# Triffin, Robert (1911–93)

Robert Triffin was at the centre of debate on international monetary reform for over thirty years. His concern was less with exchange rates, whether fixed or flexible, than with the adequacy of international reserves and the need to supplement the assets of the International Monetary Fund as 'lender of last resort' with new forms of global liquidity. The lack of adequate reserves was serious enough in the 1950s when the US balance of payments resulted in an apparently chronic world-wide 'dollar shortage'. As the dollar shortage turned into a 'dollar glut' in the 1960s, the situation should have eased but the growth of the Eurodollar market only introduced a new source of instability without instability the demand for additional international reserves. Finally, the oil embargo in 1973 brought home the full extent of the global liquidity crisis which had been building up for over thirty years.

Throughout this period, in numerous articles and books – *Europe and the Money Muddle: From Bilateralism to Near-convertibility, 1947–56* (Yale University Press, 1960), *The Evolution of the International Monetary System* (Princeton University, 1964), *The World Money Maze: National Currencies in International Payments* (Yale University Press, 1966), and *Our International Monetary System: Yesterday, Today and Tomorrow* (Random House, 1968) – Triffin had a major impact on policy by the formulation of practical proposals at every stage of the evolving situation in the international 'money muddle'. In a biographical article that he wrote for the *Banca Nazionale del Lavoro Quarterly Review* in 1981, he recommended his *Gold and the Dollar Crisis: Yesterday and Tomorrow* (Princeton University Press, 1978) as summarising, in twenty-one pages, the changes over thirty years in his prescriptions for world-wide and European monetary reform.

Triffin was born in 1911 in Flobecq, Belgium. He obtained his first degree from the Catholic University of Louvain in 1934 and then crossed the Atlantic to take an MA in 1935 and a PhD in 1938 from Harvard University. His doctoral dissertation, *Monopolistic Competition and General Equilibrium Theory* (Harvard University Press, 1940), was a powerful book, which argued that Chamberlin's theory of monopolistic competition was invalid as formulated by Chamberlin because it employed the concept of an industry in situations where each firm constituted its own industry. It won the author a post as instructor at Harvard in 1939. In 1942, however, Triffin became Chief of the Latin American section of the Board of Governors of the Federal Reserve System and changed his interests from price theory to monetary and banking reform. In 1946 he became Director of the Exchange Control Division of the IMF, then Observer and US Representative to the Intra-European Payments Committee of the Organisation of European Economic Co-operation (1948–51), and US Alternate Representative to the European Payments Union (1950–1). In 1951 he returned to academic life as Professor of Economics at Yale University where he remained until his retirement in 1977. He moved back to Belgium to teach part-time at his *alma mater*, the Catholic University of Louvain. He died in 1993.

He won the de Lavaleye prize and Gouverneur Cornez prize in 1970, the Biancamano prize in 1972, and has received honorary degrees from the University of Louvain and Yale University.

# Tullock, Gordon (1922– )

Gordon Tullock was one of the principal founders of the Public Choice Society (see Buchanan, J.M.) and he has pioneered the application of economic principles to collective decisions, thus invading an area traditionally assigned to political scientists. Co-author with Buchanan of *The Calculus of Consent: Logical Foundations of Constitutional Democracy* (University of Michigan Press, 1962), Tullock's writings have ranged even wider than those of Buchanan and he has been a central figure in the effort to revitalise old-style political anarchism as a new brand of libertarianism. Books like *The Politics of Bureaucracy* (Public Affairs Press, 1965), *The Social Dilemma: The Economics of War and Revolution* (Center for Study of Public Choice, 1974), *The New World of Economics* (Richard D. Irwin, 1975; 2nd edn, 1978), with R.B. McKenzie, *Modern Political Economy: An Introduction to Economics* (McGraw-Hill, 1978), again with R.B. McKenzie, and *Trials on Trial: The Pure Theory of Legal Procedures* (Columbia University Press, 1980) explore the economics of organisation, conflict resolution, voting behaviour, crime and the foundations of the legal system from the standpoint of the theory of public choice joined to the theory of property rights (see Demsetz, H.). *The Economics of Special Privilege and Rent-seeking* (Kluwer, 1980) develops his theory of rent-seeking, which he has done more than anyone else to incorporate as an essential feature of public choice theory.

It is not always easy to see a common thread in Tullock's work: he is almost too fertile and throws off so many ideas in all directions that the connecting links between them threaten to disappear from view. Any simple summary of his 'system', therefore, must wait on some future effort of his own. However, a common thread in his work, as in that of all public choice theorists, is the view that human behaviour must be viewed in all circumstances as a 'rational' response to the twin constraints of the physical environment and the prevailing social institutions; people will always strive to maximise their satisfactions in the face of these constraints, taking due account of the costs of alternative choices. What characterises economic analysis, therefore, is not a set of questions called 'economic activity' but a particular method of analysing any set of questions. Hence, when people make collective rather than private decisions, public choice theory asks what transaction costs, given the technical and social constraints, can cause individuals to prefer the outcomes of the ballot box to those of a market mechanism, and what are the feasible changes in the prevailing constraints which are capable of altering such preferences? The result is a sometimes startling new way of looking at old questions in political science.

Tullock was born in 1922 in Rockford, Illinois. He received a degree in law from the University of Chicago Law School in 1947 and went on to graduate studies at Yale University (1949–51) and Cornell University (1951–2). From 1947 to 1956, he was employed in the Foreign Service of the US State Department. His first teaching post was at the University of South Carolina (1959–62). Subsequently he moved to the University of Virginia (1962–7), Rice University (1967–8), the Virginia Polytechnic Institute and State University (1968–83), George Mason University (1983–7) and, finally, the University of Arizona in 1987, where he remains to this day.

He was President of the Public Choice Society in 1965 and the Southern Economic Association in 1980.

# Vanek, Jaroslav (1930– )

Jaroslav Vanek's early contributions were of a technical kind to fields like growth theory and international economics. He published an excellent intermediate text in *International Trade: Theory and Economic Policy* (Richard D. Irwin, 1962) and followed it up with another intermediate text on the theory of *Maximal Economic Growth* (Cornell University Press, 1968). And then, somewhere in the late 1960s, he had a sudden change of heart. Inspired by the experience of the Yugoslav economy, he became interested in the syndicalist concept of workers' control and worked out the pure theory of a labour-managed enterprise, using the standard tools of the orthodox theory of the profit-maximising firm under capitalism. In a treatise on *The General Theory of Labour-managed Market Economies* (Cornell University Press, 1970), he attempted to show that a competitive economy consisting entirely of labour-managed firms would have all the desirable properties of a competitive capitalist economy and even some not shared by a competitive capitalist economy, such as a strong tendency towards full employment.

Vanek's theory was, like the orthodox theory of the firm, a static equilibrium theory, which takes no account of the dynamic behaviour of firms. But it is precisely in the area of dynamic behaviour that doubts arise about labour-managed enterprises: how would a labour-managed firm handle the introduction of labour-saving technology, requiring some workers to be laid off? Moreover, even taken on its own grounds, Vanek's case involved a stark contrast between an economy made of capitalist-managed firms and an economy made of labour-managed firms; the fact that the latter is superior to the former is not itself an argument for increasing the number of labour-managed firms in the mixed economies in which we now live. Nevertheless, Vanek's writings have inspired what is now a rich literature on the theory of labour-managed enterprises (see Domar, E.D.; Meade, J.E.), which considers a number of transition paths from the present patterns of firm organisation to one in which workers would share control of firms with management; see his two-volume book of readings, *Producer Co-operatives and Labour-managed Systems*, ed. D.L. Prychitko and J. Vanek (Edward Elgar, 1996).

Vanek himself seems to have become increasingly doubtful of the value of his own general theory and in the next book, *The Participating Economy: An Evolutionary Hypothesis and a Development Strategy* (Cornell University Press, 1971), he broadens the argument from a system of labour-managed enterprises to one of producer and consumer co-operatives, in which workers and consumers participate in all vital decisions regarding production and distribution, without necessarily controlling all those decisions through elected representatives. Latterly, he has joined this argument to the thesis that solar energy is the technology of the future, which depends for its success however on the creation of 'the participatory economy'. His career provides, therefore, a fascinating example of a personal journey from orthodoxy to heterodoxy, parts of which can be charted by reading *The Labor-managed Economy: Essays by Jaroslav Vanek* (Cornell University Press, 1977).

Vanek was born in 1930 in Prague, Czech Republic, and educated in his teens at the *Gymnasium* in Prague. He obtained his first degree in statistics, mathematics and economics from the Sorbonne in Paris in 1952, which he followed with a second degree in economics from the University of Geneva in 1954. Emigrating to the USA in 1955, he received his doctorate from the Massachusetts Institute of Technology in 1957. He began teaching at Cornell University in the late 1950s, becoming Professor of Economics in 1966, Professor of International Studies in 1969, and Director of Program Participation and Labour Managed Systems in 1970, all at Cornell. He was a Visiting Professor at the Institute of Economic Science in Belgrade,

Yugoslavia, in 1972, the Catholic University of Louvain, Belgium, in 1974, a Fellow at the Netherlands Institute for Advanced Study in the Humanities and Social Sciences in 1975–6 and the Institute for Social Studies, The Hague, Netherlands, in 1978. He was a Consultant to the government of Peru in 1971 and Economic Adviser to the Prime Minister of Turkey in 1978–9. He has advised self-managed enterprises in countries all over the world.

# Viner,
# Jacob
# (1892–1970)

Jacob Viner was a leading inter-war price and trade theorist and quite simply the greatest historian of economic thought that ever lived. His *Studies in the Theory of International Trade* (Harper, 1937; Kelley, 1965) took the history of international economics, which had been worked over by many previous commentators, and placed it on an entirely new footing, sorting out misunderstandings, clarifying the main lines of advance, and in the process discovering innumerable neglected or even totally unknown articles, pamphlets, and books. Among its most famous features was a scornful rejection of the seventeenth- and eighteenth-century doctrines of the mercantilists as a series of pre-scientific fallacies.

Already in 1926, his classic article on 'Adam Smith and Laissez Faire', reprinted in his *The Long View and the Short* (The Free Press, 1958), made him a recognised expert on the eighteenth century but that was nothing compared to his astonishing book-length introduction to a reprint of John Rae's 1895 *Life of Adam Smith* (Kelley, 1965). In later years, he became increasingly fascinated by the links between theology and economics in the days before Adam Smith. *The Role of Providence in the Social Order* (American Philosophical Society, 1972; Princeton University Press, 1976) conveys the flavour of a larger work to come on the ideas of the Scholastics, Christian divines, and seventeenth-century philosophers; he died before completing it but the four chapters which have been published, J. Melitz and D. Winch (eds), *Religious Thought and Economic Society* (Duke University Press, 1978), contain many typical Viner flashes of insight, including a surprising but outright rejection of Max Weber's thesis on the Protestant ethic and the rise of capitalism. His omniscient knowledge of the literature of economics and his encyclopaedic collection of bibliographical index cards were legendary; so was his patience with young, inexperienced scholars in the history of ideas. His *Essays on the Intellectual History of Economics*, ed. D.A. Irwin (MIT Press, 1991) reprints many of Viner's classic papers.

Viner was born in Montreal, Canada, in 1892, the son of immigrant German parents. He took his BA at McGill University in 1914 and entered Harvard University as a graduate student in 1915. His doctoral dissertation on *Dumping: A Problem in International Trade* (University of Chicago Press, 1923; Kelley, 1966), written under the supervision of Frank W. Taussig, the leading international trade economist of the day, was published in 1923. It was followed a year later by *Canada's Balance of International Indebtedness, 1900–1913* (University of Chicago Press, 1924; Porcupine, 1977), one of the first attempts to provide an empirical test of the classical theory of balance-of-payments adjustments, which Viner found to be correct in all its essentials. He had already started teaching at the University of Chicago in 1916 but had left after a year for government service in Washington. Returning to Chicago in 1919, he became a full professor in 1925 at the age of thirty-two, and editor of the *Journal of Political Economy* in 1928, a task which he kept up for eighteen years. During the depth of the Great Depression 1934–9, he was a Special Assistant to the US Treasury and a keen advocate, years before Keynes' *General Theory*, of budgetary deficits and increased public spending to cure the depression. In 1946 he left Chicago for Princeton University, where he remained until his retirement in 1960, serving as Consultant to the State Department and the Board of Governors for the Federal Reserve System at various times. He was President of the American Economic Association in 1939 and received the Association's Francis A. Walker medal in 1962, awarded only once every five years. Thirteen universities in the United States and abroad awarded him honorary degrees.

Had he never written on the history of economic thought and the theory of international trade, he would still deserve mention for his many masterful papers on pure theory. 'Price Policies: The Determination of Market Price' (1921), reprinted along with his other gems in *The Long View and the Short*, more or less anticipated the whole of the Chamberlinian–Robinsonian revolution in microeconomics twelve years later. Likewise, 'Cost Curves and Supply Curves' (1931) provided the entire apparatus of short-run and long-run cost curves which are now found in chapters on the theory of the firm in every text book, and in addition sorted out the horrible confusions which Marshall and Pigou had created with their distinction between internal and external economies. Viner's original mistake in that article of asking Y.K. Wong, a young assistant, to draw the U-shaped long-run supply curve tangent to the minimum point of successive U-shaped short-run supply curves, which is mathematically impossible, has become one of those famous stories which teachers relate to add spice to their lectures on price theory.

In 1950 Viner returned to international economics with a book on *The Customs Union Issue* (Carnegie Endowment, 1950; Kramer, 1961), which has ever since supplied the starting point for every subsequent work on the economics of common markets and free trade areas. Another work, *International Trade and Economic Development* (The Free Press, Clarendon Press, 1952), attacked the big-push theories of development that were so popular in the development literature in the immediate post-war era.

*Secondary Literature*
W.J. Baumol and E.V. Seiler, 'Viner, Jacob', in D.L. Sills (ed.), *International Encyclopaedia of the Social Sciences*, vol. 18 (The Free Press, 1979); H.W. Spiegel, 'Viner, Jacob', in J. Eatwell, M. Milgate and P. Newman (eds), *The New Palgrave: A Dictionary of Economics*, vol. 4 (Macmillan, 1987).

# Weintraub,
# Sidney
# (1914–83)

Sidney Weintraub was a co-founder and co-editor (with Paul Davidson) of the *Journal of Post Keynesian Economics*, whose aim is to encourage the development of an alternative economics based on the insights of Keynes that are said to have disappeared from orthodox economics: the fundamental role of money and liquidity, the effects of pervasive uncertainty, the interrelationship between financial markets and goods markets, the nature of the labour market as a quantity-, not price-adjusting, market, and so forth. Post-Keynesian economics also goes beyond Keynes in its view of market structures as typified by oligopoly rather than perfect competition, and in its fundamental concern with questions of income distribution, particularly the share of wages and profits in national income. Post-Keynesian economics is made up of many strands and is not yet an entirely coherent and integrated structure of ideas: perhaps all that post-Keynesian economists have in common is a dislike of orthodox, neoclassical, utility-maximising economics with its textbook IS–LM interpretation (see Hicks, J.R.) of Keynes. All this is to say that Weintraub's writings are only one version of post-Keynesian economics: other versions are provided by the writings of Kaldor and Robinson, inspired as much by the ideas of Kalecki as by those of Keynes (see Kaldor, N.; Kalecki, M.; Pasinetti, L.L.; Robinson, J.).

At the outset of his career, Weintraub published a striking and still useful intermediate text book on *Price Theory* (Pittman, 1949; Greenwood Press, 1979). Subsequently, he moved away from orthodoxy in the attempt to provide *A General Theory of the Price Level* (Chilton, 1959) based on a simple model consisting of only three macroeconomic variables. *An Approach to the Theory of Income Distribution* (Chilton, 1958) and *Employment Growth and Income Distribution* (Chilton, 1966) marked an even more decisive break with orthodox economics in providing a theory of factor shares that depends, like the corresponding theory of Kaldor, on Keynesian macro-variables rather than pricing in factor markets in accordance with marginal productivity principles. Finally, in *Capitalism's Inflation and Unemployment Crisis* (Addison-Wesley, 1978) and *Our Stagflation Malaise: Ending Inflation and Unemployment* (Quorum, 1982), he argued ably for TIP, a corporate tax-based incomes policy as a method of restraining inflation. In effect TIP taxes companies that raise wages and prices at a rate that increases with the magnitude of these rises; it is an alternative to A.P. Lerner's (q.v.) proposal for the issue of tradeable 'permits' to raise wages and prices. *Keynes, Keynesians and Monetarists* (University of Pennsylvania Press, 1973) reprints a selection of Weintraub's many papers on Keynes and matters Keynesian, in particular Keynes' treatment of the aggregate demand and supply functions.

Weintraub was born in 1914 in New York City. He studied at the London School of Economics in 1938–9 but returned to the USA at the outbreak of World War II. He received his PhD from New York University in 1941. After working for the US government in the 1940s, he joined the faculty of the New School for Social Research in New York in 1951. In 1952 he became a Professor of Economics at the University of Pennsylvania, where he remained for the rest of his life, except for short teaching spells at the universities of Minnesota, Hawaii, Waterloo, Canada, and Western Australia. He died in 1983.

*Primary Literature*
S. Weintraub, 'A Jevonian Seditionist: Mutiny to Enhance the Economic Bounty', in J.A. Kregel (ed.), *Recollections of Eminent Economists*, vol. 2 (Macmillan, 1988).

*Secondary Literature*
A. Bloomfield and P. Davidson, 'On Weintraub', in H.W. Spiegel and W.J. Samuels (eds), *Contemporary Economists in Perspective*, vol. 1 (JAI Press, 1984); J. Deprez and W. Milberg, 'Weintraub, Sidney', in P. Arestis and M. Sawyer (eds), *A Biographical Dictionary of Dissenting Economists* (Edward Elgar, 1992).

# Index of Names

# Index of Subjects